Y0-BCS-987

How to Start a Home-Based
Gift Basket Business

Help Us Keep This Guide Up to Date

Every effort has been made by the author and editors to make this guide as accurate and useful as possible. However, many things can change after a guide is published—establishments close, phone numbers change, facilities come under new management, etc.

We would love to hear from you concerning your experiences with this guide and how you feel it could be made better and be kept up to date. While we may not be able to respond to all comments and suggestions, we'll take them to heart and we'll make certain to share them with the author. Please send your comments and suggestions to the following address:

The Globe Pequot Press
Reader Response/Editorial Department
P.O. Box 480
Guilford, CT 06437

Or you may e-mail us at:
editorial@GlobePequot.com

Thanks for your input!

HOME-BASED BUSINESS SERIES

How to Start a Home-Based
Gift Basket Business

Third Edition

Shirley George Frazier

The Globe Pequot Press

GUILFORD, CONNECTICUT

To buy books in quantity for corporate use
or incentives, call **(800) 962–0973, ext. 4551,**
or e-mail **premiums@GlobePequot.com.**

Copyright © 1998, 2000, 2004 by Shirley George Frazier

All rights reserved. No part of this book may be reproduced or transmitted in any form by any means, electronic or mechanical, including photocopying and recording, or by any information storage and retrieval system, except as may be expressly permitted by the 1976 Copyright Act or by the publisher. Requests for permission should be made in writing to The Globe Pequot Press, P.O. Box 480, Guilford, CT 06437.

Cover design by Nancy Freeborn
Cover photos (upper left and lower right) by Eye Wire; (upper right) by Shirley George Frazier
Text design by Mary Ballachino
Illustrations by Peggy Price

ISSN 1545-9403
ISBN 0-7627-2762-4

Manufactured in the United States of America
Third Edition/Second Printing

To my family:
husband John, daughter Genesis, mom Joan, sister Cassandra, and aunt Shirley—
the fabulous five who mean everything to me.

This book's purpose is to provide accurate and authoritative information on the topics covered. It is sold with the understanding that neither the author nor the publisher is engaged in rendering legal, financial, accounting, or other professional services. Neither The Globe Pequot Press nor the author assumes any liability resulting from action taken based on the information included herein. Mention of a company name does not constitute endorsement.

Contents

Contents

Contents

Acknowledgments

Flora Brown, my good friend and colleague, who is always ready for a midnight industry chat.

Michelle Agins, the photographic genius who captures the right look the first time.

Andrea Higbie, Suzanne Chazin, and Sari Salaverry, the teachers who brought out the best in my writing.

Laura Strom, Paula Brisco, and Shelley Wolf, true risk takers whom I thank endlessly for taking a chance to work with me.

And to all the gift basket professionals who keep this industry vibrant, engaging, and extraordinary.

Introduction

Picture this: After ten years of unquestioned loyalty, you march into the boss's office to ask for a bonus. It was you who brought in those new accounts that tripled the company's revenue. You make your case, and then it happens. The boss announces that not only won't you get a bonus, but your job is being phased out, and this is your last day. Dazed and humiliated, you take a box of empty memories out to the car and sit slumped in the driver's seat. How will you start over? All of a sudden, a beautifully stenciled delivery van pulls up. The driver takes a gift basket from the back and enters the building with a smile on her face. You gasp with excitement. "Why didn't I think of it before?" you shout out loud. "I'm creative and have lots of contacts. I'll start a gift basket business!" Three years later, you're a success and up to your designer nails in deliveries. Today is your driver's day off, and strangely enough, you have a delivery to make at your former building. On the way in, a man exits holding the obligatory "just fired" box in his hands. Your eyes meet. It's your former boss. Life is sweet.

It's a twisted tale that's very close to the way I began my career in the gift basket business. The part about being a success is absolutely true and gets better every day. The notion to enter this $3.8 billion industry doesn't hit you like an oncoming train but rather surfaces little by little from the recesses of your mind. It seems as though it was deep within you and finally rose to the top, commanding your full attention. That's what happened to me in December 1988. After I had contemplated and dropped the idea of starting a word-processing service and been on the verge of opening an intimate apparel shop, the thought of gift baskets took hold of me and never let go. John, my husband and best friend, works at a company where a female coworker was feeling sad. Being the sweetheart he is, the next day he brought her something to lift her spirits (figuratively, of course)—a mini bottle of liqueur and shot glass with rocks glued to the bottom, all wrapped in clear plastic wrap. The friend loved the gift, and everyone in the area praised John for his thoughtfulness.

Meanwhile, I was busily planning how many sizes, colors, and styles of slips and such would adorn my boutique. One look at John's gift made me drop my plans. I immediately decided to enter the gift basket business. The baskets were relatively easy to make (or so I thought), they could be created at home (no rent!), and the business would take less money to open but as much creative energy to build (which I had plenty of). My niche would be gift baskets using basket substitutes. In an industry where a basket is the mainstay, I planned to set myself apart from the competition so that the business would be different and attract more clients than others served in similar businesses. Unique and unusual containers would be my claim to fame. An upturned umbrella, a child's wagon, a rocking chair—I couldn't wait to begin.

A month later, which was three weeks into the new year, I stood in the 1200 aisle of the New York International Gift Fair, in awe of all the products gathered under the gift industry banner. There were two floors of exhibits in this 5-block-long building, plus shuttle buses that transported you to products on two piers and a permanent showroom. With so many resources and no formal training, I had lots of work to do, but I was ready for what was necessary to become successful. That was thirteen years, forty television appearances, two books, three newsletters, and countless trade seminars and magazine articles ago. I've never regretted one step or decision, good or bad, but there were times in the first years of business when I wished a resource were available to help me make better decisions and fewer mistakes. And that's the reason you hold this book in your hands today.

What happens when you decide to start a gift basket business? The first thing is that your mind goes in a thousand different directions, all in question format, which I demonstrate here with the correct answers. "Where is the resource that will get and keep me on track?" It's in your hands. "I need baskets and foods and that other stuff that makes them look nice; what is it and where does it all come from?" I'll tell you. "How do I set up shop at home and store products?" The answer is here. "Can I sell my baskets on the Internet?" You'll learn how. "Will I make money?" Yes, you really will make money, and I'll show you the formula that ensures a profitable enterprise year after year.

First we'll find out if you have the drive and determination to enter into and thrive in this business. You'll set your goals according to what you want to accomplish, keeping in mind that you're probably better at business than you think and will want to elevate your planning as you progress. Next I'll take you on a tour of the gift basket industry, and you'll start to better understand who your market is and mold your plans to meet that market's unique needs. We'll share a hands-on session of how to create a gift basket from the bottom up. You'll find resource materials in the back of this book, including industry definitions, gift basket theme ideas, and a list of major trade shows, magazines, and product sources. This book is packed with charts and forms, items that didn't exist when I started. They give you a big advantage over anyone who started years ago essentially from scratch. You'll learn how to ship, deliver, advertise, employ, compete, recover from mistakes, set up and sell on the Internet, and grow. You'll learn everything that's done in a retail storefront, but you'll do it from home, exuding the same professionalism once reserved only for big-budget retailers who can afford the rents of the region. Each day that you wake and arrive in your home workspace, taking orders and making the day's baskets, you too will say, "Life is sweet."

Treat the checklists in this book as an investment in your business. I speak from personal experience when I say that skipping an exercise could result in costly mishaps in terms of time and money.

A gift basket business is perfect for the home base. Statistics prove that most stores selling only gift baskets cannot withstand paying the monthly rent, salaries, and other fixed expenses that come with maintaining a store. Gift baskets are sold in variety stores, specialty shops, and other places where they are bought by the masses, but individuals will venture to a place where they can buy many things at one time, not just a gift basket. The main reason why gift basket professionals overwhelmingly set up shop at home is that they can perfect their craft in a relaxed environment before introducing their baskets to the world and earn a good living without the pressure of rent, salaries, and high taxes. Relaxed does not mean that you make baskets in the morning and sit down to soap operas and tea in the afternoon. This is a serious business, with income potential that has exceeded the wildest dreams of longtime designers. Working from home is a discipline all can learn and many have mastered.

Here are other reasons why a home-based gift basket business is satisfying:

- You can easily control your hours, clients serviced, and work schedule.
- No outdoor sign is needed to tell anyone that you are in business (we'll go over advertising in Chapter 7).
- Inventory is easily maintained in a temperature-controlled attic, basement, garage, closet, or spare room.
- Shipping companies pick up boxes and other packages right from your home base.
- There's no store to close if you have an appointment, make a delivery, or run an errand. You simply close the front door and forward all calls to your cellular phone or let your answering service or machine mind the office until you return.

The advantages run high, but there are also trade-offs to running a successful home-based business:

- With neither sign nor store, your marketing strategy must focus on reaching customers where they live, work, shop, relax, and surf on the Internet.
- Networking is important to find corporate customers who need baskets to maintain business relationships. You must go where they mingle to get their business.
- As a home-based professional, you must be committed to do everything for this business, even the work you don't like to do. There is no compromise.

The italicized sentences you'll find scattered throughout this book are actual comments made by gift basket professionals located nationwide. Their views reflect real-life business situations that occur every day in this industry.

Congratulations! You've decided to start a home-based gift basket business, and that's the first step. Now comes your commitment to doing the necessary work to build a successful business to call your own. Turn the page, and let's begin.

Chapter One

Understanding Your Target Market

What happens when you receive advertising by mail or e-mail that has nothing to do with your lifestyle or habits? You toss it in the garbage or hit the "delete" key. That's the result when you don't reach individuals who are in your ideal gift basket target market.

The term *target market* defines a person of a certain age, gender, and lifestyle who is most likely to buy your product. For example, an eighty-five-year-old man living in a retirement home on a fixed income is generally not the type of person who is interested in gift baskets. A thirty-five-year-old married woman with children, employed full-time, who maintains a home and has little time to shop, is a typical gift basket buyer. The differences between these individuals are obvious, and this is an example of the way you decide who is a potential buyer.

Think about the reasons why you've decided to start a gift basket business. Aside from your creativity, are there people in your circle of friends and family to whom you've given gift baskets in the past? Have individuals relayed problems in finding the right gift for other people? Are they saying that there's little time to shop or nothing unique to buy in stores? Perhaps you were part of a fund-raiser that involved creating gift baskets from scratch. Whatever the case, you've been exposed to people who buy and receive this wonderful gift, and you have an idea about who fits into your particular target market.

Use the Potential Buyers' Chart to get a better idea of the similarities between people who you believe are potential customers. Think about friends, neighbors, coworkers, out-of-state relatives, school and club acquaintances, people who provide you with services (doctors, salon owners, etc.), and house of worship members. Consult your address book and Rolodex or Personal Digital Assistant (PDA) for additional names. You won't recall everyone immediately, so expect this exercise to take several weeks to complete.

When you're finished, review the chart and search for similarities in the people you've listed. Are there more men or women? Are they in a certain age group? Is there a higher percentage of single or married individuals? Do they travel for business or pleasure, have children, or eat out often? When you narrow your focus on the type of people you will pursue to buy your baskets, you have a better chance of selling to those who will buy versus targeting people who aren't interested. In time you will find that your market will change, but right now you want to get a sense of whom to approach when you're ready to sell.

Gift basket statistics aren't easily found, but they do exist. Here's a sample of the most important facts taken from various surveys conducted between 1995 and 2000:

- Women, ages twenty-eight to fifty-five, with a household income between $35,000 and $75,000, are the most frequent buyers.
- The average price of the best-selling basket rose from $30 in 1995 to $48 in 2000.
- Companies account for 37 percent of all sales.
- The top three themes are happy birthday, thank you, and congratulations. The top three holidays are Christmas, Valentine's Day, and Mother's Day.
- Gift baskets are the third most popular gift, outranked only by flowers and gift certificates.
- Southern states account for 33 percent of sales, followed by the West (25 percent), Midwest (22 percent), and Northeast (20 percent).

Gift baskets are enjoying increased popularity in stores. A 1997 survey commissioned by *Gifts & Decorative Accessories,* the leading gift trade magazine, revealed that gift baskets were the number one product added to stores, rising from 2 percent in 1991 to 7 percent in 1996. In a 2001 survey, gift baskets were ranked as having the third-best selling price of all store merchandise (behind art and rugs). Don't let this information stop you from going

Potential Buyers' Chart

Name:	
Location (City, State)	
Age	☐ 21–30　　☐ 31–40　　☐ 41–50　　　☐ 51–60 ☐ other (specify) _____
Marital Status	☐ single　　☐ single living w/partner　　☐ married ☐ divorced　　☐ widow/widower
Relationship to me	☐ relative　　☐ friend　　☐ neighbor　　☐ coworker ☐ other (specify) _____
Employed	☐ yes　　☐ no　　☐ self-employed ☐ full-time　　☐ part-time
Recreation	☐ bowling　☐ movies　☐ dining out　☐ clubs/dancing ☐ cooking　☐ travel　☐ home entertainment ☐ other (specify) _____
Internet access	☐ yes　　☐ no
Person receives gift baskets	☐ yes　　☐ no
Person orders gift baskets	☐ yes　　☐ no
Other characteristics	
Comments	

into business. Check your local stores. Do you notice more gift baskets than before? Statistics are a measure of overall trends, but they don't always reflect what's happening in your town. Remember why you've chosen gift baskets, and let nothing sway your decision.

Now let's uncover more about the people and places that buy this joyous bundle of goods.

Defining the Market

Your marketing strategy (advertising, networking, and other forms of selling) is key to what turns prospects into clients and leads into sales. To successfully sell gift baskets, you must first understand the definition of marketing as it relates to the gift industry. Marketing is the total organized sales approach—paid or bartered—used to:

- Develop a client profile (who the best candidates are to buy your baskets)
- Assess how to turn prospects into clients (what you do, say, and send to make them buy)
- Keep them buying and telling others about you (how to make them repeat customers and your biggest cheerleaders)

These three components are separate in deed, yet fit together like puzzle pieces to complete the picture. Marketing is neither difficult to accomplish nor overwhelming to achieve, but developing your marketing approach will take time. Since your strategy begins with identifying your client, let's begin there.

Who Is the Typical Gift Basket Buyer?

When I began selling gift baskets in 1989, I had a simple marketing strategy—simple because I did not do my research. My target market had three characteristics: They (1) walked, (2) talked, and (3) called occasionally to buy a basket. Since parrots and some robots fit two-thirds of this brilliant equation, my unsuspecting sabotage kept sales slim to none. So much for that strategy.

Every industry has a core group of loyal buyers, and gift baskets are no exception. Earlier I introduced you to some of the industry statistics. Now let's review the five main buying groups: (1) individuals, (2) independent professionals, (3) corporations, (4) nonprofit organizations, and (5) institutions.

Individuals

The average buyer is female and usually (but not always) a white-collar professional. She'll fall into one of three categories:

1. Because of job and personal demands, she has no time for an extensive gift search and prefers working with a company that will create and deliver gift baskets with one phone call.
2. She likes to shop by phone and considers Internet purchasing to be an integral part of her life. No matter where she lives, gift baskets fit this category.
3. She appreciates gift baskets' individuality. A totally new creation is prepared each time she orders.

There will be others outside of this profile who will also become loyal customers, such as blue-collar professionals, who are avid gift basket lovers; men ages twenty to fifty, coming on strong as frequent buyers; and teenagers seeking baskets for Mother's Day, Valentine's Day, and the holidays, sometimes spending more than adults. Individuals often volunteer information when ordering. They mention a son's Little League practice or affiliation with a professional group. These are important profile-building facts that help you find more prospects and sales. Well-crafted surveys also uncover new ways to find buyers; we'll discuss such surveys later in this chapter.

The sample Customer Profile Form shows what information is needed to complete the buying profile and understand how to serve these customers better. For example, if one customer gives her husband a birthday gift basket in June, you note this in the "Gift Basket Orders" row and send her a reminder postcard next May to encourage another sale. Keep the forms in a binder, separating clients alphabetically by last name. These data can also be tracked on your computer by using a data management software program such as ACT! or Goldmine.

Customer Profile Form

Name:	
Home address:	City:　　　　　　　　　　　　State:　　　Zip:
Telephone:	(　　　)
Fax:	(　　　)
E-mail:	
Approximate age:	
Birth month:	
Marital status:	☐ single　　　☐ married　　☐ living w/ partner ☐ widow/widower　☐ divorced
Holiday celebrated:	☐ Christmas　☐ Hanukkah
Spouse:	
Children's names, ages:	
Employer:	
Work address:	City:　　　　　　　　　　　　State:　　　Zip:
Job title:	
Telephone:	
E-mail:	
# of gift basket orders:	
Date of last order:	
Occasion:	
Memberships:	
Hobbies:	
Referrals:	
Comments:	

Independent Professionals

Professionals with private practices make up another group of individuals who buy gift baskets. Many of them are in and around your town—for example, doctors, dentists, chiropractors, attorneys, accountants, veterinarians, consultants, surveyors, contractors, computer specialists, therapists, insurance agents, landscapers, real estate agents, cleaning services, and others. These are people who provide the types of services that are required periodically by you and others in your circle of friends and family.

> *Lots of doctors order healthy snack baskets to send to colleagues who refer patients.*

Independent professionals are usually in business for themselves and need gifts to thank others in their field for referrals, to give office staff for special occasions and holidays, to introduce themselves to other businesses with which they want to have relationships, and to increase their sales overall through periodic gift giving.

Gift basket professionals make sure that the people who render services to them know about their gift baskets. From there, the designer educates each prospect on how the product opens new doors of opportunity that increase her or his client list and boost sales.

Independents love ordering gift baskets for other reasons. Gift baskets can help:

- Mend past ties
- Express remorse
- Congratulate (baby, wedding, etc.)
- Welcome a customer to the area, new home, new job, etc.
- Seal the deal (new/renewed contract)
- Show appreciation

These reasons are what private practitioners want to know about your gift baskets. It doesn't matter to them that you have a business. What they care about is how your gift baskets enhance their personal and professional lives. You will sell many gift baskets to this large segment of buyers if you tell them how gift baskets bring joy and comfort in good and bad times.

Gift basket professionals find it much easier to talk about their baskets directly after service has been rendered to them by an independent professional, right before leaving the person's office. This is when you'll have the prospect's undivided attention and be able to leave your business card or make a follow-up appointment to return with some sample baskets to show the prospect, staff members, and any clients who may be sitting in the waiting area.

Other selling opportunities within this group include making presentations to their associations and to other groups with which the independent professional belongs.

You'll find more ideas for selling to these service providers, who are discussed as part of the corporate market, in Chapter 6.

Corporations

A corporation is layered with multiple opportunities: (1) Executives represent company-wide orders, (2) departments represent vendor and staff orders, and (3) individuals represent personal orders. Making contact with corporate personnel through mail, phone, e-mail, or speaking with them at social and business functions quickly increases your chance to sell. Corporations buy gift baskets for births, bereavements, new employees, relocation, and every occasion and holiday.

Articles published in sales and marketing trade journals throughout 2003 highlighted the following industries as frequent corporate customers:

- *Communications giants.* Companies that provide telephone services are big fans of gift baskets. These businesses are located in every state, and each is usually staffed with a human resources department. This is where all employee activity is centered, including the giving of gifts for birthdays, new births, get well, and other sentiments. What's favored most by this group is that the gift basket designer always creates something different for each employee, no matter how many times the same theme is used.
- *Office-supply companies.* These corporations are retailers that you find on major highways across the country. This is where you purchase paper, pens, computer supplies, and general office products. While we are buying small items, the sales ex-

ecutives of these supply firms are visiting large corporate offices in an attempt to secure corporate accounts. After meeting with a purchasing agent, many of these executives send gift baskets to their contact, which is also shared with the department staff. The sales executive not only sends gift baskets to get the account but also to celebrate business anniversaries and major holidays. The office-supply business is very competitive, and giving gift baskets to potential clients is considered a critical factor to stay ahead of the competition.

- *Concierges.* This business, usually associated with lodging, is branching out of hotels and rooting itself in the country's largest corporations. It's tough for corporate employees to manage personal needs within the hour lunch break. Corporate concierges make employees' lives easier by finding and scheduling services, rentals, and reservations and by ordering gift baskets. The big money is made not only by selling employee baskets but also in making sales to departments such as purchasing and human resources. The latter buys abundantly for out-of-town guests.

- *Interim housing units.* Corporations greet executives at temporary lodging sites with dinner and snack gift baskets. A few years ago, one gift basket professional recounted in an article how one of her clients purchased Italian dinner baskets filled with pasta, sauce, breadsticks, olive oil, and biscotti for delivery to a housing unit where executives lived while visiting or relocating. There are magazines, such as *Corporate Choices,* that list where housing units are located in each state. Check your local library and the Internet for this and other temporary housing journals.

Other corporate customers include:

- *Hotels.* Dignitaries, newlyweds, and convention visitors are a few reasons why hotels are still atop the list. Sales and marketing executives and the concierge are the best buyers.

- *Real estate companies.* Welcome and thank-you baskets are purchased often. Small and large companies have equal needs but differing budgets, which sometimes means using less-expensive containers than baskets for lower-priced orders. Talk to building managers and sales executives.

> *I made contact with a real estate company owner who asked
> me to bring gift baskets to his weekly managers' meeting.
> That was three years ago, and the sales haven't stopped yet.*

- *Contractors.* Regional landscapes are changing every day, thanks to the national home-building boom. Try contacting owners and their assistants.
- *Interior decorators.* Versed in creating new living and work spaces, they usually order higher-priced gift baskets to thank customers and referrals. Principal designers and owners are your target.

The marketplace is filled with corporate sales opportunities in addition to those listed above—for instance, new car, car repair, and custom car service providers; home-based businesses in all industries; radio, television, and cable station executives; entertainment firms; Internet and software companies; beverage giants; and pharmaceutical companies. What types of firms are in your region? Have new companies recently opened for business? Watch for corporate changes through newspapers, television news, business journals, and Internet stories from reliable sources. You'll always find basket-selling opportunities when such companies want to introduce themselves to a new client, say thank you for previous business, or reestablish a relationship with an inactive client.

> *I was a part of a craft show in the cafeteria of a large com-
> pany. Not a lot of sales that day, but the exposure brought
> me lots of corporate work that holiday season.*

Bad news also brings potential sales. Corporations often use baskets as peace offerings to customers to make amends for errors or negative press coverage. Establish a relationship with the company's public relations department before a crisis strikes. (Chapter 6 will take you step-by-step into the world of corporate sales, from targeting prospects to postsales maintenance.)

Nonprofit Organizations

Donations are an organization's major source of fund-raising. Private and nonprofit groups alike use gift baskets as a sales tool before and after donations are received. Frequent gift basket buyers include Rotary Clubs, Kiwanis Clubs, men's and women's groups, Boys and Girls Clubs of America, the United Way, Planned Parenthood, the Boy and Girl Scouts, local churches, PTAs, youth groups, seniors' clubs, and so forth. Again, newspapers, television news, and reliable Internet sources report who's fund-raising or planning an event and often quote top executives in charge.

> *I always find new customers through donations to a police auxiliary league. The strategy is inexpensive and helps me show off my baskets year after year.*

One fabulous fund-raising event is the annual black-tie affair. This event shows your most spectacular basket donation to supporters who will remember your name and tell friends, family, and colleagues. Ask the person in charge if you can attend the event as a corporate sponsor or organization guest, even if the value of your donation is $50. It's an evening of mingling with people who mix charity with business, where the principle of "not what you know but who you know" opens the door to more sales and publicity.

> *Donations are great for advertising, and they're also a tax deduction!*

Find organizations you'd like to help. Contact these groups about their fund-raising activities to ensure that your basket donations are worth investing time and money. Send a letter of introduction after the initial contact, along with pictures and information explaining the benefits of your baskets. Your letter should include your Web site address for the person in charge to see gift basket photographs and a page explaining your company's mission and buying benefits. More on Internet selling is covered in Chapter 7. Act quickly on every opportunity, or you may find the door to prosperity closed.

Once you donate, other groups will beat a path to your door for more donations—a practice that can drain your business dry. Control the frenzy before it starts by setting a donation limit. Two baskets per month costing $50 retail or one at $100 is an affordable limit for most professionals. The donated amount is the basket's retail price. In reality, your cost (the wholesale price) is about one-third of the retail price.

Be choosy about donating. Not all organizations are composed of members who would normally buy baskets. If you reach your monthly donation limit and other organizations call, tell them that you cannot donate this month but to call again in the future. If a charity is important, by all means allow yourself an exception to that month's donation limit, as long as future opportunities are worth the effort.

Institutions

Hospitals, colleges, universities—these are the groups that come to mind when hearing the word *institution*. They all perform public service activities, solicit volunteers, and often thank customers and patrons with token gifts of appreciation.

A hospital's public relations department, human resources team, and volunteer staff coordinator, for example, have budgets with monies for promotional products, and that's where your baskets enter the picture. Hospital gift shops also have opportunities, as occasional subcontractors are needed to make and wrap small gifts and baskets. Colleges and universities solicit donations from alumni and outside sponsors. Wealthy individuals often leave endowments for a new building or wing, and they are thanked with enormous gift baskets filled with foods and gifts fit for a king.

Guarantee Their Satisfaction

No matter which market you approach, each one asks the same "WIIFM" questions, translated as "What's In It For Me to buy your baskets?"

- Do you save me time? Money? Help increase my profits? Make my life better?
- Are you prompt? Efficient? Reliable? Discreet?

No customer cares how it's done. All customers simply want the solution—gift baskets made and delivered to satisfy their need whenever a special event or crisis occurs. If you complete this flawlessly, in the eyes of the client, and contact him or her occasionally by mail, phone, or e-mail (only after receiving permission), you've built the beginnings of a relationship full of repeat orders and referred business.

Place clients' names in your computer database or other filing system, and send periodic postcards, newsletters, and flyers with ideas and reasons why your baskets are the only ones to choose. This type of marketing plays a key role to make your gift baskets a product that no one dares to do business without.

Matching Your Baskets with Customers' Needs

Each group has buying preferences. Some will trust your judgment on product selections for their baskets, while others will want to know every product chosen, colors used, and other enhancements to ensure that the basket is made according to their specifications. Television detective shows and mystery novels cast the main character as a keen detective, a supersleuth who asks probing questions that lead to solving the crime successfully. The questions you ask won't be similar to those in a mystery show or novel, but you will have to ask the buyer in-depth questions to understand what he or she searches for to express the right emotion through giving a gift basket. Questions about age, likes and dislikes, allergies, color preferences, recreational activities, and job functions get to the heart of what theme and products will please the recipient.

While it is true that you cannot please everyone, you can attempt to please as many clients as possible, using the following strategies:

- Make your inventory a mix of low-, medium-, and higher-priced products. Some clients will order $25 baskets with basic goods, and others will spend $100 or more for upscale specialties.
- Geography also makes a difference. Real estate companies in one region may prefer state-made products to welcome the new home owner, while those in another region may prefer a variety of products that simply say "Welcome to your new home," not caring where the products are made.

- Look at competitors' baskets for design ideas. Don't copy their baskets; view the arrangements for inspiration to carve your own niche.
- Have a test-tasting party, inviting friends, family, and colleagues whose judgment you trust. Limit the tasters to no more than twenty-five people within the age range of your target market. This event can be done at home or another comfortable location where tasters can give on-the-spot feedback through completed questionnaires and open discussions on product flavor, preference, and packaging. Buying samples for the test group will cost a lot less than buying a case of products that won't sell in your baskets. The tasting is fun and productive and gives you insights into buying options to succeed in this industry.
- Matching client preferences also includes offering engravable keepsakes, using personalized ribbon, fulfilling multiple orders, and asking about food preferences (kosher, low- and no-fat, allergy concerns). Further, clients will request basket variations on themes and products that you've not yet considered. When asked about the availability of an unusual product, respond by saying, "Let me call you later today with an answer"; then conduct your research and return the call. Keep this new information handy in a labeled folder so that when it's needed again (and you will need it), you'll have the information at your fingertips.

Customer Service That Keeps Them Buying

You took the order, created the baskets, and made prompt delivery. Now what? Will a simple thank-you card keep the client ordering? This is the third step in marketing, where supporting the relationship with thoughtful contact and promotional ideas makes a favorable impression and attracts repeat sales.

I couldn't believe the poor service I received at a gift store. It's hard to understand how seemingly successful companies thrive when salespeople are rude and obnoxious.

In this age of fluctuating customer service, I'm sure you remember situations in some stores when the word *service* seemed obsolete. Too many businesses still act as though customers should be satisfied with ignorance. As a home-based business, you must take the high road, offering the kind of fabulous, unexpected service that will amaze the client. Here are methods that will put your company on a pedestal (Chapter 11 goes into further detail on keeping the client satisfied):

- Send clients periodic cards for birthdays, congratulations, well wishes, buying anniversaries (the first time they purchased from you, etc.), and other sentiments. If appropriate, add a coupon to the card for a percentage off their next order.
- Cut out and mail clients articles of interest to their profession or lifestyle. Attach your business card with a note stating, "Thought this might be of interest to you." Think of how much business you'll gain for the price of an envelope and a stamp.
- Mail Thanksgiving or Happy New Year cards instead of traditional Christmastime holiday cards. Clients can probably build a house with the amount of holiday cards received each season. A Thanksgiving card stands out because it is sent before the holiday rush, and a New Year's card stays on the client's desk for months, whereas holiday cards often are discarded on January 2.

> *Exceptional customer service is how I distinguish my company from the rest. I go to the limit to service customers because I want to keep their account.*

Finally, the sample Customer Survey Form shows how easy it is to prepare a questionnaire focusing on facts only a customer can give. Follow these tips to create your own survey:

- Decide what information is most important, and frame your questions to get the best and most precise answers.
- Ask no more than ten questions, and use only one page. Clients will look at the survey and immediately decide whether or not they'll participate. Also choose questions that require more than a "yes" or "no" response. After each question, list the three to five best answers and add a line at the end of each question for a custom response.

Customer Survey Form

Dear Friends:

Moore Baskets appreciates your patronage and wishes to serve your needs efficiently. To help us enhance our service to you, please complete and return this brief survey by Friday, June 10. Timely return automatically enters you in our drawing to receive a breakfast basket of baked breads and juice delivered every Monday morning for one month. All information will be kept confidential.

1. What feature(s) do you like most about Moore Baskets? (Check all that apply.)

   ☐ Product variety/selection   ☐ Reliable shipping
   ☐ Prompt service
   ☐ Other (specify) _____

2. How can we improve our service to you? (Check all that apply.)

   ☐ Product personalization
   ☐ Event reminder service
   ☐ Updates through electronic newsletter
   ☐ Other (specify) _____

3. Why do you choose to call Moore Baskets for gift baskets? (Check all that apply.)

   ☐ Service accommodates my busy lifestyle
   ☐ Large assortment of choices
   ☐ Lack of variety at/poor service from other stores
   ☐ Other (specify) _____

4. Your position:

   ☐ CEO, president, owner   ☐ Department manager
   ☐ Vice-president   ☐ Purchasing agent
   ☐ Other (specify) _____

5. Industry profession:

   ☐ Hospitality   ☐ Telecommunications
   ☐ Home interiors   ☐ Pharmaceutical
   ☐ Real estate   ☐ Other (specify) _____

6. Age:

   ☐ 21–30   ☐ 41–50
   ☐ 31–40   ☐ 51 or over

Thank you for responding. To enter our drawing, please complete the information below and mail it in the enclosed envelope (or fax or e-mail it to us) for delivery by Friday, June 10.

Name: _____   Company: _____

Address: _____   Suite/room:_____

City: _____   State: _____   ZIP code: _____

- Give a deadline to increase the urgency, and offer an incentive (gift) for on-time responses. There's no need to mention the type of gift, which can be a key chain or small notepad. Whatever you choose, try to send a gift that's labeled or engraved with your company name and phone number or Web site address.
- Include a self-addressed, stamped envelope.

Mail the form to a customer after the first order. It can also be mailed to customers who haven't ordered in six months or to prospects with the best potential for future orders. Some designers post surveys on their Web sites for easy customer access and submission. After recording your first sale, review the research used to identify the client to help you win more sales from similar prospects. Persistence, patience, and good target marketing form a solid foundation for a business that you'll be proud to call your own.

Target Market Checklist

	Completed
1. Complete as many copies of the Potential Buyers' Chart as needed to identify individuals most likely to buy your baskets.	_____
2. Define the characteristics of the five major buying groups that make them more or less likely to buy your gift baskets and state why.	
Individuals	_____
Independent Professionals	_____
Corporations	_____
Organizations	_____
Institutions	_____
3. List local nonprofit and private organizations for possible sponsorships and promotional exposure with basket donations.	_____
4. Conduct an informal survey, in face-to-face contact and through questionnaires, asking potential customers what snacks and gifts they would like to see in your gift basket designs.	_____
5. Decide and list how you will stay in touch with customers when you have concluded the sale.	_____

Chapter Two

What It Takes to Succeed

A Plan of Action

Have you ever compiled a list of weekend chores? Asked a friend for directions to his house? Assembled a piece of furniture? These examples have one thing in common—they all require a formal list of instructions for successful completion of the task.

Being successful in business is no different, and that's why developing a business plan is a crucial step. The business plan charts the course and guides your decisions on what to do, how to do it, why it must be done, results, and alternative plans when you hit a roadblock. A business plan is easy to assemble, with components separated into basic steps that answer the following questions:

- *Start-up rationale.* Why is the gift basket business for you? What, if any, experience do you have in the industry? What goals do you expect to accomplish by entering this field?
- *Marketing.* Who will you sell to and why are they the best candidates? What methods get their attention and the sale? How will you service them when the sale is complete?
- *Competition.* What regional gift basket and competitive product companies exist? What are their strengths and weaknesses? How do you plan to compete with them for clients?

- *Financial.* What money sources are available to you to start your business? How will the capital be used during the first few years of operation?
- *Gift basket planning and control.* What gift basket themes will be offered, and what inventory will be purchased?
- *Office and workspace planning.* Where in the home will you set up the office and design area? What products and equipment will be needed to advertise, mail invoices, calculate sales and expenses, and complete other paperwork? How will you answer customers' calls if you are working at a full-time job?
- *Expansion and growth.* Where do you see your business in five years? In ten years? What marketing techniques will you use to increase customers and sales? How will you manage growth of your home business?

Taking the time to construct a detailed business plan, you (1) plan to win (no successful person goes into business without doing his or her homework), (2) plan the way (it's better to have directions than to be lost with nowhere to go), and (3) plan for life (if you'd work for the success of another company, why wouldn't you do the same for yourself?).

Current gift basket designers cite the lack of creating a business plan as the number one mistake they made when starting their businesses. Many of them state that a written plan would have helped them understand that this business is not just about being creative. The ability to sell, market, purchase and maintain inventory, and stay organized goes far beyond gift basket making. Don't let the pretty side of this business fool you. Gift baskets are business first, creativity second. I urge you to view the task of creating a business plan as a critical part of your success.

Look over the Sample Business Plan, which begins on page 22. It's a fictional but true-to-life account of Jane Moore, a single woman in her mid-thirties working full-time for a real estate firm. Jane has made a few gift baskets in the past for friends and family. Since then, others have asked her to make baskets for birthdays and similar occasions. She's not interested in selling real estate and knows her job reaps no future rewards, but because Jane works in the industry, she reads real estate articles and sees the ongoing demographic changes. A new train station brings more people into town, and some of them have even decided to live there. On her lunch hour, she walks past five new businesses, including a gym, hotel, and a restaurant that caters to local businesses. The library has expanded to include business journals and Internet-accessible computers. These facts play an important part in Jane's decision to start a gift basket business. Her apartment is small, but she's decided to start this business and work on a plan to relocate to a larger home if business grows sufficiently. Jane will begin her research on the Internet at the library, first to find industry information and then to write a business plan based on regional statistics, market trends, and sales opportunities in and around town. That will give her a good foundation to begin her life as a successful gift basket entrepreneur.

Jane's plan is documented in writing because she knows that her goals must be outlined in an orderly manner. Her procedure is written in plain English. Terms such as *paradigm shift, upside momentum,* and *strategic alliance* are found in formal business plans presented to outside investors and financial institutions, but this version is for Jane and family members who may want to invest in her business.

(More information on constructing cash-flow projections and other financial documents is discussed in Chapter 9.)

Three-hole punch your plan and put it in a binder. Add tabs to separate each section. Your business plan is now an official document that you will proudly review daily and update according to research and priorities.

Appropriately named, the action plan described near the end of the Sample Business Plan moves the owner into the decision-making process to complete the goals stated throughout the business plan within a specific time frame. These time frames can be broken down by days, weeks, months, and quarters and also completed on an ongoing basis. In this plan, completion of goals is stated in months and quarters: first quarter = January–March, second quarter = April–June, third quarter = July–September, and fourth quarter = October–December. Each goal is researched, findings documented, and decisions made to reach sound business solutions. As each goal is completed, other goals take its place and the cycle of business growth continues.

When you commence business, consult your business plan every month to check your progress. If the plan is too grand or not aggressive enough, your efforts can always be stepped up or scaled down.

Honestly Assessing Your Abilities

How do you respond to ongoing life pressures, to abrupt changes or disappointments, and to the challenge of doing something new? These are but a few of the many challenges you

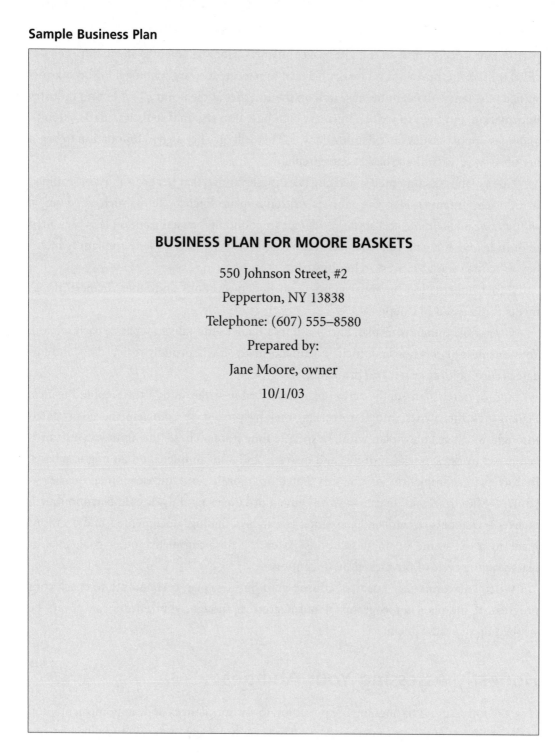

BUSINESS PLAN FOR MOORE BASKETS

550 Johnson Street, #2

Pepperton, NY 13838

Telephone: (607) 555–8580

Prepared by:

Jane Moore, owner

10/1/03

TABLE OF CONTENTS

Reasons to Start This Business

I enjoy making gift baskets and feel that this business will allow me to achieve personal and professional success while controlling my own destiny.

Friends and family like my baskets and have recommended me to others who appreciate my work. I am also a member of several business groups and see opportunities to sell gift baskets to other members.

Many new homes and buildings are under construction in the area. Plans are also under way for a new convention center, which will bring in more people and attract new businesses, all with the potential to become clients.

The only retail companies in the area selling gift baskets are a small candy shop and two florists that sell competing products. The Yellow Pages includes eight listings for home-based gift basket companies, but there is little evidence of them doing business in and around town. There is plenty of room for me to successfully sell baskets, attracting area customers and providing services to make them loyal and frequent buyers.

Credentials

Although I have made gift baskets in the past, I have yet to attend classes for training on how to make a professionally-styled gift basket. My design style is attractive, but formal training will assist me in producing better, more creative designs in less time and give me added confidence.

Last year I attended craft store classes on floral arranging and bow making. This training has benefited and will continue to benefit my gift basket creativity. I also plan to attend a gift basket conference, which will help me learn more about the industry and boost my confidence.

I understand computers and software through my work at a real estate agency and a home computer. My experience in organizing work schedules and solving customer problems in person, by phone, and through e-mail gives me an advantage in providing good service to future clients. The formal presentations I make each week at my job have given me confidence to speak in public, which will be necessary when showing my baskets to potential corporate clients.

I also require training in small business management to gain insight into general setup information, research sources, recordkeeping, state laws, taxes, and more. These details are provided for a nominal fee by SCORE, the local Small Business Development Center, and periodic small business and tax workshops sponsored by the state.

Plans to support and strengthen my credentials are listed in the subsequent Action Plan.

Marketing Plan

Lots of changes are happening in the community and surrounding towns, confirming why people will buy gift baskets:

Regional construction is enormous. Real estate managers give only key chains to each new tenant and homeowner. They may have interest in giving welcome baskets or small gifts in tote bags.

Construction companies need baskets to say thank you to clients and enhance other business relationships.

Many professionals have businesses in the downtown area or at home. The newspaper publishes a weekly list of new companies and upcoming business meetings that seems to increase each week.

I plan to introduce my gift basket business to individuals, acquaintances, and small businesses that are familiar with me. This includes my friends, church members, officers at my local bank, doctors and dentist, a local jeweler, my pet's veterinarian, business group associates, my mail carrier and post office tellers, the apartment's landscaper and window-washing service, and the dry cleaning store's owner. I will ask each person if he or she currently uses or is interested in buying gift baskets for personal or business use, plus inquire about other people who would be interested in my baskets. Their feedback will give me a good idea of the sales potential before branching out to service the rest of the state and developing plans for nationwide sales.

The town has a population of 10,000 residents and 150 service-related businesses. Both groups are good buying prospects because:

- Individuals give to each other for all occasions and often ship gifts to family and friends during the holidays.
- Professional businesses are always referring customers to one another. With more businesses moving in, there will be more reciprocal goodwill gift giving.

The businesses in this town and the surrounding area with the best potential for buying are:

Two landscaping companies
One corporate cleaning service
Two restaurants that host business meetings
Four real estate agencies, competing heavily through newspaper ads
One women's club
More than thirty doctors and dentists in private practices

Two hospitals
Twenty-five accounting and legal firms
Two hotels and one bed-and-breakfast
One chamber of commerce and three business organizations
Approximately fifty home offices

Each group offers individual and corporate basket sales potential. The following outlines my potential buyers list and methods to get each group's attention.

Description of Potential Buyers

I have compiled a sketch of individual buyers using 2000 census charts, data published in local newspapers, membership records from organization directories, and details of personal observations about company employees and store customers in and around town. Gift basket buyers include:

- Women, age twenty-one to fifty-five, single with no children, living alone or with a partner in a condo or townhouse. Such a buyer is a professional who frequently works overtime, travels often by air for business, and makes time for long weekend getaways. She exercises frequently as a member of a local gym. When she's not eating out or ordering takeout, she enjoys cooking and entertaining friends at home. This is a woman who understands and uses the Internet regularly.
- Women, age thirty to fifty, married with children in all age ranges, living in a single-family home. This kind of buyer is a professional who works as little overtime as possible and travels by air to company meetings. This busy woman has very little time for herself, usually prepares meals at home, and picks up takeout on weekends while completing chores. She uses a computer more frequently at work, and her children surf the Net at home.
- Men, age twenty-five to forty, single, living alone in an apartment or townhouse. Such a buyer is usually a professional, is a member of the local gym, and occasionally needs specialty gifts for women. He also has an expense account and buys thank-you gifts for staff and clients. He appreciates discretion, is an avid computer user, and uses his free time to travel, meeting other singles who use discretionary funds on gifts for themselves and others.
- Men, age thirty to forty-five, married with young children, living in a single-family home. This type of buyer is a professional who works overtime frequently and travels by

air on business. He dabbles on the Internet but doesn't have as much experience as his secretary/assistant, who is in charge of ordering the department's gifts.

This sketch, along with the comments I will incorporate from individuals, will help me determine who are the most likely individuals and businesses to approach for publicizing and selling my baskets.

Promotions

I believe that commuters who listen to three types of morning radio shows are potential clients. One station plays soft jazz, another has a country music format, and the third plays light music (a blend of 1960s–1980s hits). I will make appointments to speak with the stations' morning show producers and propose a barter arrangement that satisfies my need for publicity while providing the station's employees with break-time "rewards." In exchange for the on-air host mentioning my business and describing the bartered basket, the station's employees will share the baskets' contents. Not all radio stations accept barter agreements, so approaching three stations will increase the odds of gaining one relationship.

Several nonprofit organizations host black-tie events held throughout the year. Creating an elaborate gift basket for each event's silent auction is a small expense that will introduce my business to wealthy professionals. I will call each group and speak with the organizer to learn how I can be a part of the festivities. A photograph of the basket, organizer, and me will be taken for submission to newspapers.

Each year, the board of education holds a reading contest for elementary school children. Three winners receive a variety of prizes, and I plan to offer three gift baskets in varying sizes as part of the package. The winners will be rewarded, and my business will be showcased to teachers; principals; librarians; office workers and other administrative employees; cafeteria, maintenance, and security personnel; and parents; most of whom are part of my buyers' profile.

Other types of gift basket promotions are possible through restaurants catering to office personnel during Administrative Professionals Week and hotels that lodge convention travelers and bridal parties.

These ideas cost only the wholesale value of the products used, a few telephone calls, camera film, and postage.

Advertising

I will inquire about the cost of advertising in the newspapers and business journals that professionals read while traveling to work. My preliminary research shows that newspaper advertising doesn't work for gift basket companies, but I might consider ads for holidays and special occasions.

Next I will explore advertising under two Yellow Pages listings, one each under "Fruit" and "Gift Baskets" to double my exposure.

If the radio station promotion doesn't work out, I will ask each for a media kit with advertising rates. After reviewing the expense and area demographics, this type of advertising may prove its worth.

My computer software gives me many options to create my own stationery and business cards on quality paper purchased from a local office-supply store. Using my computer and printer with color options will make the stationery look more professional. However, if this does not work, I will explore buying stationery from a local printer or source found on the Internet.

I plan to develop flyers by computer to mail directly to professional prospects, human resources personnel, and charity organizations. Gift basket flyers and other literature must specify that the right is reserved to substitute equal- or greater-value merchandise for any order if products are unavailable due to stock or seasonal fluctuations.

Office-supply stores and stationery mail-order catalogs sell customizable doorknob hangers. They are a worthwhile expense as long as no town laws prohibit me from this kind of solicitation.

Postcards seem to be a favorite sales tool of seasoned professionals. I plan to request literature for evaluation.

Rolodex cards will accompany flyers mailed to companies or be distributed at chamber of commerce gatherings and other events. A mail-order stationery catalog received on the job has a nice selection, as well as other interesting advertising specialties.

A few businesses are using magnetic billboards and window decals as promotional advertisement on cars and vans. I will check the cost of these products and also check with my attorney for any liability concerns in case I am in a vehicular accident.

Web Site

My research into setting up a Web site and why businesses maintain a Web presence convinces me that I should place my company on the Internet.

At present, there are thousands of gift basket Internet sites. Many of them are slow to load because of photographs, and others don't have order capabilities. I plan to create a Web site using tools that make pictures load faster, add informative text and basket descriptions, include interesting facts and ideas, and market my site to local businesses and professionals who will come to town for conventions.

I also plan to create a monthly newsletter, which will be promoted on my site and in printed literature. The newsletter will contain personal and business ideas that draw the reader to my site to see and order baskets.

Preliminary research has been completed regarding Web site setup. Moorebaskets.com is available and will be registered through a low-cost domain name registrar. I wish to protect my Web name, so I will also register morebaskets.com so that competitors don't have access to this variation. My Internet service provider (ISP) has comparable Web-hosting rates to five other service providers. My final decision will depend on the ISP's reputation, support and service features, customizing options, and the availability of on-line customer ordering.

Although I can afford to hire a Web designer, I plan to create the site myself. Before starting, I will list on paper everything that will appear on my site, decide which software package will be used to design the site, and find an adult school course for design instruction.

Customer Follow-Up

After finalizing a sale to individuals or corporations, I will:

Send a thank-you card.

Send the client a birthday card each year. When completing the sale, I will ask the client for his or her birth month and log it in the database.

Mail an informational postcard every two months informing the client on new themes, new products, and holiday specials.

Ask the client for permission to subscribe her or him to my free, on-line newsletter for gift-giving ideas.

Watch the newspapers for articles on each client's industry and mail them to the client when appropriate as a constant reminder of my gift baskets.

Competition

Several stores sell either gift baskets or competitive products:

In town:
One card store
Two florists

Within 30 miles:
One discount variety store
Two department stores

Three card stores
Three florists
Eight gift basket professionals with Yellow Pages ads

On the Internet:
Two gift basket businesses in town with post office box addresses
Six gift basket companies advertising in the Yellow Pages and four hosting Web sites may be a sign that potential individual and corporate gift basket buyers are underserved.

Competitors' Strengths and Weaknesses

Retailers have a common strength. They have stores where customers come in, view merchandise, and make purchases. However, the service in most area stores borders on neglect. In just one of the five stores visited was I greeted at the door. In two stores, I paid for merchandise while the clerk was on the phone. In two other stores, I was thanked for my purchase.

The home-based gift basket companies had a lot of excuses for the baskets I pretended to want. Two companies' phones were answered by machines that identified a residence, not a business. Before one machine disconnected me, I could hear a baby crying in the background (I called again to leave a second message). They both called me in the evening. Neither had any printed sheets or pictures of their selections. One referred me to her Web site, which had badly scanned pictures and many misspelled words. Neither could ship my basket to another state without approximately three days' notice.

I sent an e-mail message to two other Internet gift basket sites and asked a few questions about one of the baskets, including how quickly it could be delivered. One answer was e-mailed two days later. The other answer took a week to arrive. In Web terms, that is a slow response rate, and I plan to provide my clients with a faster response time.

Not knowing how these companies thank or keep customers, if at all, I plan to send thank-you cards after each purchase. I will ask each customer for his or her birth month and send a birthday card at the beginning of the appropriate month. This is a quick and inexpensive way to stay in touch with them.

These facts are added incentive for me to provide customers with 100 percent better products, service, and dependability than most area stores, home-based businesses, and Internet sites currently provide.

Financial Plan

My salary is $45,000 per year, with a savings of $2,500 held for emergencies and an untouchable 401K plan. Listed here are my monthly salary and approximate expenses to show any monies left over to use for financing.

Monthly Income and Expenses:

Income
Salary (after taxes and health insurance): $3,000

Expenses
Rent: $1,000
Food (including takeout): $250
Car payment: $350
Gas for car: $100
Car insurance: $200
Utilities: $90
Telephone: $50
Cellular phone: $50
Credit cards: $150
Laundry and dry cleaning: $30
Miscellaneous (clothes, toiletries): $100
Recreation (movies, clubs, theater): $100
Internet fee: $20

Total: $2,490
Remainder/(deficit): $510

[*Author's Note:* It never seems like this much is left over each month, does it? Monitoring your financial habits, another daunting but necessary task, shows your spending patterns and money on hand during the month.]

I will open business checking and savings accounts immediately after registering my business with the proper agencies. I am determined to save $400 to place in the savings account each month to finance the gift basket business. My car payments end in three months, and I am able to trim my miscellaneous and recreation costs, which will allow me to save while covering unexpected expenses.

I will request credit history data from three major credit reporting firms and review the data for discrepancies and repair.

Alternative Money Sources

Bank

My current bank is friendly, and I am satisfied with their services. Officers and tellers know me well, which makes it easier for me to ask loan officers about building reputable credentials to apply for a future loan. Creating a Cash-Flow Projection Statement, which is included in this Business Plan, is a good way to convince my banker that I'm serious about building a profitable business.

Credit Cards

Two credit cards will be designated for business use only. Charging no more than a total of $250 on both cards each month is an affordable limit to repay without incurring interest charges.

Other Banking Needs

While at the bank, I also will inquire about a Visa/MasterCard/Discover merchant account, since clients expect payment options other than cash and check. I will also inquire about accepting credit cards at other banks and through joining industry associations.

I also will contact American Express to receive a merchant application, as this company requires applicants to call them directly.

Basket Themes

To satisfy my prospects and ensure that my business starts profitably, it will be wise to create a mix of all-occasion and special holiday themes, including:

Birthdays
Thank yous
Valentine's Day
Administrative Professionals Week
Mother's Day
Father's Day
Get well wishes
Happy Holidays
Congratulations (new baby and other good fortune)
Welcome to new home

Other themes can be created, by request, using the same items in the aforementioned designs.

Products

The products (inventory) to be purchased to start business successfully are:

Foods
Cheeses (nonrefrigerated)
Crackers (different flavors)
Coffee
Tea
Bottled water
Beef sausage (shelf stable)
Assorted nuts
Biscotti (two flavors)
Cookies (chocolate chip, shortbread)
Caramel popcorn
Jelly beans
Mints
Chocolates
Ready-to-make soups

Gifts
Puzzles
Paperweights
Notepads
Pens and pencils
Candles (votives and tapers)
Body lotions
Moisturizing creams
Soaps
Bath gels
Potpourri

Basic Supplies
Baskets—assorted sizes
Cellophane—30 inches by 100 feet, clear and printed
Basket bags

Clear tape and double-sided tape

Floral foam

Bamboo skewers

Tissue paper

Silk flowers

Star spray

Decorative picks

Premade bows; ribbon and curling ribbon

Balloons—assorted sizes

Education

One to two gift basket videos showing design basics

One bowmaking kit to learn how to make bows

Purchasing Plan

Gift trade magazine advertisements led me to order additional product catalogs by mail for future product selections.

I will call to register for the upcoming New York and Philadelphia gift shows, where products are displayed and reps answer questions on-site.

Through research and the creation of a buying chart, several gift basket product suppliers have been selected as sources of the initial merchandise. Other interesting products are available through manufacturers that sell one or two specialty products.

[*Author's note:* A sample Buying Chart is given in Chapter 4.]

I have also learned, through research, that some designers have made the mistake of purchasing what they prefer rather than buying what's best for customers. This expensive lesson will be remembered before I commit to a purchase.

As products arrive, I will check each shipment for damage and freshness dating. If no date is indicated on the package, small rectangular labels purchased at an office-supply store will be coded with a freshness date (e.g., March 28, 2004 = 03284).

How to Start the Business While I'm Working

My work schedule at the real estate agency is Monday to Friday, 8:30 A.M. to 4:30 P.M. It takes me twenty minutes to commute from work to home. There is occasional overtime, and the extra money can be used to increase my capital. Knowing that it will take many months of diligent work, research, and promotion, I plan to schedule my weekdays as follows:

1. Wake up at 5:30 A.M. Since my best work is done in the morning, I must rise early to succeed in the long run.

2. Complete preparations to get ready for the full-time job by 6:15 A.M.

3. Work on gift basket business from 6:15 to 7:45 A.M., including reading the paper, checking and updating my daily planner, recording telephone numbers to make calls, reviewing Web sites to prepare my own, checking my e-mail, and planning other work to complete during lunchtime.

   a. Eat breakfast, work on personal bills, sort laundry, and do whatever else is needed each morning.

4. Leave for job at 8:05 A.M.

5. Listen to a motivational tape or compact disc in the car to keep a daylong winning attitude.

6. Lunchtime. Depending on the day's schedule:

   a. Make business calls to wholesale companies and other sources on cellular phone.

   b. Check business phone and return as many calls as possible.

   c. Borrow/return library books or do research.

   d. Visit stores to see competitive baskets and products, noting interesting basket items and logging manufacturers' phone numbers to call for catalogs.

7. Return home around 5:00 to 5:30 P.M., depending on after-job chores. Listen to the tape or disc again while driving.

8. If possible, return phone calls from afternoon messages.

9. Enjoy dinner.

10. Complete other chores as needed.

11. Update the day's progress on computer.

12. Plan tomorrow's tasks and document them in the daily planner.

13. As inventory arrives, check items for any visible damage and store them.

14. Start experimenting with my own basket design style a few nights each week, using the recently purchased videotapes as a guide.

15. In bed around 11:00 P.M., reading a book (business manual or fiction) for about a half hour before retiring.

Office Setup and Structure

My apartment consists of one bedroom, a kitchen, a dining room, a living room, and a bath. The dining room will be converted into an office. Inventory and office supplies will fill the two storage closets. If more space is needed, especially for the inventory, there are two options:

- Use two portable screens to act as a makeshift wall in the living room to store additional inventory.
- Ask manufacturers to hold my purchases and ship on request (ask companies whether they can do this and whether extra shipping charges apply, before placing an order).

Once the dining room is converted, move the computer out of the bedroom and into the new office.

Business Registration

After researching federal trademark records on the Internet to see if the company name I choose is in use by another company, I will register the company with county and state officials. Next, I will request the paperwork from the city clerk and state tax department, complete the forms, have them notarized, and submit them for processing.

Mail

Because I do not want to encourage home soliciting, I will rent a post office box to serve as my business address. Mailbox centers are another option, but the higher rate that they charge is better spent on inventory.

Food Health Laws

Health department rules state that a business selling food out of the home is allowed to proceed (1) if the food for sale is packaged according to FDA regulations and the home-based retailer never touches the food directly or (2) the home retailer obtains a food handler's license from the county health examiner after full inspection of the home work area. Since I will only use prepackaged foods in my baskets, I can proceed with my business.

Insurance

General liability business insurance must be obtained. Since I have apartment renter's insurance, I will call the insurer to ask about coverage for a home-based business. If none is available, I will seek coverage through other carriers that advertise in craft and gift basket magazines and on the Internet, or ask friends and other professionals with home-based businesses for referrals.

Office Needs

Last year I purchased a new computer with a modem and software for business use, which includes word-processing, spreadsheet, and database capability. I also plan to purchase desktop publishing software to create advertising materials and financial management software to record sales and expenses.

My current printer has color or black-and-white printing options and also makes copies, scans, and faxes. It's still considered new and does not need replacing.

My dining room table will become the work surface for creating gift baskets. I plan to replace the tablecloth with a heavy-duty cutting surface to protect the table.

Since I live alone, I will use my home phone for business, changing the outgoing message to reflect a professional environment. I will call the telephone company and have one extra phone line installed for a fax machine. Separate lines are needed to function properly as a true home business.

External Communications

Once advertising begins, calls will come to the home office while I'm working at the other company. My best options for doing business while on the job are:

Option 1:
I will have call forwarding installed on the business phone and use it during the day to forward calls to my cellular phone. My cellular carrier gives me a voice mail option, so I can leave a friendly, detailed message on the system about hours of operation and when I return calls. This approach will let customers know when they can expect to hear from me.

I will do my best to return the phone call quickly using my cellular phone either outside the office building or in the car.

Option 2:
If calls become too frequent and I still can't afford to leave the job, I will investigate employing an at-home person, training him or her on telephone order taking, and transferring my business phone to this person's home telephone line on weekdays.

The person will call me for emergencies; otherwise, I can call him or her three times a day for morning, afternoon, and after-work messages. The person's salary can be a combination of a base rate per hour plus commission on each order taken.

Shipping and Deliveries

Shipping

With more professionals moving into the area, ABC Delivery and General Express have become visible around town. Calls placed to both companies on shipping prices and arrival times will reveal approximate shipping costs and customers' charges.

The price of boxes and bubble wrap for shipping baskets will be compared at several local, catalog, and Internet-based suppliers before final purchase.

Deliveries

At first, basket deliveries will be difficult if not impossible for me to do, especially during the week. Weekend deliveries are more probable. I don't properly service my car and must begin a maintenance schedule for my own safety and to drive confidently to customer appointments.

The wise choice is to set up an account with an affordable courier whose time is flexible, whose fee is reasonable, and who is able to accommodate my sporadic needs. Each floral competitor has a delivery van. The companies are very competitive, and newspapers report that the tires of each other's vans are mysteriously slashed on occasion. These reports convince me not to approach either firm about renting their services to deliver baskets.

Expansion

Within one year I expect my gift basket gross profits to total approximately $9,000, as shown on the proposed cash-flow statement. The income will be made by serving:

- Individuals working in various office settings
- Corporations that use baskets for their clients and staff
- Independent professionals who thank staff members for their hard work and colleagues for referrals
- Organizations that depend on corporate support and need baskets to thank the corporations for donations

As with most companies, I expect not to make a profit the first year. The costs of a start-up, inventory-driven business are expensive, but the future benefits are rewarding. In the second year, inventory and advertising products are well in place to attempt making a profit, no matter how small.

When I have established myself as a profitable gift basket professional with a growing list of clients, other ideas will be incorporated to sell gift baskets throughout the state and country. My plans include:

1. Moving my residence from the small apartment to a townhouse, where two rooms will be converted into a larger office and workspace.
2. Having the part-time employee "graduate" from taking phone orders to being an office helper.
3. Adding pages of photos to my Web site, using it as my prime source for promotion. With more of my prospects using the Web at home and work, my site will eliminate the expense of creating a printed color catalog.
4. Installing a toll-free number if at least one-third of my clients are located out of town.
5. Leasing a van for basket deliveries.
6. Introducing pet, aromatherapy, and a new line of men's baskets.
7. Courting new clients, such as hospitality employees and civil service workers, two additional groups that buy gift baskets but have little time to shop due to work schedules.
8. Resigning from the real estate firm when my efforts consistently pay my personal expenses, provide overage for salary and retirement savings, and allow for saving enough income to cover one year of personal and business expenses.
9. Continuing my education as needed.
10. Consulting with an industry adviser for answers to technical questions and to conduct better business overall.

Action Plan with Completion Dates

Credentials

1. Find and enroll in a gift basket design class. Check adult school course listings at the library, in newspapers, at community colleges, and on the Internet. Also check on the location and price of future gift basket conferences—1/04.
2. Enroll in adult school classes to strengthen my entrepreneurial skills and heighten my success aptitude—first quarter '04.
3. Investigate and sign up for upcoming business workshops sponsored by the state, SCORE, and the Small Business Development Center—first quarter '04.

Marketing

1. Begin a word-of-mouth advertising campaign by announcing my gift basket business to individuals, acquaintances, and small-business owners who are familiar with me. Create and distribute business cards, encourage these people's opinions, document their comments in my database, and decide who will receive initial advertising messages—fourth quarter '03–first quarter '04.

2. Call the three radio stations to gauge their interest in a barter agreement for employee snack gift baskets in exchange for a radio promotion. If a barter agreement is not possible, request a media kit to review paid promotion rates—11/03.

3. Contact the organizers of annual black-tie fundraisers to explore how my business can be part of next year's festivities—first quarter '04.

4. Find out from the board of education when the next reading contest will be held and if gift baskets would be welcomed as a prize. Over time, search for appropriate products for these baskets—1/04.

5. Contact sales and marketing managers at area restaurants and hotels to propose working together to promote our respective businesses through providing gift baskets for their guests—first quarter '04.

6. Call the telephone company and inquire about Yellow Pages ad prices—10/03.

7. Check town solicitation laws regarding doorknob hangers. If no restrictions, purchase hangers, customize, and distribute—fourth quarter '03.

8. Purchase Rolodex cards, thank-you cards, and birthday cards, and also purchase premium paper in several colors at the office-supply store to create flyers—fourth quarter '03.

9. Call attorney regarding liability concerns using magnetic signs and promotional decals on my personal automobile. If OK, research both products and order when ready—first quarter '04.

10. Order gift basket postcard samples and information—11/03.

11. Clip interesting articles and send to clients—ongoing.

12. Register my chosen Web site name with a domain name registrar—fourth quarter '03.

13. Compare Web-hosting services and choose one to use to support my Internet site. Research which Web site software will be easiest to use, and make sure that the software is compatible with the chosen Web service—first quarter '04.

14. Subscribe to several free, on-line newsletters that are gift basket and non–gift basket related. Review each to decide what my newsletter will include. Create a mock issue and edit as needed. Collect e-mail addresses and launch newsletter when Web site is on-line—second quarter '04.

Competition

1. Visit competing stores to view gift baskets and other merchandise. Check basket prices and in-store products for ideas and basket design styles—11/03–ongoing.
2. Continue to watch the growth of Web sites on the Internet, specifically any that appear from my town and surrounding areas—ongoing.
3. Document how companies in other industries win accounts despite the competition, and use their experience to stay ahead of my own—ongoing.

Financial Plan

1. Request personal credit reports from three agencies—12/03.
2. Open business savings and checking accounts at my current bank or at another establishment that offers merchant accounts—first quarter '04.
3. Deposit $400 in the savings account each month for business capital—ongoing.
4. Consult with a loan officer on borrowing options and credential updating—fourth quarter '03–first quarter '04.
5. Create a cash-flow projection statement—fourth quarter '03–first quarter '04.
6. Call American Express to request merchant account application—11/03.

Purchasing Plan

1. After reviewing samples, subscribe to gift trade magazines—first–second quarter '04.
   a. Order catalogs from manufacturers advertising goods and services—fourth quarter '03–ongoing.
2. Attend trade shows to view products, ask questions, and get catalogs—first quarter '04.
3. Buy products after conducting thorough research and planning purchases on a buying chart—first–second quarter '04.
   a. When products arrive, inspect inventory for damage and freshness before stocking on shelves. Label any products needing freshness dates—ongoing after first purchase.

Office Setup

1. Check federal records on the Internet for business name duplication—fourth quarter '03.
2. Get business registration papers from county and state officials. Complete and return them promptly—fourth quarter '03.

One-Year Cash Flow Projection Statement
Moore Baskets
October 2003–September 2004

	OCT	NOV	DEC	JAN	FEB	MAR	
Income							
Sales	$125	$300	$1,550	$775	$820	$265	
Shipping/Delivery	25	80	32	16	43	53	
Total	$150	$380	$1,582	$791	$863	$318	
	Small-business sales	Hostess & new home	Christmas holiday	New Year's	Valentine's Day	Everyday themes	
Expenses							
Post office:							
Postage	$28	$53	$62	$40	$71	$23	
Box fee		55					
Delivery:							
Courier					50		
ABC Shipping			20	10	15		
Boxes		30			40		
Shipping supplies		20			20		
Business name registration	35						
Notary public	2						
Liability insurance	350						
Office equipment:							
PDA			150				
Fax machine		150					
Storage bins	25			10			
Office supplies	20		10		25		
Advertising:							
Yellow Pages						40	
Rolodex cards		45					
Doorknob hangers				28			
Postcards			95			95	
Other						10	

	APR	MAY	JUN	JUL	AUG	SEP	TOTAL
	$650	$875	$1,050	$800	$275	$560	$8,045
	30	40	24	318	35	133	$829
	$680	$915	$1,074	$1,118	$310	$693	$8,874
	Admin. Prof. Day	Mother's Day	Father's Day; weddings	Hotels & conferences	Everyday themes	College/ back to school	
	$42	$50	$40	$38	$33	$35	$515
							55
	45					30	125
	6	28	12		14	58	163
			25			30	125
			10			15	65
							35
							2
							350
							150
							150
		10					45
			35			18	108
	40	40	40	40	40	40	280
		45					90
			28				56
					95		285
			23			10	43

One-Year Cash Flow Projection Statement
Moore Baskets
October 2003–September 2004

	OCT	NOV	DEC	JAN	FEB	MAR	
Subscriptions:							
Trade magazines		50					
Newspapers	30			30			
Education				100		200	
Software/books	75		200		25		
Travel:							
Mileage (@ .36/mi.)	16	18	23	14	32	20	
Tolls	2		6	4	8		
Parking			5	2	7		
Meals				15		25	
Car insurance (½)*				75	75	75	
Communications:							
Telephone	45	40	50	42	45	43	
Fax line installation		125					
Cellular phone	43	53	44	48	52	48	
Fax	15	14	23	26	19	16	
Utilities (¼ elec. bill)**	10	13	15	12	18	16	
Banking:							
Bank service charge	12	12	12	12	12	12	
Check printing		85					
Merchant account fee				25	30	22	
Internet:							
Monthly fee	20	20	20	20	20	20	
Web site w/cart				35	35	35	
Donations					75		
Inventory	580	273	420	128		106	
Monthly expenses	$1,308	$1,056	$1,155	$676	$674	$806	
Monthly profit/(loss)	($1,158)	($676)	$427	$115	$189	($488)	

* Car insurance—car driven 50 percent for personal use, 50 percent for business.

** Four-room apartment with one room used for workspace = ¼ of bill allocated for business.

	APR	MAY	JUN	JUL	AUG	SEP	TOTAL
							50
	30			30			120
				200			500
							300
	25	30	13	42	35	22	290
	7			8			35
	3			5		4	26
			5	30			75
	75	75	75	75	75	75	675
	40	45	38	33	35	40	496
							125
	42	44	45	44	38	40	541
	14	23	28	25	19	16	238
	15	12	12	16	15	14	168
	12	12	12	12	12	12	144
							85
	28	33	22	23	21	24	228
	20	20	20	20	20	20	240
	35	35	35	35	35	35	315
		100		85			260
	48		212		380		2,147
	$527	$602	$730	$761	$867	$538	$9,700
	$153	$313	$344	$357	($557)	$155	($826)

3. Convert the dining area into an office and basket design workspace—first quarter '04.

4. Call apartment renter's insurance company to find out whether or not additional coverage for home-based businesses is available. If not, seek insurance through other reputable sources—fourth quarter '03.

5. Investigate the cost of buying a fax machine, and make an appointment for the installation of a separate telephone line—fourth quarter '03–first quarter '04.

6. Recheck the health department's laws on operating a business at home using prepackaged foods—first quarter '04.

7. Open post office box for business mail—fourth quarter '03–first quarter '04.

8. Ask friends, family, and associates to refer at-home telephone sales help candidates—as needed.

Shipping and Deliveries

1. Call shippers and couriers for rates—fourth quarter '03–first quarter '04.
2. Make an appointment for car service with either a recommended mechanic or my car's service dealer—fourth quarter '03.
3. Find and compare costs of box and bubble-wrap suppliers before purchasing—first quarter '04.

Expansion

Review and update expansion plans at least every three months, or as needed.

will experience that pave the road to success. There isn't one businessperson on earth who hasn't been disconnected, been let down, or had an unpleasant surprise, yet each has learned to take it all in stride, knowing that with every step the businessperson comes closer to reaching his or her intended destination or one that's better than originally planned.

Review this self-analysis and see how your personality compares with the traits exhibited and religiously practiced by today's successful gift basket professional.

Patience and Temperament

In this business you wait for clients, wait for deliveries, and wait for payment, and that's just for starters. Do you have the tolerance to wait patiently without erupting like a seething volcano? Balloons will break en route to the client, and unsecured baskets will grow wings and fly through the air from the back to the front seat of your car when you stop suddenly at a red light. Mood swings due to personal conflicts cannot be reflected in your attitude toward clients. Exasperating times will and do occur more often than not, but these can be handled positively as you begin to master good planning and budgeting skills, dashed with a healthy dose of on-the-spot meditation.

Organization

Do you have the ability to maintain an efficient, orderly system to find a document at a moment's notice? This is not a business where paperwork has the option to run amok, only to be found when it's least needed. The same applies to maintaining an orderly design workspace. If you find your legs tangled in a mass of curling ribbon, that's a sure sign that chaos has entered the building. Quickly usher it out by putting an end to the mess before it's completely out of control.

Discipline

This is the ability to instinctively develop fine-tuned habits of performing tasks within a given amount of time. There's no more dancing to the beat of an employer's time clock. You must set and keep generally accepted business hours while being available to speak with clients who expect you to accommodate their needs at a moment's notice. Grouping separate tasks to do in a set period, rather than performing one thing that takes eight hours, increases the success ratio over time.

Determination

Nothing worthwhile comes easy in life no matter how simple it looks, and gift baskets are no exception. What will you do if the phone doesn't ring as often as expected or if marketing efforts don't immediately bring sales? Consistently employing an "I can" attitude and methodically planning new actions to target the marketplace are the stance all winners embrace, and so should you.

Personality Plus

It's more than just a term in a high school yearbook. Mingling among throngs of new people in social settings who are prime buying candidates will be part of your business's claim to fame. Since prospects don't line up on doorsteps begging for baskets, the extrovert gift basket professional busily connects with contacts who need gift baskets for personal, professional, and organizational use. Striking up conversations with prospects on subjects you have in common is key to the successful sell. Limiting your apprehensions about meeting new people makes this task a smooth-sailing event.

Instinct

Clients, through no fault of their own, don't always express their needs succinctly. It's up to you to guide them through the initial meeting and order process, giving them useful ideas through understanding their unique gift-giving needs to ensure that the right basket is given for each event or occasion. This skill takes practice; however, an open mind and an eagerness to assist the beleaguered client make this process easier. As my good friend and colleague Flora Brown, of Gift Baskets by Flora, explains, "I hear what they don't say." Develop your inner sense of understanding, and reap the waiting rewards.

If your personal assessment suggests you're doing well in most areas, that's a big step in preparing yourself for the years ahead. If help is needed to strengthen these characteristics, find tips to elevate them through speaking with others who regularly deal with similar situations. In no time you'll find yourself moving triumphantly through the challenges of owning a thriving business.

Love and Support from Family and Friends

You're about to give birth. It may be the first time or the fourth (three prior children are at home, in college, or on their own). Like all babies, this one needs changing, it needs love, and, yes, it will keep you up at night. Over the years, you'll worry about the direction it's taking and be proud when it makes the "good news" headlines.

If you're single with no children, you're free and clear to start the business at home as you wish. Having a family and starting a business require a mix of consideration and compassion for the pending changes at home.

Family support has a dual role. Family members will want and need to be included in your decision to start the business and be kept up to date on its progress. As this business is a new addition to the family, it will compete for your attention. Everyone at home will feel the strain as you work on this new "bundle of joy." Lessen the burden by introducing the "baby" as one that will increase your personal satisfaction while keeping you closer to home.

Your own understanding of how family members feel is important to winning their support. Some families will welcome the change with open arms, while others will be apprehensive and downright defensive, feeling like a "foreign object" is invading their turf. They're afraid of encountering disruptions to the home schedule, entering a quiet house if they're used to your presence, and being faced with frozen dinners and take-out meals every other night. The threat of change creates a tornado of tension, stress, and emotional upheaval. Understanding your family's concerns starts by including them in tasks that you know they'll enjoy. Introduce your plans by sharing a vision on their important roles as volunteers:

- *Taste testers.* Everyone likes tasting new foods and snacks and giving his or her opinion. As products arrive, announce the taste-testing schedule for one night each week until the work is complete. Remind family members that it's a tough job, but somebody has to do it.
- *Evaluators.* Men can rate the men's-based gifts, baskets, and containers. Their feedback can help you choose products in catalogs before shipments arrive. The same applies for women rating women's gifts if you are a man starting a business. Children can rate gifts for babies and other youngsters.

Although your buying decision is final, the family will enjoy their consulting positions and look forward to seeing what's in each new box.

Set specific hours for working on business. Answer the business phone only within those hours or you'll find home life disrupted by clients calling at 11:00 P.M. Post the hours in your phone message, on flyers and other literature, and in a visible area in the home. Your family will soon accept the schedule, and clients will also learn to respect the hours of operation.

Your list of personal and professional chores will quickly become unmanageable if you're not using a daily planner. As an investment in time and sanity, the daily planner should be consulted every morning and last thing at night. Every deadline, appointment, and important person must be logged each day. A typical planner contains (1) a monthly calendar, usually separated on two facing pages, with boxes for entering appointments and other vital information; (2) a daily schedule to plan the day's chores and a "completed" box to check each item when accomplished; (3) a telephone directory, listing everything from your best client to the local pizza parlor; (4) a notes section, to jot down thoughts or important telephone numbers to call later; and (5) other sections, as needed. The planner, whether a book or electronic device, is your unpaid assistant, working twenty-four hours a day to ensure that neither family nor business suffers in the hectic months ahead.

Friends will also go through changes. Your announcement soon separates true friends from the rest. Friends give praise and cheer, saying that it's about time you took the plunge. The rest won't believe you can succeed, will doubt your abilities, and will become jealous. It's a tough decision, but you must decide if pessimistic people are part of the support team or a strain on your will to succeed. Starting a business is hard enough without having someone constantly reminding you of past mistakes. Tell the nonbelievers that you're so busy with your plans that you won't have time to call them. They'll find fault with this too, but it's OK—you expect it. Just as you've found the courage in deciding to start a business, so too must you summon the same strength to leave negative people behind.

Also, think twice before revealing your plans to coworkers. Gossip spreads through an office like wildfire, and you may find yourself butting heads with a boss who is not pleased with your plans. Keep your new business separate from your current employment, and find the freedom to accomplish your goals without additional job stress.

A Winning Attitude

Relentless pursuit and determination to succeed—this is a phrase that sums up the spirit of a winner. Some are born with it, and others develop the drive over time. The winning attitude builds itself differently in every person but brings us all to the same conclusion that it's time to be the boss. Here are ways to stay positive as you proceed:

- Listen to motivational tapes. Empower yourself every day when you shop, commute, wait in line, wash laundry, exercise, and perform routine tasks.
- Join business groups. Attend a few meetings before deciding which ones help in gaining new clients and meeting other successful people. Also, make sure that you agree with the group's overall mission.
- Watch positive infomercials. Why not listen to a free motivational message? Buy the product if you choose, but just listening energizes you.
- Read about successful entrepreneurs, and mold their message of success for your use.
- Keep the winning attitude alive twenty-four hours a day by focusing on the positive side of every situation—for example, the glass is half full, not half empty; you have a flat tire, but it's a beautiful, sunshine-filled day; and you didn't sell the client a gift basket, but with a better approach next time you *will* make the sale. Switch the winning attitude on each morning like an automatic pilot. If you have a partner, you will motivate each other, but when you're a sole proprietor, you must be committed to making motivation a daily habit.

Building a Superb Reputation

We are all judged by our actions. If you promise to mail a package or call someone, do it in a timely fashion. Your reputation precedes you and lasts long after your career is over.

If a friend borrows money but never repays you, what does her reputation become? What would creditors think if they had to call you each month for payment? To build a good reputation:

- Request your credit profiles from Experian (800–397–3742), Equifax (800–685–1111), and TransUnion (800–888–4213). You can also request a profile on the Internet at www.experian.com, www.equifax.com, and www.transunion. com. Although you cannot completely delete negative credit, check your credit history for discrepancies and to review what a bank and other creditors read to determine if you are a good credit risk. Don't wait until you submit a loan application.
- Check yourself. Are you like the fictitious borrowing friend? Do you pay your bills on time? If you have difficulty remembering due dates, your daily planner will keep your payments on track. Enter due dates on the calendar, and prepare bills at least five days before they're due.
- Treat everyone with respect, even your competitors, who may one day recommend clients to you or do another valuable favor. New business comes from everywhere. From a taxi driver to an ambassador, treat everyone as you want to be treated.

Preparation, support, a good attitude, and a great reputation—every success story shares these traits. Join the club, and work to succeed on your own terms.

What It Takes to Succeed Checklist

1. Prepare a business plan, including:
   - Your goals and credentials _____
   - Marketing plan _____
   - Competition research _____
   - Financial plan _____
   - Gift basket themes and purchasing _____
   - Dividing time between employment and start-up _____
   - Office and workspace plans _____
   - Shipping and delivery schedule _____
   - Cash-flow projections _____
   - Expansion details _____
   - Action plan with completion dates _____

2. Introduce your family to your plans to start a business. _____
   Offer them "positions" as taste testers and evaluators. _____

3. Purchase a daily planner book or electronic device to track personal and professional tasks. _____

4. Choose friends wisely and tell them about your business carefully. _____

5. Perform a personal assessment of your:
   - Strengths—List what makes you a candidate to become a successful gift basket professional. _____
   - Weaknesses—List the situations and activities that frustrate you and how to keep minor problems from derailing your business. _____

6. Strengthen your winning attitude.
   - Listen to motivational tapes. _____
   - Read success stories. _____
   - Watch positive television shows. _____
   - Join business groups. _____

7. Create a better personal reputation.
   - Request and edit your credit profiles. _____
   - Pay bills on time and stay true to your word. _____
   - Treat everyone respectfully. _____

Chapter Three

Home Office and Workspace Setup and Structure

Choosing a Business Name

Naming a business is monumental. It should be an easy task, but between having a unique, memorable name and staying within guidelines, name selection can be tough. When I attended a How to Start a Business class years ago, the instructor said that a company's name should reflect the business itself so that people would easily know what's for sale. At the time, I wanted to open an intimate apparel boutique and remembered thinking that the name Lane Bryant did not identify it as a full-figured women's clothing store. What about the name Payless, whose title assumes you won't pay much, but for what?

Those stores are nationally known because of aggressive advertising and mall presence throughout the country. If they were regional stores like Safeway or Winn-Dixie, you'd have no clue of their industry if you were living outside the selling region.

A business name can be as simple as Gift Baskets by [Your Name] or something more elaborate, reflecting the service or a theme, such as All Occasion Baskets, Solutions in a Basket, A Basket Because, Baskets to Remember, Attention to Detail, or Sentiments.

The name you choose must (1) make a personal statement, (2) be easy for customers to remember, and (3) not resemble another company's name, with the exception of the word *basket,* the common denominator that links thousands of businesses in this industry.

Give the name proper consideration before committing it to business cards and state registration. Ask trusted friends and family for their opinion, but take it with a grain of salt. If you truly love the name you choose, that's the one to use.

It is also very important that the business name be spelled correctly. There is no excuse for distributing promotional materials with incorrect spellings. Unfortunately, correspondence will sometimes be mailed with a spelling or punctuation error due to haste or ignorance. I've seen the word *conscious* become *concous,* and I have spelled *savvy* as *saavy.* What is the image of a company that spells its name wrong or whose correspondence is riddled with errors? Even before a prospect sees the baskets, the perception is that the gift baskets are sloppy, the company won't deliver properly, and the business won't last. I once created a fabulous brochure with a terrible mistake—one of the words on the front flap was incorrectly spelled. I missed it, and so did the computer's spell check (technology is truly wonderful). The fifty brochures were mailed before the error was caught. Applying the only logical solution, I reprinted the brochures and mailed them again with a note stating, "Whoops! We made a slight error on our first brochure. Please discard it and replace it with the enclosed one. Thank you." Check and correct all spelling, because your business depends on it.

Should You Consider a Trademark?

Dear   :

Your company name [name of company] is in violation of trademark infringement against our client, who has legal claim as the sole bearer of this name under the laws of the U.S. Department of Commerce, Patent and Trademark Office.

You are advised to immediately cease and desist using the name [name of company], striking it from all stationery, literature, and materials in your possession. We expect confirmation of the termination by mail within thirty days of receipt of this letter. Failing to comply with this request will result in costly legal consequences.

Call us at (707) 555–6868 with any questions. Thank you for your cooperation.

Sincerely,

Would receiving this letter ruin your day? Of course, and possibly ruin the time and money invested in everything registered and personalized with that name. Before making the ultimate commitment, it's best to research the name to ensure no chance of trademark infringement. A trademark, as defined by the U.S. Department of Commerce, Patent and Trademark Office (PTO), in Arlington, Virginia, is a name or combination name and design (logo) that identifies a company or an individual acting as a company. Trademarks are researched by either a hired attorney or an individual. The search is available at any federal depository library located in all fifty states (call 800–PTO–9199 [800–786–9199] or 703–308–4357 for the nearest location), or you can search the PTO's Internet database at www.uspto.gov/main/trademarks.htm.

If you decide to apply for a trademark, your options are twofold. First is to request the forms from the PTO, reviewing them thoroughly before you start. The language is straightforward, and PTO staff are available to answer questions. If errors are found on the completed submission, the PTO sends back notice of the problem(s) and the probable solution(s). Edit the submission and resubmit the paperwork. Second is to enlist the paid services of an attorney versed in trademark procedures. The same error notice and resubmission apply here too, except the attorney handles the work.

The PTO's current trademark application fee is $335. This is a minimal charge when you add up the cost to change your name, stationery, business cards, Web site address, and promotional products, not to mention your priceless reputation. Approval can take up to two years or more in some cases. Once approved, the trademark is enforced for ten years, then updated according to PTO rules. Even if no one currently uses your business name and you don't apply for a trademark, someone else can trademark the name years later, giving him or her the legal right to have an attorney send you that wonderful cease-and-desist letter.

Existing in every state are gift basket businesses using untrademarked, duplicated names. If you are running a business that you expect to keep for life, research the business name and consider obtaining a trademark.

I almost cried when I saw the name of my business on someone else's card. I immediately looked up the name and got a trademark. Now no one else can use the name.

Local Name Registration

Once the business name is chosen, it must be registered with the proper city, county, and state officials. As each state has different requirements, ask local county officials about the procedures, which may include a small registration charge. Any form needing a notary's stamp is usually completed free of charge by your bank. The sample Generic County Registration Form gives you an idea of the generally asked questions.

State registration is usually more lengthy but easy to complete. Some of the questions are: (1) Is the business seasonal? (2) What is the business structure (sole proprietorship, corporation, etc.)? and (3) Will you collect sales tax? After the form is reviewed and approved by the state, you receive a business license with your name, business name and address, and tax identification number (TIN). A sole proprietor's identification may consist of the owner's Social Security number divided like this: 555–555–555/000, or your state may issue a different type of business ID. Once the business license is issued, you'll need a resale form to accompany the license. The resale form will enable you to buy gift basket products without paying state sales tax. Each state has its own resale form, which is available through your state's tax department or other issuing authority and can be duplicated as needed for purchases. The resale form comes with instructions that explain how to complete it before submitting it for purchases from a manufacturer or retail store. Make about twenty-five copies of this license and place them in a secure file to use as needed. It proves that you are a registered business authorized to purchase tax-exempt merchandise from manufacturers, representatives, and other sellers.

Sales Tax Collection

Gift baskets are considered luxury items, and as with all luxuries, they are taxed when sold. The entire basket price is calculated for sales tax, not each basket's components. If a customer orders one or two individual items, sales tax is charged for each product, just as in a department store. For example, if you work in New York City and sell a $50 gift basket, the sales tax percentage added, according to New York State law, is 8¼ percent; $50 + $4.13 (8.25 percent of $50) equals a total sale of $54.13. Accordingly, if a client orders three packages of his or her favorite truffles at $4.00 each, the total sale is $12.99 ($4.00 x 3 = $12.00 + $0.99 tax).

Generic County Registration Form

State of _____

County/municipality _____

The undersigned hereby certifies that _____(name of person)_____ is conducting business

under the name _____(business name)_____ ,

which operates as a _____(sole proprietorship, partnership, corporation)_____ under the laws of the

above-named state. The business is located at _____(complete street address)_____ ,

____(suite/room/apt)____ , _____(city)_____ , ___(state)___ , __(zip code)__ . The nature

of this _____(product or service)_____

business is _____(explain fully)_____

_____ .

The names and addresses of all owners of the above-named business are as follows:

Name   Address (if post office box, also list street address)

_____   _____

_____   _____

_____   _____

The representative of this business declares that the above information is true and correct.

_____

Signature

_____   _____

(print name)   Date

Signed in the presence of:

_____

Signature of witness

Witnessed this _____ day of _____ , 20____ .

_____

(print name)

Your state's tax division should have a handy booklet that explains the intricacies of sales tax collection.

Upon registration, a coupon book of sales tax remittance forms will be mailed to you. These forms are completed according to each state's laws, clearly explained in the documents accompanying the coupon book. In New Jersey the ST–51 form is filed monthly if a merchant (also known as the business owner) collects sales tax of $500 or more; otherwise, the ST–50 quarterly form is filed even if no sales tax is collected for the period, or the merchant is subject to fines and penalties for not filing. Two reasons why no sales tax is collected in some months are (1) a person just registered the business and has not begun to sell merchandise and (2) all sales for the period were based out of state, whether physically in another location or sold to clients by phone or fax or on-line. Currently, sales tax is collected on in-state sales only (the state where the business is registered). Some states would like Congress to change this law, as they feel cheated because merchants do not collect sales tax for all states or on Internet sales. For now the in-state tax law stands.

Zoning Issues

Your town has zoning laws set up for every street. This means that the block you live on is designated either residential only; a mix of residential and professional business offices (doctors, dentist, etc.); or a mix of residential, professional, and retail. If your block has private houses and no businesses, you probably think that the zoning law is just for homes, but you could be wrong. Doctors could have set up practices on your block long before you arrived, and the street may be zoned for offices. There's only one way to know, and that's to contact your town's zoning department.

The purpose of calling the zoning department is to find out if you can legally set up shop at home. Ask questions to find out the parameters for doing business on your block without volunteering information that you are considering starting a business. The worst-case scenario is that you're told that the block is zoned residential only, absolutely no businesses, even home-based ones without a sign. Don't panic. Let's sort through the options that keep you on track.

Making the Best of Your Home-Based Location

It's a sure bet that some businesses currently operate at home with no knowledge of city laws, block zoning, and so on. Some may not want to know the law for fear of having to close business if they are deemed illegal, but ignorance is not bliss. Neighbors or rivals can report you to local authorities, who will investigate and send their version of the dreaded cease-and-desist letter if they find any violation. Instead of letting things get out of control, be proactive. Find out the zoning rules as part of your action plan, and treat this as just another procedure.

Decide whether you are more comfortable asking questions about your block's zoning ordinance by phone or in person. In either case, you must ensure that all questions and answers are clearly understood by you and the zoning official. Ask if there are other city blocks that were zoned residential only and were changed to business/residential. If so, find out the details: (1) What are the procedures for pursuing the change? (2) Is a lawyer needed to present the case to the zoning board? and (3) How long does the process take from petition to decision? Each response will lead to other questions. Don't leave the office until you understand every option. Remember to keep a winning attitude. (See Chapter 2.) The advantages are that your gift basket business adds sales tax revenue to state coffers, does not allow visitors to the residence and therefore adds no extra block traffic, supports community organizations and charities through donations, causes no pollution or damage to existing structures, and is not a nuisance. If you are planning to take your cause to the zoning board, this is your best ammunition. The action taken is up to you. Knowing local laws and the options ahead of time to avoid future problems lets you continue opening for business on schedule.

Working with an Accountant

Choosing an accountant is a critical step in weaving your way through the maze of bookkeeping basics and IRS laws. How do you find an accountant who specializes in small business?

- Through recommendations from other small-business colleagues, by phone, at meetings, or at social functions

- By contacting state accounting associations for referrals
- Through bookkeeping and accounting teachers at adult schools (some teachers are CPAs)

A certified public accountant (CPA) is a person who, after passing stringent state testing, is granted a license to practice accounting, which includes performing audits and issuing financial statements. Decide if you want to work with a state-licensed professional or a public accountant, who possibly knows the same information but has not yet passed the state test.

When you've located a contender, his or her credentials must be thoroughly checked just as you would do for any other business entity entrusted to provide an important service. When I sought an accountant, one introduced herself at a business meeting. As she continued the introduction, she mentioned her political aspirations. Up went the red flag. I envisioned her attending to her own career and not to my account. My search then led me to a CPA I had met years before who in the interim had added more experience to her impeccable track record of working with small businesses. She is a professional who speaks with me whenever I need help, never talking above my level of understanding. Her fee is reasonable, and over the years I've been satisfied with her knowledge and advice.

State accounting associations offer pamphlets on choosing a CPA; such literature includes questions to ask and more sources for retaining help. In addition, without becoming a full-fledged accountant, it is wise to enroll in a basic bookkeeping course. Knowing a debit from a credit helps you correctly maintain sales and expense records and other important documents.

Choosing a Business Structure

Gift basket businesses are sole proprietors, partnerships, corporations, or limited liability corporations (LLCs), and a knowledgeable accountant will steer you through the business structure decision. Sole proprietors are the biggest industry group because this structure is the easiest to set up and maintain.

A *sole proprietor,* also known as the owner of the business, has complete control over the day-to-day business operations. There is no "salary," but the owner may draw funds from the business income for personal needs. The business owner is taxed on all income derived from selling gift baskets, basket components, and anything else sold under the business umbrella.

A sole proprietor's business is funded through the owner's personal assets and outside credit sources, which include loans from banks and family members. Many sole proprietors work alone, employing family or outside help if needed during the holidays and busy times. This business cannot be transferred to a new owner; rather, the business is sold and the new owner opens a brand-new business under his or her control. If the owner dies, the business ceases operation, with all assets transferred to the owner's estate. Unlimited risk for losses incurred is the sole proprietor's responsibility, and all personal assets (car, home, bank account, etc.) are subject to seizure if the business closes with outstanding debts. Still, this form of business ownership is the most preferred nationwide.

Partnerships are formed by two (or sometimes more) people, most often when one person likes creating baskets, while the other is versed at keeping the books, negotiating, or performing other service-based skills. Agreements are strongly recommended, as they state each partner's level of participation, direct who controls each aspect of the business, determine each partner's share of profits and losses, and specify how the business will be terminated if a partner leaves or dies.

As with a sole proprietorship, each partner may draw down funds from business income, which is deducted from that month's receipts. Profits are distributed to each partner according to the terms stated in the partnership agreement. Additional capital is found through new investments of cash from either partner or through the admission of a new partner. If an additional partner is admitted, a new partnership agreement must be drawn. Each partner is personally responsible for the debts of the business.

> *My mother and I are partners. If something goes wrong, we*
> *motivate each other and keep the business going strong.*

> *I had a partner who was good at selling—her own baskets!*
> *The relationship was undermined from the start because she*
> *was my friend and I didn't insist on having a contract.*

Home Office and Workspace Setup and Structure

Gift basket professionals also incorporate for legal purposes they feel protect them against losses a sole proprietor or partners may incur. A *corporation* is recognized as an entity separate from the personal assets of the owner(s), which means that all liabilities (payments to creditors, legal problems, etc.) are limited to the corporation's assets. Stocks or bonds can be sold to the public to raise cash, but in doing so the owner(s) must explain the business's direction to the stockholders. A corporation's owner can also be an employee and draw a taxable salary. The corporation's life is unlimited, still operates after an owner's death, and is easily transferred to another person, with no effect to the business.

A *limited liability corporation,* also known as an LLC, is an ownership option that many gift basket professionals consider. Unlike the sole proprietorship, an LLC is seen as a more effective way to limit the liability of your assets in case of lawsuits. Business owners complete the same year-end federal tax documents as a sole proprietor. Some states do not recognize LLCs as business entities, however, so you should consult your attorney to determine the best business structure for a small business in your state.

Although sole proprietorships and partnerships are more risky because of personal liability, they will continue as the dominant industry structures guided by some basic rules:

1. Follow health regulations (never touch foods being sold to the customer, unless you secure a food handler's permit from your local health department).
2. Insure the business (against unavoidable injuries, etc.).
3. Trademark your name.
4. Be aware of zoning laws.

Choosing an Attorney

Attorneys are sought mainly for small-business legalities you neither have access to nor can stay up to date on. Issues such as liability for reselling foods that may harm a recipient (allergic reactions, early or unknown spoilage and other illness-related problems) are a valid concern. A rule of thumb is to purchase prepackaged foods and other edibles with stamped expiration dates (or dates you adhere by label after purchase), never touching the food except for the outside wrapping. Each state has its own laws pertaining to food resale restrictions, and an attorney, preferably one in your state who is versed in small-business issues and liability law, will have the information you need.

Attorneys can also help you incorporate your business, if you so choose, or trademark the business name. While you are busily completing gift basket orders and deliveries, an attorney can be at work for you to keep your business legally working in good order.

Contact your state bar association for small-business attorney referrals, and ask friends and family members for recommendations. Legal help is also available through several industry associations that often provide assistance through a phone-based service. For a monthly fee, charged by credit card, a legal service lets you call whenever necessary to ask business-related questions.

Insurance Needs

A general liability policy for a gift basket business provides $1 million of coverage and costs several hundred dollars per year. It is available through industry and business associations and independent carriers. Also check your existing homeowner's, apartment dweller's, and car insurance provider for riders to existing coverage for home-based businesses and car deliveries.

> *I had insurance the first day I opened for business. My homeowner's policy did not protect me in case of a lawsuit, so I checked around for a good rate before settling on a carrier.*

If anyone other than you or a bonded courier delivers your baskets, beware. It's commendable to have a neighbor or friend volunteer to make a delivery and a few dollars on the side, but if an accident occurs en route, you become involved, and that opens up a whole new area of responsibility.

Why a $1 million policy? This set figure is what insurance carriers have mandated for gift industry businesses. Anything less and you'd still pay a premium equal to or a few dollars less than the $1 million amount. This coverage insures you against people who slip and trip on your property if they are coming to your home for business reasons. A client may not be coming for a basket pickup, but a copier salesperson might slip or the shipping delivery person might trip. Sure, such persons can put in a claim through their companies, but they hurt themselves on your property. What can go wrong definitely will go wrong, so prepare for the worst and put your mind at ease with a policy that protects your home and business inside and out.

Finding Space in Your Home

Tax season is so predictable. It's the time when television news producers search the depths for the most frightening home office deduction story they can find, following it up with "expert advice" and a dos and don'ts list for maintaining an office at home.

The IRS home office rules state that the home office deduction is allowed if you use an area at home exclusively and regularly for business. Contact the IRS (800–829–1040) to have home business information sent to you, or visit the IRS Web site at www.irs.treas.gov for home office deduction details. Discuss your office setup with your accountant to ensure that the home structure and taxes associated with your new business are within IRS guidelines.

Finding space in your home is a matter of where you live and the extent of the living quarters. Some dwellers have extra space in the attic or basement, while others live in one- or two-bedroom apartments, knowing that it will be a challenge to organize space but are willing to sacrifice for success. Here are questions to consider: (1) If there is no extra room available, can you section off part of another room with movable screens to create a separate, extra room? (2) Can unused furniture be stored or sold to create new space? and (3) Is it time to rearrange your home for better efficiency?

Organizing Your Workspace

I don't want my business taking over my home like others say has happened to them.

How do you see your gift basket workshop? A collection of meticulously woven baskets hanging from hooks or stored on racks, waiting to be chosen for the next creation? Do flowers and star spray sparkle in the sunlight streaming through a large and inspiring picture window? Everything gradually takes its place as each shelf, table, and hook is installed. Nothing is set forever, as new tools are added and regularly used items are moved to better locations. Consider installing lots of shelves, whether the steel floor models or wooden planks attached to walls. Let's review some other ideas for coordinating an efficient workspace.

Baskets

Baskets can be stacked from floor to ceiling, placed on shelves, or strung from the ceiling supported by hooks and wire.

> *My baskets hang from floor to ceiling on a lattice. It keeps*
> *them neatly organized and out of the way until used.*

Shred

A medium-size box placed under the worktable holds individual clear plastic bags of different shred colors. This way, a handful is easily grabbed and brought above the table to line the waiting basket. When you are buying ten pounds of shred, the boxes act as their own storage container. Sometimes the boxes are too bulky to place under the worktable, so fill clear plastic bags with enough shred for about ten baskets (that's twelve handfuls), place these in a box as mentioned above, and store the large boxes in another area. Write each shred's color on the outside of the ten-pound boxes to keep from guessing which color is in each box.

> *My shred is placed in a four-compartment bin. That way, I*
> *have less to store in the workspace. The rest of the shred is in*
> *plastic garbage cans waiting to refill the smaller bin.*

Cellophane, Bags, Shrink, and Shells

Cellophane mailed from a manufacturer is usually shipped in a cardboard tube that doubles as a storage container. Use the tube box or purchase a small tabletop rack to hold one roll or a floor model that holds eight to ten rolls. Retail stores also sell opaque storage containers that hold approximately twenty rolls in an upright position.

The shrink-wrap machine is placed on its own table or atop the worktable, pushed to the side until needed. This is one piece of equipment that should always be accessible. Crimper and other tools are handily hung on the wall above the machine. Basket shells (clear cellophane bags that slip over the finished basket and are shrunk into place) and basket bags (clear or printed cellophane bags closed above the basket and tied with a bow) are stored flat and placed in a container under the worktable. Keep cellophane, shells, and bags covered so dust does not settle on the film.

Enhancements and Support Materials

Enhancements are added to the basket for a touch of elegance around the foods and gifts. Popular enhancements are bows, balloons, twisted tamboo grass (curly ting ting), flowers, star spray, fans, picks, and pinecones. Shred is also considered an enhancement.

Support materials are placed in the basket opening and act to stabilize the foods and gifts. Such products include Sahara foam, packing paper, newspaper, Styrofoam peanuts, and tissue paper. Supplies are best stored on shelves or in shallow boxes to always see what's available.

Foods and Gifts

This industry thrives on foods that need no refrigeration, so they, as well as gifts, are taken out of shipping boxes and stacked on shelves. Foods can also be stored in clear, lidded plastic containers that are purchased in discount stores. This gives the foods added security from bugs and other types of infestation. Manufacturers are offering more shelf-stable cheeses and other nonrefrigerated foods—a blessing that allows a wider choice for clients. If any products need refrigeration, a health department examiner may advise you to store refrigerated items in a unit other than the family refrigerator.

Expiration Labeling

Most manufacturers stamp expiration dates on the back, side, or bottom of a package. When you receive a shipment or make a purchase from a local wholesaler, check to ensure that freshness hasn't expired. Be careful not to buy products at local stores that aren't stamped, since you cannot be sure when the item was produced. If the freshness date is missing from shipped products, consult the catalog for information or call the manufacturer for assistance. You can then purchase labels at an office-supply store and attach one label to each product bearing your own expiration code. Use a pen to write a date only you can understand (e.g., 11013 = November 2003 expiration; 11 is November, 01 means the first day of the month, and 3 stands for 2003).

You'll find more information on buying and freshness in Chapter 4.

Maintaining Product Catalogs

Heed this warning: Stacks of catalogs pile up faster than losing tickets after a lottery drawing. As catalogs arrive, keep them in one place to review when you're ready. Use an old box, putting them in a pile on a countertop or in a corner on the floor. Review catalogs at least weekly to keep the stack low. After review, clip or tag pages to call manufacturers and place orders; then put the catalogs away or file them for future use.

Choose an easy-to-follow, organized system to file and retrieve catalogs. Storage options and ideas that professionals use with great success are:

• *Storage bins, purchased in office-supply or discount stores.* The bins come with clear or colored tops. Catalogs are stored alphabetically or by product type. The latter method is preferred by most professionals, who use labels like Food, Baby, Fragrance, Baskets, Enhancements, Wedding, Variety, and Miscellaneous. Use cardboard to separate the bins into sections, cutting your own tab on one corner like a manila folder, high enough to separate each section. Write the section's name on the tab, using a black felt-tip marker. Depending on thickness, about thirty catalogs will fit in each bin. Stack bins atop one another and store them away from the workspace area.

> I bought plastic crates at an office-supply store and separate everything by item with file folders. The biggest folder is for baskets. When a new catalog arrives, the old one gets thrown out. The best thing is that the crates are stackable.

- *Steel filing cabinets.* These are also purchased in office-supply stores, but bargains are found at thrift stores, yard sales and flea markets, and close-out retailers. Hanging file folders are good to separate catalogs, moving back and forth on the inside steel frame. Folders are available in 2- and 3-inch bottom widths, which are recommended to hold thick books. Again, catalogs are stored alphabetically or by product type.
- *Other catalog containers* to consider are milk (plastic) and vegetable (wooden) crates.

> Milk crates separate my catalogs by product, and each one
> has a label on the front telling me what's in each crate. I also
> use the computer to list the catalogs alphabetically and spec-
> ify which heading I can find a catalog under.

Professionals regularly use database management systems, such as ACT!, to create and maintain a list of wholesalers and popular products for gift basket designs. Using this type of system makes it easier to retrieve catalogs as needed.

Projecting Your Best Professional Image

Your company's image must mirror the client's view of himself or herself. He or she is the epitome of a winning attitude, polished appearance, and community respectability. To see yourself as the caviar of companies when your telephone and fax machine still share one line or as you continue making excuses for avoidable problems spells disaster for your image and long-term sales potential.

There's no compromising on the tools needed to conduct good business. Install the priorities first, then invest in the other essentials as quickly as possible.

Stationery

Components include letterhead, second sheets, envelopes, business cards, and trifold brochures. Stationery is purchased through a commercial printer or mail-order stationery company or designed on computer by you or another professional, using plain or colored paper and appropriate software.

Promotional Products

Picture brochures are an important sales tool, promoting gift baskets by using pictures and text. A brochure can be one glossy page displaying baskets and other gifts with text and order form on separate paper or a multipage catalog combining photographs, text, and an order form saddle-stitched in the center.

A Web site is another component, which showcases your basket designs to a worldwide audience twenty-four hours a day. It is your number one promotional product if a picture brochure is not within your budget or isn't desired, or if your designs change so frequently that a brochure would become obsolete within months.

Rolodex or rotary-file cards are given to every corporate client, with the tab marked "Gifts" or "Gift Baskets." Print cards in groups of 100 at first, graduating to 500 at a time when you're satisfied with the card's design and message. Corporate clients each receive three cards (unless they request more): one for the office, one for their assistant, and one for their home. Even in today's fast-paced, technological environment, corporate clients still use these cards.

Postcards are a high-response advertising vehicle, printed by a commercial company specializing in photo cards with back-side text. Such cards relay a visual message for instant customer response. Nonpicture postcards have also proved to be an effective sales tool.

> *Postcards worked well for my sales and were cheaper than the cost of putting together a brochure.*

As *ancillary products,* consider purchasing writing instruments, notepads, cubed paper, and anything else to personalize with your company name for desktops in corporate and residential environments.

Stamps, Meters, and Internet Postage

Sort through your personal mail. What gets opened first—bills, checks, or junk? Does the priority depend on whether a stamp or a meter was used for postage? Probably not, and this is the same logic used to decide whether to use stamps or a postage meter.

Meter leasing is available through independent carriers. Some companies waive leasing fees for the first three months. After that, the fee is based on the average quarterly postage used, as documented in a postal log completed each time you refill the machine at the post office. So, in addition to paying for postage, you're billed a fluctuating lease fee.

Internet sites also make mailing easier by allowing you to stamp mail through your printer. Companies such as Stamps.com and SimplyPostage.com let you place postage on your envelopes or onto labels for larger packages through Internet access. These services were highly praised during the Internet boom but have fallen out of favor in recent years. Postage affixed by computer comes at a premium above the price of a stamp, is convenient for some, but still has no bearing on what gets opened first.

Using stamps for business mail is just as popular as small-business meter use. Stamped business mail is not viewed negatively or as unbusinesslike. In fact, it may be opened quicker than metered mail and is definitely opened before bulk-rate mail. It's all a matter of preference.

Mail Delivery

Carefully consider where business mail is delivered. Once you register the business name, the street address becomes a soliciting target. Salespeople may visit your home unannounced, attempting to sell their merchandise. A small home mailbox or slot will be inundated with business mail, especially if you're ordering catalogs. If you are living in a complex, neighbors might see the extra mail and question your activities, leading to un-neighborly relationships.

Post office box rental charges are paid annually and are quite reasonable. A mail center, another option, usually charges higher rates than the post office but offers incentives like United Parcel Service (UPS) shipping and delivery and use of the mail center's street address (versus a post office box address) and will tell you by phone if there's mail in your box and from whom. Post office and mail center boxes are viewed as equals in stature, so your choice depends on price, services needed, and address preferences.

Telephone Systems

Answering Machines

- *Dual-tape answering machine.* One tape greets callers, while the other records the message. This replaces the one-tape option, where the more messages taped, the longer the wait after the tone. The dual-tape system is fast becoming obsolete, due to updated technology.

- *Digital (tapeless) answering machine.* This system records messages digitally, so messages are never lost because of a broken or worn tape. This technology is often linked with a handy multiple mailbox telephone, which separates customers' orders from catalog requests, personal calls, and other client services.
- *Local telephone company's voice mail system.* It's affordable and also available with multiple box capabilities, though it will cost more on a per-month basis than using an at-home machine. Local companies may offer a one-month free trial.

Answering Service

Consider this option if you prefer a live operator minding your phones while you're out of the office. Ask colleagues for recommendations, and check the Yellow Pages. Answering services usually offer a free month of service for evaluation. If you choose this service, visit the company and introduce yourself to the operators assigned to your calls. Thank them in advance for efficient service, and sweeten the introduction with a box of chocolates or assorted cookies.

> *Answering services in my area are too expensive for me, and you pay for all calls, the wrong ones too. Instead, I use an answering machine with caller ID to alert me if the caller is a salesperson or a possible client.*

Fax Machines

A plain-paper fax is the best technology for today's businesses. Other fax machine options include (1) thermal paper fax, an option too old to consider unless someone gives you a free machine as a starter; and (2) a computer fax modem, popular, but may be ineffective if your computer is inoperable.

"I'll turn on the fax" is becoming a less-acceptable phrase in business. To the company attempting to send a fax, it means a loss of time and money, added aggravation, and an automatic downgraded opinion of your business. The preferred fax machine installation uses a dedicated line, which means calling the phone company for the separate line and a telephone number for fax use only. The phone company installs the line, charging a flat service rate plus extra for each additional fifteen minutes of work above the allotted time. You can also purchase an installation kit from the phone company and do your own wiring or have an experienced person do the work. However, if a non–phone-company representative installs the wiring, it may not be guaranteed against service problems, so check with the phone company before the work is done.

Computer, Software, Backup, and Printer

Computer

Buying a computer today is an easy and affordable task thanks to technological advances. Advertisements bombard you in print, on radio, and on television hawking the latest equipment and features. A computer purchase is a wise investment in your business, allowing you to perform tasks electronically and surf the Internet daily. If you cannot buy a computer outright, Gateway, Dell, Compaq, and other industry leaders offer low monthly price deals that everyone can afford.

Software

Gift basket professionals use word-processing (letters), spreadsheet (sales/expense analysis and inventory tracking), database management (clients' names and addresses), desktop publishing (newsletters and flyers), presentation (for corporate client meetings), and Internet or on-line service access software. If you're unfamiliar with software packages, ask colleagues for recommendations before buying, see in-store demonstrations, or call software companies for demo disks, and attend classes as mentioned under "Education" later in this chapter.

Backup System

Disaster planning is no longer reserved for big companies only. All important computer documents should be copied on a backup system. A visit to a local computer store reveals all of the internal and external options. Some computer manufacturers will install internal systems, while retailers provide excellent external equipment. Your system should back up files on a weekly basis, at minimum. If you value your business, you will install this system.

Printer

Laser or ink-jet printing are the best options to consider. Many are inexpensive and print in both black-and-white and color. Hewlett-Packard makes printers by which all others are measured, but many brands are acceptable. Again, talk with colleagues and experienced professionals about choices, and see product demonstrations.

Shredder

Shredders are as necessary as the office desk and chair. They confidentially discard information meant for your eyes only. A shredder protects your business and your customers' sensitive information from the person walking past the garbage or from your closest competition searching for secrets. It's not a paranoid purchase, just sensible and affordable protection.

Price shredders at local office-supply stores and through mail-order companies. A combination crosscut shredder and wastebasket, dicing five pages at a time, is adequate. Once you've used a shredder, you'll wonder how you lived without it.

Wireless Communications

Cellular Telephone

As technology continues to evolve, product prices decrease dramatically. Skyrocketing cellular telephone sales are one of the main reasons why states must add new area codes. Consider purchasing a cellular phone to speak with clients while you're on the road, to call clients who can't or don't hear the doorbell, to make calls when you're in traffic or will be late for an appointment, and to feel safer while traveling and keep in touch with family.

> *When I'm out on business, I have my office phone calls forwarded to my cellular phone. It doesn't cost much and keeps me in touch with clients wherever I am.*

Don't give the phone number to anyone unless it's essential to do so. Cellular phones are such an important tool that more-experienced professionals often use this phone as their main line, bypassing the cost of maintaining a land line.

Paging System

Pagers are also great for client access and as an alternative to a live operator if you won't be using an answering service. They are equipped with number and text message capability and can be programmed for regional or national coverage.

Education

Enroll in courses at adult schools, colleges, and other centers that improve your professional and organization skills. In class there are others to meet for future business opportunities. Courses to consider include Image Enhancement (wardrobe and appearance), Presentation Skills, Recordkeeping, Computers and Software, Negotiation Skills, and Desktop Publishing.

Internet courses have also risen as a popular way of learning. From the comfort of your home, classes are led by experts who teach the aforementioned subjects and gift basket business skills.

Laying a firm foundation increases the rate of business prosperity tenfold. Make the commitment to set up your business on solid ground.

Home Office and Workspace Setup and Structure Checklist

<u>Completed</u>

1. Decide on a name for your business. _____

2. Use the nearest federal depository library or the PTO Internet site to complete a trademark search. _____

3. Register the company name with the correct county and state departments. _____

4. Contact the local zoning department about your street's zoning restrictions. _____

5. Ask friends, family, and business sources for small-business accountant and attorney recommendations. _____

     Make appointments to meet with accountants and attorneys for assistance choices. _____

     Decide on a business legal structure. _____

6. Call insurance companies for estimates on product liability and car delivery insurance. _____

7. Decide on the best location for the office at home. _____

8. Purchase accessories to maintain workspace order. _____

9. Investigate and purchase equipment and supplies needed for the home office.

     Telephone with answering machine _____

     Fax machine and installation _____

     Stationery _____

     Promotional products _____

     Cellular telephone and pager _____

     Computer, software, backup, and printer _____

     Shredder _____

10. Research and register for helpful educational seminars. _____

Chapter Four
Selecting Your Inventory

Your business is starting to take shape. The business plan is prepared, and you have determined the market to target, have set up the office and workspace, and are registering with the proper officials. Now it's time to select merchandise, find its sources, and perfect the choices on a buyer's chart. Before you make your first purchase, let's cover some basic buying strategies to develop good budgeting and purchasing habits.

Checking In with the Health Department

Certain specialty gift baskets contain gardening tools, baby items, or just gifts, but the majority contain food, the all-important component that entices every client. Local health department rules for the handling and stocking of foods vary from state to state. The best thing to do for your clients' and your own protection is to use only prepackaged foods, snacks, and beverages in your baskets so that your hands never, ever directly touch any product. Every cookie, cake, nut, and mix is to be packaged in cellophane, boxes, or bags by the manufacturer before shipment to you. When the products arrive, inspect every package thoroughly for damage and spillage.

When checking state and local health department rules for reselling prepackaged foods and snacks in baskets, the questions to ask are:

- Does the health department restrict home-based businesses from buying prepackaged foods for resale in baskets?
- Are there any inspection requirements?
- Is a permit required?
- Are any fees involved?

States have laws that cities sometimes take months or years to adopt or even consider—which is why both the city and state departments of health are called for the rules. As with zoning issues discussed in Chapter 3, ask questions without giving your name or exact details about the business. This is not to imply that you are attempting to get around the laws; you are merely trying to get all the facts, prepare a plan of action, and follow the right procedures without being targeted unjustly for inspection.

> *In my state a health license is needed if we wrap or prepare food, but we use only foods prewrapped by the manufacturer.*

Gift baskets are a worldwide industry, but many health departments across the country have not adopted rules or regulations to accept gift baskets as a home-based business. The industry provides a worthwhile service for other businesses, brings joy to shut-ins and those recuperating, and donates to charities that help the needy locally and nationwide.

Profitable Occasions and Events

There are as many reasons to create gift baskets as there are people who buy them. Messages centered around traditional selling occasions that are a good starting point to introduce the business are:

- Happy Birthday
- Congratulations (wedding, promotions)
- Thank You
- Welcome (new job, new home/apartment)
- Good Luck
- Bereavement

- Get Well
- Thinking of You/Miss You/Love You

  Special events include:
- Father's Day
- Mother's Day
- New Year
- Administrative Professionals Week
- Valentine's Day
- Christmas/Hanukkah/Kwanzaa

The most popular occasions, as determined by basket sales over the past few years, are Christmas, Valentine's Day, and Mother's Day. Holidays like Easter and Halloween are not listed, but some clients may request baskets for children or religious items for adults.

Most of the inventory can be used for every occasion, with notable exceptions for custom themes. The differences in what's offered are decided by the client's price range and preferences, together with the receiver's dietary restrictions and color choices.

A Shopping List for Success

What are the main components to create standard, themed, or custom gift baskets? Even though you may decide, in the future, not to use all the products listed, read on to familiarize yourself with the basics.

Baskets

Baskets are manufactured throughout the world. They are small-, medium-, and large-size; are round-, oval-, rectangular-, and square-shaped; are one-color or multicolor; are made with and without handles; and come in styles too numerous to mention. Start by using basic baskets, such as those with handles in various shapes and colors. Also try nonhandled styles to create a simple yet elegant gift covered in shrink-wrap or tied with printed cellophane and fastened with a large bow.

Containers

Gift baskets are converted into custom packages when containers are the base. They make the product unique and set your business apart from the rest by offering more than generic baskets. My business specializes in using containers to give the recipient a new vessel to keep in bathrooms, bedrooms, or anywhere else in the home; I have used children's wagons, rocking chairs, and upturned umbrellas as part of the package. Other containers to consider are miniwheelbarrows, fabric-covered boxes, shoes, ice buckets, teacups and saucers, silver trays, golf ball buckets, doll cribs, and pen-and-pencil cups. The container used is limited only by your imagination.

Shred

Positioned around the rim of the basket or container, shred creates an attractive, seamless bind between basket and products. Because shred is made from various fibers, there are many types to choose from, such as tissue, sizzle, parchment, and excelsior. It's available in a variety of colors and a multicolor mix called fiesta or confetti.

Bows, Balloons, Ribbon, and Raffia

What else ties a look together better than the adornment found around a basket? Bows are purchased premade or made from flat ribbon to create as you wish for themed basket co-ordination; either version comes in many widths, sizes, and colors and is usually found at the top of the basket as the finishing touch. Balloons are a low-cost addition that brighten the gift and increase the retail cost; they come in all sizes, shapes, and colors. Curling ribbon is made in two widths, $\frac{3}{16}$ and $\frac{3}{8}$ inch. Available in a rainbow of colors, it generously adds volume, as streams of curling ribbon cascade from the top of the basket down to the bottom. Raffia is a long, strawlike natural material; it gives baskets an environmentally friendly appearance and is a decorative alternative to ribbon.

> *Individuals want balloons more than corporate clients do. The markup is great, and they don't take up much space in the workroom.*

Cellophane

This plastic material closes the basket and its contents together. It is available in several sizes, with 100 feet long and 20 to 40 inches wide being the most common. Clear cellophane (also called cello) is an all-purpose standard, but the printed version is popular now that more manufacturers offer stylish designs. Printed with petite red hearts, fruit, flowers, white lace, or spiderwebs, to name a few patterns, cellophane is an easy-to-use last touch before adding the bow and is the preferred choice for hand deliveries. Cellophane also comes in opaque red, yellow, and green, though these colors are mainly associated with pre-made store Easter baskets and grocery fruit arrangements. These opaque colors prohibit customers from viewing the contents, and that decreases sales.

> *In five years of business, I have never used shrink-wrap, and
> I mail baskets around the world without a problem. I buy
> cello at floral suppliers, who have the best prices in the area.*

Basket Bags

Professionals use basket bags because they provide a quick-and-pretty closure for any container. These bags, made from cellophane, are sealed on the bottom and sides, leaving the top open for basket insertion. When the basket or container is placed in the bag, the designer closes the top with a bow or raffia. The bag is then folded close to the container and taped. Basket bags are available in many sizes and in clear and printed styles.

Shrink-Wrap

Shrink-wrap tools include the basic machine, a crimper (also called a hand trimmer), which creates a closed, cellophane-type shell around the basket, and a heat gun, which shrinks the film, or wrap, in place. Known for its crystal-clear appearance, shrink-wrap is made in different gauges (thicknesses) and is widely used to ship baskets around the world, stabilizing products as they travel. A popular choice for shipping is to first shrink-wrap a basket for stability, and then wrap it in printed cellophane for style and an enhanced appearance.

I use nothing but shrink-wrap. It keeps everything together,
and I feel more confident that the basket will get there intact.
A video that came with the machine helped me perfect my
technique.

Enhancements and Labels

Enhancements are anything that creates visual appeal: flowers, star spray, twisted tamboo grass (also known as curly ting ting), tissue paper, birds, butterflies, and more. These are the products responsible for creating a one-of-a-kind basket.

Labels are affixed to the cellophane, basket bag, or shrink-wrap, usually on the lower side of a basket. Not all companies use a label, but those that do add enhancement either through an unusual label design that draws attention or through the printed message, such as "Designed especially for you by [your business name]."

Paper, Peanuts, or Foam?

Baskets and other containers have fillers that stabilize the creation so that the products don't sag or tip over the container. What's used to fill the container varies depending on your preferred style, which is updated as better techniques are learned through workshops, videos, books, or consultations. Among the products relied on as filler are printed or un-printed newspaper, plastic peanuts, old cellophane, and Sahara (gray) foam. Talk to professionals and you'll hear many ideas on what works best. In Chapter 5 we'll proceed step-by-step with ideas to sturdily fill the container.

The peanuts and paper I use to fill the basket come from the
boxes I receive when shipments arrive.

Tape and Other Sticky Stuff

Transparent tape acts as a chameleon, blending into whatever it binds, while double-coated tape connects bamboo skewers, product, and shred together, as explained next under "Bamboo Skewers."

Glue dots bond food and gift packaging together inside of a basket or container. The dots are clear, circular in shape, and very tacky, yet are easily removed by the gift receiver when the gift is opened. Glue guns and sticks are very affordable and easily keep products in place or hold wavy ribbon in place on the outside of cellophane. Both are found in many craft and floral supply stores. Glue sticks are inserted into the plugged-in gun, which heats up and turns the stick into melted glue. A quick application to the intended surface makes a fast and tidy bond.

> Tape is handy, and the glue gun is good for adhering boxed packages. To hide the tape, I usually use tissue paper and shred propped up around the products.

Bamboo Skewers

These wooden sticks are an inexpensive brace, securing products in baskets and keeping them upright. Since a whole stick is too long to use on one product, the sticks are usually broken into thirds. The small skewer, about 4 inches in length, is attached to the lower edge of a product with transparent tape. Two inches of skewer are taped onto the product's back side, and 2 inches hang below. Double-coated tape is placed directly on top of the transparent tape. The last step is to press enough shred on top of the double-coated tape to hide the skewer. The skewer, attached to the product, is inserted into the Sahara foam, which is already in place inside the basket. Now the product is secured upright in the basket. An example of this technique is shown in Chapter 5.

Gifts

As mentioned in Chapter 1, anything can be labeled a gift, but here the gifts you choose must be the appropriate size to place in the basket, so choose whatever fits on desktops, on kitchen counters, on vanity tables, or in cars and whatever matches the theme and preference of the client. Browsing through catalogs and reviewing your business plan offer more suggestions and ideas to select quick-selling gift products.

Foods

Delicious, aromatic, flavorful, and intriguing, foods and snacks are the all-appealing pleasure added to 99 percent of today's baskets. Manufacturers continue to create spicy, exotic, and wholesome goods to enhance baskets made for choice-conscious consumers. Popular themes are Southwest, Texas, and other regional specialty flavors; couch-potato snacks; take-an-office-break items (flavored coffees and biscotti); and indoors-at-the-movies fare (popcorn and chocolate-covered anything). Concentrate on choosing foods that are appropriate for most themes rather than selecting goods that are chosen for one-of-a-kind baskets.

Where to Buy Products

Gift Basket and Gourmet Trade Shows

Industry trade shows are held nationwide, usually at convention centers, permanent showroom buildings, and larger hotels. Attending a show is exciting and fascinating. It's the time to see new products and industry favorites and to attend seminars to learn sales techniques, see product demonstrations, and interact with other industry professionals who seek similar solutions. The shows feature a mix of everything, including museum collections, floral products, and giftware from other countries. These shows are open only to the trade, which means that you must have business identification (sales tax certificate, business card, and business check) to attend. Gift basket shows focus on baskets, products, education, and camaraderie with other professionals looking for new ideas, alternative building techniques, and the latest sales tools. Gourmet shows highlight industry foods, accessories, and packaging. Lots of gift basket foods, snacks, and beverages are found here.

Many exhibitors now accept major credit cards to pay for purchases. Show specials offer free products or freight if you buy at the show. Take advantage of these discounts if the deal is good. (Some of the regional trade shows and permanent showroom buildings are listed in the Appendix, as are gift trade magazines, which publish a full calendar of shows and events at least once a year.)

Manufacturers

Manufacturers, also known as vendors, are the products' makers. Buying directly from them means that you pay the lowest cost for the product because there is no middleman. The only exception is that some distributors (discussed later in this chapter) sell manufacturers' products at the same low price and don't require a high minimum purchase. When placing orders, shipment is quick (as long as it is in stock), so if you use a post office box address, give the manufacturers your street address to avoid delays.

Manufacturers' Representatives (Reps)

As the title suggests, representatives are hired by manufacturers to sell their products in markets where the manufacturer has no presence. Be advised that most reps sell at different minimums, according to each manufacturer's purchase requirements.

Distributors

Are you searching for companies that sell many of the products and supplies you want with no- or low-minimum terms? Distributors answer the call, providing quality snacks, beverages, baskets, ribbon, shred, and more. There are many distributors throughout the country, which means that freight charges are reasonable no matter where you live. Several companies are listed in the Appendix.

Catalogs

If you cannot attend trade shows or if a certain company is not exhibiting at a show you visit, catalogs are the next best way to identify basket products. Some companies mail free product catalogs, whereas others now charge a fee. The options are:

1. Pay the cost; you've heard that the company has some interesting products. If there's a charge, most companies will deduct the catalog cost from the first order.

2. Ask if the company will be displaying its product line at a local trade show. Then you can view the merchandise to see if the firm offers anything useful.
3. Look for the company's Web site on the Internet, which is often more up to date than a catalog.
4. Decide not to get the catalog at this time and continue searching for companies that offer free catalogs.

Warehouse Clubs

Discount warehouses, with names such as BJ's, Costco, and Sam's, are another source for products. They are sometimes mistaken as competition because they sell gift baskets during the holidays. This misconception is explained further in Chapter 10. Each fee-based club sells products in bulk to all members and does not charge tax on items that businesses will resell. If snacks, cookies, and gift items are what you seek, this is another place to find them.

Floral Wholesalers

These suppliers are found in the Yellow Pages under "Floral Suppliers" and at gift trade shows. Floral suppliers sell baskets and enhancements, silk flowers, balloons, bags, ribbons and premade bows, cellophane, tissue, and much more. Local providers sell to businesses on a wholesale basis and require each buyer to register with them before purchasing. Usually the supplier needs a completed resale form and a copy of your business license. A resale form, which floral management will provide during registration, documents your intent to resell the purchased products.

Retailers

Certain retailers sell products and enhancements at a bargain price. Such retailers are 99-cent and dollar stores, craft stores, office-supply houses, grocery stores, and party suppliers. These stores will sell to you tax-free as long as you present your credentials before the purchase is rung. Simply tell the cashier that you are reselling the items, and have your business license copy ready for presentation. Always carry copies of these documents in your daily planner or a car compartment, as purchases are sometimes made on impulse.

> *I bring my resale license when I buy from retailers, and they make a copy of the license for their records. Some of them have their own forms that must be filled out the first time you make a purchase.*

Buying in Bulk Versus Retail

Running a business means that you buy as many products as possible in bulk to ensure that you are paying the least cost to make the highest profit. Buying at full retail price eats into your revenue. Bulk purchases are better for several reasons:

1. Bulk offers the lowest price directly from the manufacturer, unless a retailer's price is so low that it rivals the manufacturer's cost.
2. Manufacturers guarantee product freshness. Unless products are already tagged, retailers do not know when a product will expire.
3. If a client wants multiple baskets with similar products, bulk purchasing almost guarantees that adequate quantities will be on hand. Retailers are not obliged to hold products off the selling floor for your exclusive use.

The sample Buying Chart on the next page shows how to plan your purchases before buying. The chart helps determine product selections and how much cash or credit is required for the inventory. Products are separated by category. The "C" between "Price Each" and "Baskets" stands for Corporate, and an "X" is placed in each row where the product doubles as a corporate item.

Obtaining Credit

Each time an account is established with a new vendor, you build a reputation that allows the issuance of credit from that vendor and other companies. At first you will pay for purchases by check, credit card, or COD (cash on delivery). Try not to order COD because it

Buying Chart

Company: Moore Baskets

Market: Individuals and corporations (local real estate, software, and tourist needs at hotels and resorts).

Mfr./Vendor	Description	Quan.	Price Each	C	Bskts.	Cont.	Food	Gifts	Enhan.
	Baskets								
BB Baskets	Small	6	$1.80		$10.80				
Basketique	Medium	6	2.50		15.00				
Basketique	Large	6	4.20		25.20				
BB Baskets	Odd-shaped	3	3.20		9.60				
	Containers								
Tooloose	Medium fabric-covered boxes	6	$2.50			$15.00			
Tooloose	Children's wagons	6	5.00			30.00			
Shiny Times	Silver trays—oval	6	1.90			11.40			
TeaTime	Large teacups/saucers	12	3.00			36.00			
	Food								
Snack Tyme	Champagne crackers	6	$0.99	X			$5.94		
Food Stuff	Truffles (6/bx.)	12	1.20	X			14.40		
Food Stuff	3 oz. chocolate popcorn	6	1.50	X			9.00		
Food Stuff	3 oz. cheddar popcorn	4	1.30	X			5.20		
Food Stuff	3 oz. pretzel sticks	4	1.60	X			6.40		
Snack Tyme	4 oz. biscotti	6	1.20	X			7.20		
Snack Tyme	6 oz. assorted nuts	6	0.90				5.40		
Snack Tyme	4 oz. choc. chip cookies	6	0.75				4.50		
Pantry Place	Sparkling ciders—small	3	0.99				2.97		
Pantry Place	Coffee	4	0.75	X			3.00		
Food Stuff	Tea (12-bag boxes)	4	0.60	X			2.40		

Buying Chart

Mfr./Vendor	Description	Quan.	Price Each	C	Bskts.	Cont.	Food	Gifts	Enhan.
Pantry Place	Cocoa	4	$0.50	X			$2.00		
Pantry Place	Cappuccino	4	0.60	X			2.40		
Food Stuff	8 oz. pancake-mix bags	6	1.30				7.80		
Food Stuff	Sm. syrups—asst. flavors	6	0.80				4.80		
	Gifts								
Read n' Write	Notepads (large)	6	$1.10					$6.60	
Read n' Write	Notepads (small)	6	0.90	X				5.40	
Cooks Delight	Linen napkins	3	0.75					2.25	
Cooks Delight	Oven mitts	3	2.00					6.00	
Scentsatious	Hand lotions	4	1.25					5.00	
Scentsatious	Bubble bath	4	1.30					5.20	
Heads Up	Stationery sets	4	2.20	X				8.80	
	Enhancements								
Floral Barn	Shred—4 colors (10 lb. ea.)	4	$10.00						$40.00
Floral Barn	Curling ribbon—12 colors	12	1.45						17.40
Floral Barn	Sahara foam (24 bricks/bx.)	1	12.50						12.50
5 & 10	Bamboo skewers (100/pk.)	1	1.00						1.00
Supply City	Cellophane (2 rolls—30-by-100)	2	3.15						6.30
Supply City	Clear tape (5 rolls)	5	2.60						13.00
Supply City	Double-coated tape (5 rolls)	5	2.75						13.75
Supply City	Glue dots (1,000)	1	22.00						22.00
	Subtotals				$60.60	$92.40	$83.41	$39.25	$125.95
	GRAND TOTAL								$401.61

adds a charge to your order. After three orders have been placed, call the customer service representative or appropriate department and ask how you can establish a net-thirty account. That means the merchandise will be shipped to you without advance payment, with full payment due within thirty days of the shipping date printed on the mailed invoice (not the date the goods are received).

The vendor will request a credit sheet, which is similar to the sample Credit Reference Sheet shown on the next page. Such a sheet is printed on letterhead and lists references that will acknowledge a current financial relationship with your company. The DUNS number shown on top is issued free of charge by Dun & Bradstreet, the information services firm providing business information reports to companies who make marketing, insurance, and other credit-based decisions. Dun & Bradstreet will register your company after asking general business questions, such as the owner's name, the year business commenced, and projected revenue. This is a simple procedure, and you will not be asked to provide personal evidence, so confidentiality is maintained.

Businesses acquire a DUNS number to register their business through an objective information source. A DUNS number is not a requirement, but it helps you further establish your company as a bona fide business. Obtaining a DUNS number is a wise investment. Call Dun & Bradstreet at (800) 234–3867 for registration details or apply on the firm's Web site at www.dnb.com.

Vendors usually like to see five or six companies listed on the Credit Reference Sheet to verify creditworthiness. If you can provide only three, do so. The companies listed are those you purchase from now, whether by check or credit card or on account. If you are turned down, explain to the vendor's credit representative that you intend to purchase products often, and ask if there's any other way a net-thirty account can be opened. The worst you'll be told is to reapply in the future. That's a viable option to exercise in the coming months with all the companies with which you intend doing business.

Understanding Buying Terms

Just as you check the return and exchange policy at retail stores, so too must you understand each vendor's purchasing terms before buying inventory. Along with studying the definitions given in the Glossary, here are questions to ask before making initial purchases:

1. What is the minimum purchase amount or case quantity?

MOORE BASKETS

CREDIT REFERENCE SHEET

DUNS NO. 55–555–5555

Bank

Prospect Heights Bank
1010 Broadway
Pepperton, NY 13840
(607) 555–8080
Checking Account #48-368437-0

Credit References

BB Baskets
618 Western Boulevard
Seattle, WA 98120
(206) 555–1282
Account #418635

Floral Barn
511 Parkview Place
Los Angeles, CA 90047
(213) 555–2000
Account #002-839

Pantry Place
222 West 128th Street
St. Louis, MO 51888
(314) 555–3404
Account #30-694

Scentsatious
820 Boulevard
Columbus, OH 28360
(614) 555–2789
Account #SB013

Supply City
68320 Rio Grand Avenue
Baltimore, MD 30280
(303) 555–1606
Account #7045

550 Johnson Street, #2, Pandora Station, Pepperton, NY 13838
Telephone: (607) 555–8580   Fax: (607) 555–8585

2. Can a case of products be mixed (different flavors, products, etc.)?

3. What is the shelf life (for foods)? Is the expiration date marked on the package?

4. What is your return policy? Is there a restocking fee (a percentage or flat fee charged for returning products)?

5. How do I receive credit for damaged or missing goods?

6. Do you accept credit cards as payment?

7. What if the quality isn't what I expected? Can I return the product for exchange or refund?

Although it's not always feasible, question 7 brings up a good point: why it is important to see products at gift and gourmet trade shows. Catalogs are sometimes deceiving—a product may look good on paper but not look or taste good in person.

Most vendors list their terms in each catalog. If terms are 10 percent net-thirty, that means you receive 10 percent off the total purchase cost if the bill is paid within thirty days of the invoice date. These terms are usually reserved for repeat buyers.

Free Samples for the Asking

When buying foods, ask the vendor to include an extra bag or a few free samples of the purchased product for client tasting. This will allow you to save all purchases for client orders instead of using your stock as samples. As the product's maker, manufacturers store sample goods for shows and in-house demonstrations. Some catalogs indicate that a sample product is included with each purchase, and others offer it only with the initial order. Always ask for samples, no matter what the catalog says.

Retailers and discount warehouses have no samples in their stockrooms. Only manufacturers and some reps have access to extra products and will most likely send you samples as you become a steady client. Don't be afraid to ask. What better way is there to get the client's order than to please his or her palate?

Co-op Buying Opportunities

Ever wonder how some stores can sell a product for much less than other stores? *Co-op* is short for "cooperative," and stores that sell the same products can lower their costs by buying inventory together in one large order. Gift basket professionals are also taking advantage of co-op opportunities. Co-oping calls for unselfishness and putting competition on hold so that the buying members can purchase goods at a lower cost than they would usually spend if buying individually. Co-op buying also takes away the worry about meeting a vendor's high minimum, because the total order will easily take care of the minimum requirements.

Some of California's professional gift basket groups purchase through co-ops, as do groups in other states where camaraderie comes first, fueling the entrepreneurial spirit of achievement. Ask some of your competitors if they are involved in co-op buying. If not, then you know that the opportunity exists to start a co-op, but only if everyone involved can be trusted to order together and pay the bill accordingly.

Home-Based Holds on Wines and Alcohol

Liquor licenses cost hundreds of dollars to purchase, and cities and towns issue only a certain number of licenses each year. Couple this with the fact that you are a home-based business whose local health department can barely keep up with small-business changes, let alone allow you to sell alcohol. In assessing the types of baskets you will create for clients each month, ask yourself: (1) How many baskets will I make containing alcohol? (2) Is a liquor license worth the fee? and (3) Am I ready to be responsible for the laws associated with selling alcohol?

> *I don't bother with alcohol, because it's against the law in most states if you're home-based and because there are too many stipulations: If you're caught, you're fined; if you deliver a basket and leave it with a minor who happens to drink it, you're really in trouble. It's just not worth the problems.*

Another concern is shipping baskets that contain alcoholic beverages. Some states allow this practice while others prohibit shipping alcohol across state lines. These rules are exasperating for those who have licenses, let alone the home-based designer.

There may be special situations where you consider adding alcohol to a basket. Some states have rules saying that alcohol can be added if the client brings the bottle to your workshop. Others want that, plus the client has to physically place it in the basket. These situations may not be special enough. Do you think the client has time to come to your office with alcohol and put it in the basket? This defeats the home-based concept of service. Leave wines and alcohol in the liquor store, and tend to your core clients. Also, remember that the market offers great substitutes. Sparkling ciders and juices are extremely popular. Look for products with interesting labels, flavors, and bottle shapes.

Selecting the proper inventory takes preparation to make the best decisions that result from understanding your market and its needs.

Selecting Your Inventory Checklist

<u>Completed</u>

1. Call local health department to determine existing home-based gift basket business restrictions. _____

2. Decide how many gift basket themes you will create and market successfully. _____

3. Call trade show producers to register for future shows you can attend. _____

4. Prepare a complete list of products you are prepared to purchase to start your business. Check the list carefully. _____

5. Find local florist suppliers in the Yellow Pages and visit them. List useful products and document their costs. _____

6. Order product catalogs and select appropriate products. _____

7. Order gift basket supplies. If food: Ask manufacturer to send tasting samples with order. _____

8. Ask competitors if they consolidate their purchases or know of any co-op groups. _____

9. As deliveries arrive, check the packing slip against your order. Ensure that products are not damaged, that products are date-coded (if food, or code yourself), and arrange products on shelves in workspace. _____

10. Call Dun & Bradstreet and apply for a DUNS number. _____

Chapter Five

Gift Basket Design Tips and Techniques

W̶e've arrived at Design Central, where your hands-on gift basket class is about to begin. This chapter will take you step-by-step through one of the many methods of basket creation, making you an instant designer or at least a more knowledgeable one than you are now. Every professional uses similar techniques fused with tricks learned over the years that work best for him or her. While practicing this craft, you'll also incorporate special touches to make beautiful baskets in your signature style.

It's also important to study other design methods by attending conferences, watching videos, and speaking with colleagues who've learned through trial and error and through varied training sources.

Before beginning, have all basket-making products together on the worktable (Figure 1). The tools that you'll use in the lesson are: a medium-size basket or container; foods; gifts; enhancements; shred; Sahara foam (one brick); one sheet of tissue paper (any color); basket filler (printed or unprinted newspaper); cellophane; clear (transparent) tape; double-coated tape; a long, sharp knife; four bamboo skewers; and a nonstick pull bow.

Step 1: Filling the Basket

The Sahara foam is the hidden object that sits in the basket, horizontally stabilizing foods and gifts for all to see. The foam must fit snugly into the basket and be level with the basket's rim.

Place the foam in the basket to determine how to carve it (using a knife) to fit the basket's shape by trimming and shaving it on the top, bottom, or sides. Figure 2 shows a precarved foam brick. Its sides have been trimmed to fit the depicted basket, which is wider at the top and gradually decreases in size toward the bottom. Be careful not to trim too much before remeasuring the foam in the basket or you will have to start again using another brick, saving the smaller one for the next creation.

Figure 1

After trim and fitting, the foam is placed on a double layer of tissue paper (one piece folded in half). Trim the tissue lengthwise (parallel to the center fold) so that 3 inches of tissue are on either side of the foam. Wrap the foam in the tissue

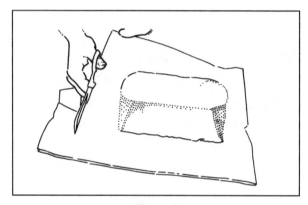

Figure 2

paper, taping the top overlap and folded ends (Figures 3 and 4). The tissue is doubled so that tape can be applied (if needed) to hold the products in place on top of the foam. When the recipient tears the tissue by taking products out, another layer keeps the foam covered and the residue out of the recipient's eyes and off his or her clothes. Also, the tissue paper's color doesn't matter, as the shred and enhancements will mask a noncoordinated color.

Next, fill the bottom of the basket with your choice of filler. Push the filler down for a firm fit (Figure 5). Now return the foam inside the basket (Figure 6). If the basket has so much filler that the foam cannot sit properly at the rim, either mash the filler farther down into the basket or remove a portion so that the foam fits in place. After the foods and gifts are secured, shred will fill the additional spaces between the foam and basket. The inner basket base is complete.

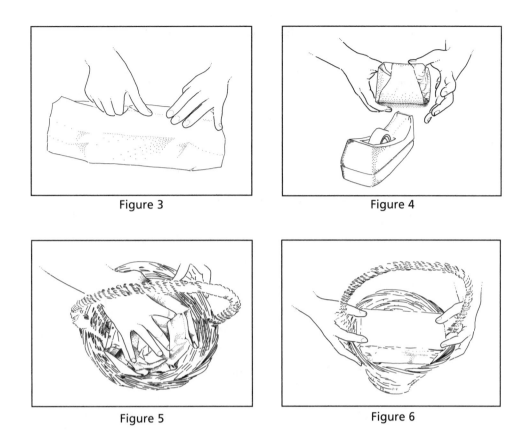

Figure 3

Figure 4

Figure 5

Figure 6

Step 2: Planning the Product Placement

With the products (foods and gifts) you've chosen to fill the basket in front of you, assess where each product will be placed before the arrangement is completed. Follow this guide:

- Product placement starts in the middle, with other items secured around the centerpiece product.
- Larger items go in the back, smaller in front (graduated method of allowing all products to be seen).
- Bottles are centered and placed slightly toward the back (if placed at the very back, the basket will tip over due to the concentrated, heavier weight).

- Some baskets are styled with all products facing front, while others place products for viewing on all sides.

  I prefer turning the basket's products so they are viewed all around the basket, but because they require a good number of items, I reserve this look for baskets $50 and up. Customers love it and frequently order the larger baskets to get this styling.

- Products do not have to be symmetrically placed. For example, if a tall item is on the basket's left side, another tall product is not necessarily needed on the basket's right. Enhancements also do not have to be symmetrical; place them where you wish.

Figure 7

Because this is your design, do what appeals to your sense of style. Colleague and customer critiques will guide you through adjustments. Figure 7 shows one type of placement strategy. The middle bottle can be tilted because the handle and curling ribbon will be used as anchors. A no-handle basket calls for an upright bottle.

Step 3: Product Anchoring

Choose the first product and a bamboo skewer for midbasket placement (Figure 8). The first product, a medium-size bottle, needs a skewer two-thirds long for secure anchoring. In most cases, bamboo skewers are broken into thirds so that three separate products use each piece.

Break the size of bamboo skewer needed, putting the rest aside for later use. To break the skewer, either snap it between both hands, using thumbs and index fingers, or cut it with scissors (Figure 9). Place the skewer lengthwise on the product and hold it in place (Figure 10). The default placement is in back of the product, but if for some reason the product is so large that it hangs off the foam in back, place the skewer on the product's side or front. Ultimately, the skewer will be masked for nondetection.

Figure 8   Figure 9

Figure 10 shows about 2 inches of skewer on the product and 3 inches below (a smaller, lighter product requires about 2 inches below). Now place a piece of transparent tape lengthwise on the skewer and product (Figure 11). The tape covers the length of the stick directly on the product plus ¼ inch above the stick. Now put the same-size length of double-coated tape directly on top of the transparent tape. Press a small amount of shred onto the double-coated tape, which acts to mask the skewer. The product is ready for placement into the foam inside the basket. The skewer will break the tissue paper's seal as it goes into the foam (Figure 12). If you don't like the placement (product tilting back, not centered, etc.), pick the product up and reinsert it as many times as needed until you are satisfied.

Because the bottle is set slightly tilted, its neck must be anchored to the handle. Tie and knot curling ribbon around the bottle's neck, then tie and knot the ribbon around the handle, curling the ribbon's ends with scissors (Figures 13 and 14).

Products can also be stabilized with tape set on the bottom of the product down to the tissue-covered foam. Place approximately 6 inches of transparent tape evenly from the product to the tissue paper (Figure 15).

Not all products need a bamboo skewer for stabilizing. Some items will fit and stay in place between the basket and foam snug enough not to move, as shown by the boxed product placed in back of the bottle (Figure 16). This is an ideal point to place a glue dot between the box and bottle for extra security. The next product, a whimsical book on dieting, is wrapped with cellophane to protect it before a bamboo skewer is taped to its back. The picture of the book shows how to press the shred on top of the double-coated tape to mask the skewer (Figure 17).

Gift Basket Design Tips and Techniques

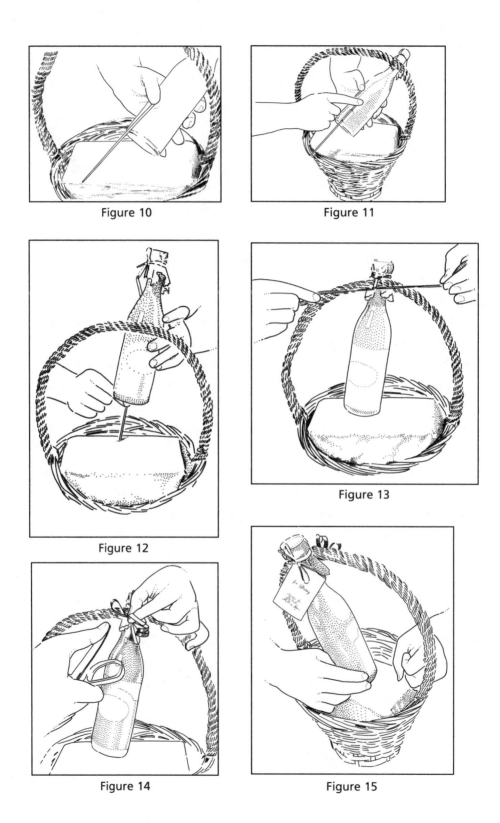

Figure 10

Figure 11

Figure 12

Figure 13

Figure 14

Figure 15

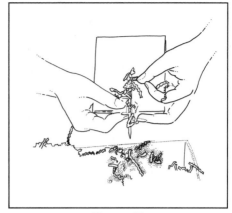

| Figure 16 | Figure 17 |

Choose the next product. Repeat from the process in step 3 until all products are anchored. Is your basket design as you had originally envisioned it? Is it better? Your work of art is almost complete.

Step 4: Finishing Touches

Shred is added in and around the openings on top of the covered foam and between the products. Depending on the shred used, a little or a lot is needed to add depth to the basket. Shred is about ½ inch high atop the foam throughout the basket so that it does not cover the product names or overwhelm the contents (Figures 18 and 19).

Enhancements are next. Use whatever fits the theme, placing flowers, birds, ting ting, ivy, star spray, and other adornments throughout the basket. This sample basket shows how to add star spray and ting ting.

Star spray is purchased tall and straight. Place it in the basket as is or add dazzle by curling the long grass, using the scissors' edge (as done with curling ribbon). Wind the wired stars around a pencil or marking pen, then gently pull the stars upward for height before basket inclusion (Figures 20 and 21). Treat star spray with kindness; the stars will come out of the casing if pulled too firmly.

Ting ting is shipped in long, thick bundles. To shorten, break the ting ting by hand or cut it with scissors. As with star spray, place where preferred in the basket, again breaking the tissue's seal and bringing the bottom down into the foam (Figure 22).

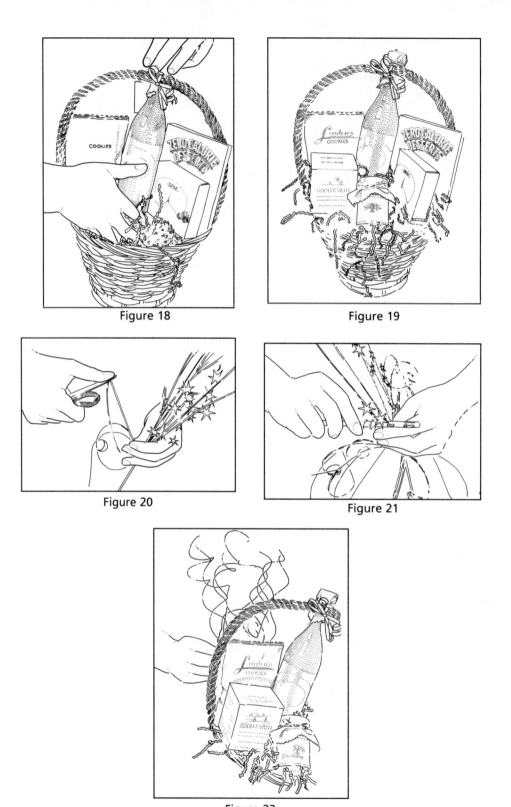

Figure 18

Figure 19

Figure 20

Figure 21

Figure 22

| Figure 23 | Figure 24 |

Shorter enhancements are nice to place in the basket's front and between products. Don't forget to add a business card or other promotional piece inside the basket between the shred and the container.

You've created a great design (Figure 23). Now on to the finish.

Step 5: Wrapping the Creation

The basket is ready for cellophane closure. Roll the clear cellophane out across the clean work surface. Place the basket on top, bringing both ends of the cellophane about 8 inches above the basket (Figure 24). Measure the cellophane all around the basket, ensuring that the sides and top are evenly distributed (bring the sides of the cellophane up to touch the basket's sides to measure uniformity). Have the bow made and ready for placement. There are two popular ways to apply cellophane, and each is described in turn.

Method 1. With edges together, hold one side of the cellophane at the top, about 6 inches from the edge. Bring the cellophane sitting flat on the table (the small piece of cellophane that winds from front to back) straight up to the basket's side (your hand is now

Figure 25

Figure 26

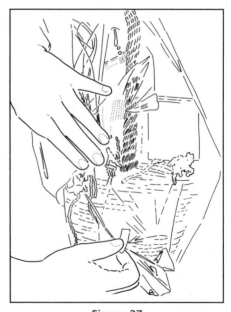

Figure 27

touching the side of the basket) (Figure 25). Holding it in place, fold the lower cellophane at the back of the basket toward the front (around the basket), then fold the front cellophane toward the back (in the opposite direction) (Figure 26). Let go of the cellophane at the top and hold the three-corner side wrapping in place. Put a piece of transparent tape at the point where all three pieces meet (Figure 27).

Figure 28

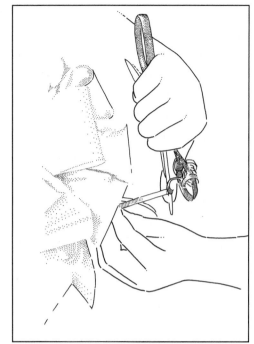

Figure 29

Repeat method 1 to complete the other side. If there's an extra person at home, have him or her hold the top of the cellophane while you work on the sides.

When both sides are complete, gather all cellophane at the top and hold it between your index finger and the thumb of your hand (right-handed persons should use their left hand, vice versa for left-handed persons). Firmly pull the top cellophane upward with your free hand to smooth the cellophane's appearance around the basket (Figure 28). When you're satisfied with the look, place the bow in front of the basket at the neck and bring each narrow ribbon on either side under your hand and to the back. Let go of your grip around the cellophane and tie the ribbon twice to make a knot. Here you can gently pull the cellophane once more at the top to again smooth the appearance. Add more curling ribbon around the neck if desired and curl with scissors (Figure 29). The ribbon will fall like locks of hair around the cellophane. Trim the extra cellophane above the ribbon by gathering it between your index finger and thumb about 4 inches from the top and cutting in a fanlike circle to make the cellophane more uniform and stylish. Figure 30 shows the finished creation.

Gift Basket Design Tips and Techniques

Method 2. The second wrapping technique is similar but shown using a smaller popcorn basket. Again, gather the cellophane at the top of the basket, holding it between your index finger and the thumb. Pull the cellophane above with all-around firmness (Figure 31). Place the bow around the neck and tie twice in back, making a knot. The cellophane on either side of the basket is out and open.

Working on one side, hold the two cellophane edges together and fold the cellophane end over end in 1-inch folds toward the basket's back until it's flush against the side. Tape in place. Repeat on the other side (Figure 32).

In both methods, there are extra cellophane creases and gaps to hide at the bottom of the basket. Hold the basket up at eye's view with one hand. With about 6 inches of transparent tape in hand, place 1 inch on a crease. Pull the tape down and under the basket for a clearer, more polished look. Repeat where needed around the basket bottom. If desired, place a promotional company label on the cellophane in front or just off to the side.

One extra design (Figure 33) uses a fabric-covered box as the base, a teacup and saucer on top, and a cappuccino mix inside the cup. The stacking technique is achieved by placing graduated items above the larger base. A glue dot is placed between the cup and saucer to bind them together. Shred is placed around the cappuccino mix inside the cup. Cellophane ties the entire gift together, restricting movement between the products. Close the cellophane, top with a bow, and trim the uneven cellophane on top.

Congratulations! Your basic gift basket is complete and ready for sale.

Design and Construction Changes

Here are ideas and other techniques to help you with more gift basket designs.

Basket Bags

The popularity of basket bags has made encasing much easier for today's professional and is a wonderful alternative to cellophane and shrink-wrapping. When the basket is complete, it is inserted into the top of the bag. A bow is used to close the top entrance, and the extra bag protruding from the sides is folded toward the back of the basket in small folds, then taped in place.

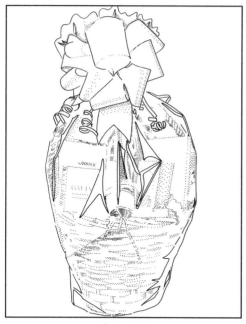

Figure 30

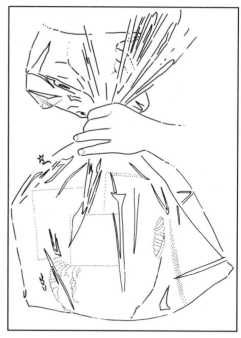

Figure 31

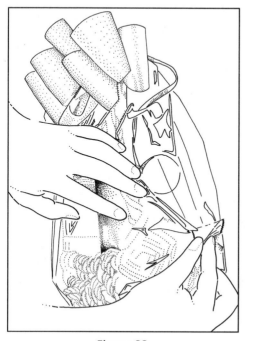

Figure 32

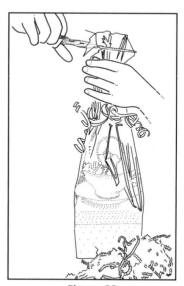

Figure 33

Sahara Foam and Large Baskets

If one foam brick is too small for a large basket, join two bricks together using wire pins bought at any floral supply store. Insert each prong of the U-shaped wire pin into the side of each brick. Then trim the bricks as needed for a snug fit and cover in tissue paper before continuing. You should need no more than four pins per two bricks (two each on the top and bottom).

Extra Bamboo Skewers

Sometimes a bottle or larger package is too heavy or wide for one bamboo skewer. When necessary, tape two skewers to the product, about 1 inch apart from one another and so that they project 3 inches below the bottom of the bottle.

Product Stacking

Foods and gifts are placed not only individually in baskets but also on top of each other. One example is the tall gift with the fabric-covered box. Another example is a basket using several flat-topped products that give a slight boost to smaller products sitting on top. The box of tea in the main basket design is one such product that can become a base to a supporting item. Use one of the following to bind two products together: (1) double-coated tape, (2) transparent tape evenly attached between the two products, or (3) glue dots.

Flower Wrapping

Any silk plant or flower that is manufactured on a vine, such as ivy, is perfect for wrapping around a basket's handle. The vine is usually supported by internal wire, so circular wrapping is quick. Wrapping is also popular around the basket's rim by attaching flowers using separate strands of wire twisted on the inside of the basket or by using a coordinating curling ribbon concealed by shred on the inner basket. When wire is used, it is first bent into a U-shape. The ends are inserted between the basket slats from the outside and twisted on the inside.

Other Enhancements

A bow's tail hanging down the front of the basket can support a gift tag. After writing the client's sentiment, staple the tag onto the tail.

A balloon, another enhancement, is usually placed at the top in the center of the cellophane. No matter how snugly the ribbon is tied, a supported balloon will fit. Inflate the balloon, twist the knot around a balloon cup, and insert the matching tube into the bottom. The tube's length can be shortened by breaking it like a bamboo skewer. Then insert the tube through the gathered cellophane center and down into the wrapped basket until the balloon sits on the cellophane. As the tube enters the designed basket, guide it around the products to ensure that nothing comes unglued, untaped, or unmasked. If the tube is too long (the balloon sits too high above the cellophane), pull the balloon and cup off the tube (still inserted inside the cellophane), break off the excess, and replace the balloon.

Quick-Change Artistry

By now you know that more than just baskets are used in creating packaged gifts. The fabric-covered box is great for inserting gourmet-flavored teas and coffees, notepaper, or matching coasters. Instead of using the featured cappuccino mix, sugar-coated or chocolate-covered spoons are a nice touch in the cup. Fit a piece of Sahara foam in the cup, cover with tissue, insert the upright spoons (handles are halfway down in the foam), and surround with coordinating shred. Add enhancements, gather the cellophane at the top, and tie on a bow.

A Word about Shrink-Wrap

Although shrink-wrap is not shown in the drawings, it is as popular as cellophane and basket bags and possibly more widely used because stores use shrink-wrap to protect baskets from the many customer hands that poke and pry into the basket on the selling floor.

The best way to understand how to use shrink-wrap is to attend a gift trade show and ask the representative to demonstrate its use. Shrink-wrap machines are sold in several widths; the wider the machine, the more choices of gift basket sizes to wrap. Chapter 4 includes more detail on shrink-wrap equipment and materials. Don't rush into a buying decision. Collect information on manufacturers' prices and added buying incentives, such as a discounted starter kit of shells, a free crimper, or a how-to video.

Style by Trial and Error

Experiment with your style of gift basket creation as much as possible. The time to wonder if a bottle is secure or to find out that hot glue melts packaging or enhancements is not while making a client's order. Try your style on a medium- and a large-size basket. If those work well, smaller sizes won't be a problem. The section "Tracking Production Time," later in this chapter, explains why early experimentation is so important.

After securing a few products, tip the basket sideways (parallel to the table). Does anything move, twist, or turn? If so, does the product push other items out of place? The point is to stabilize products securely without gluing or taping so much that the gift is welded together and the recipient must cut the product out of its wrapping to eat or otherwise use it. Take your time, find the preferred comfort level to style great baskets, and put a streamlined method of creating in place for the business to come.

Themes, Colors, and Other Considerations

Custom baskets are created for many themes. What would you use in a basket for a second marriage, which incorporates a different mix of products from those given to a new bride, or the birthday of a person who loves anything shaped like a star? These are some of the questions clients will ask that challenge your theming capabilities. Some clients will want a fixed-price basket and leave the selections up to you (most gift basket professionals love this type of client), while others will want a certain theme and price and must scrutinize every item selected (like doctors, I've been told that former gift basket professionals make the worst clients). Such detail can be methodical and a bit overwhelming, but in providing exceptional customer service, you'll tell clients what's available, ask them what the recipient likes or prefers, and come to an understanding of the right blend for the occasion.

Pleasing everyone who calls is a tall order not easily accomplished, nor should it be your absolute priority. About 1 to 3 percent of all calls each year won't be fulfilled due to competition, lack of product selection, and clients' indecision. If 1,000 sales calls are received in a year, up to 30 may be unfulfilled. The good news is that 970 calls will have produced sales.

Another type of theming is the use of coordinated colors. Black and white, blue and silver, yellow and green, and red, white, and blue are examples of color coordination uniquely detailed through product packaging, shred, and enhancements. Even a natural-colored basket is a candidate for coordination by painting it with a nontoxic, odorless spray.

Last, but not least, are three more facts to consider when selecting products and styling your baskets:

1. Beware of buying too many seasonal prints. When the holidays end and you still have cookies prepackaged in cans printed with Christmas motifs, you'll have to either eat the cookies or give them away because you can't sell them next year. Buy a few prints if necessary, but make most of your holiday and special-occasion purchases a selection of colors appropriate for all-occasion sales.

2. During the summer months, or if you live in a year-round warm climate, chocolates may not be a smart purchase. Imagine being the recipient of a melted, gooey mess. If the client says that chocolate is a must, select products that won't melt. Chocolate sauces in jars, chocolate pasta, and chocolate cheesesticks are wise and delicious substitutes.

3. Foods should never share the same basket with strongly scented candles and bath products. Fragrances absorb into edibles, creating a flavor that sends taste buds into shock.

4. When putting two drinking glasses together inside of a basket, secure them by placing glue dots directly between the glasses. This padding will allow the glasses to share the same space without breaking en route to the recipient.

Maintaining Bug-Free Baskets

It is extremely important to inspect products when they arrive and again before placing them in baskets. If your home has a bug problem, use large plastic storage containers, found in discount stores, to hold all products, and keep the opaque lids snapped shut. Then put the containers on storage shelves. There's no time or extra money available to discard and replace products that should have been protected on arrival.

A manufacturer may also play host to bugs that are found only after your careful merchandise inspection. Years ago I recruited my family for a popcorn taste test. Before opening a light caramel flavor, I happened to glance at the product through the clear packaging. It was small, but inside the bag was a thin worm about 1 inch long. It was the same color as the popcorn, so it was hard to detect, but thankfully I saw it. There could have been a hole the size of a pinprick in the bag, or perhaps the product was not as fresh as it should have been. Nevertheless, the bag was discarded. Today I'd bring the problem to the manufacturer's attention, request a credit toward my next order, not buy the product again, or all of the above. This is not a bug example to turn you against popcorn (there are some fabulous flavors on the market that are irresistible). Bugs feast on all types of foods, so inspect the products carefully.

Gift basket professionals love to line fireside baskets containing an assortment of snacks, spreads, and hot beverages with pinecones found in backyards, woods, and parks. Cones add a rustic, homelike appeal. However, the bugs that call these cones home seem to enjoy making a special appearance that the recipient will never forget. To avoid that situation, bake the cones for ten minutes in a 350-degree oven or for two minutes in a microwave oven before adding them to a basket. After baking, the cones are ready for use as is or can be lightly sprayed with gold paint to add highlights and a warm, golden touch.

Keeping Wrapped Baskets Dust-Free

When returning to your office after hours of showing baskets at shows, fairs, and other events, open cellophane exposed over time to air particles becomes a magnet for dust and flying debris. By the time those same baskets are transported to the next event, they're a dusty mess and must be rewrapped before showing again. The cellophane or shrink-wrap is taken off, the bow reworked, and new cellophane used to cover the basket.

Re-covering baskets uses your time and money. Even if cellophane costs 12 cents per use, rewrapping a number of baskets each month adds up over time. Keeping wrapped gift baskets dust-free is easy, especially when you take just a few minutes to cover and care for them the moment you return from a sales event.

Reserve at least one storage shelf or additional table for wrapped baskets, or install another shelf specifically for these arrangements. Cover them with one extra-large, lightweight drop cloth. Lightweight, scarflike material surrounds the baskets without weighing the top down into the basket's midsection. When the cloth is removed, the baskets should have a showroom shine. If you're not satisfied, give the baskets a quick sweep with a lambswool duster to remove microscopic particles trapped on the cloth's underside. Dust penetrates everything, but lambswool removes dust from blinds like magic, so it will perform miracles on cellophane, basket bags, and shrink-wrap.

> *A summer sheet is placed on my baskets when they arrive in*
> *the office after an all-day display. If that's not good enough,*
> *I'll use my shrink-wrap heat gun to blow off the excess dust.*

If you must remove the cellophane, save the covering to use as filler material (rather than newspaper) within another basket design.

Pricing Your Baskets for Profit

A basket's wholesale price (the price it costs you to make the basket) is calculated by totaling each and every product used, no exceptions. From there a simple formula is applied to calculate the retail price. We'll use the sample basket created in this chapter as a visual aid.

The total wholesale basket cost is $14.98, which is tripled to calculate the retail price (the price a customer will pay for your gift basket). The sum of $44.94 ($14.98 x 3) is rounded to $45.00. The triple pricing formula is used by professionals nationwide because it justifies both product and labor markup. If you are to profit, your retail basket cost has to reflect more than just a doubling of the wholesale cost, and tripling your inventory costs assures profitability.

Some professionals practice what is known as triple-plus pricing. This is the ability to overtriple the wholesale price, which can be mastered only after years of research to find wholesale sources with the lowest-priced, high-quality products. For example, a basket that wholesales for $10 can be sold for $40. It will take time for you to sell your baskets at this markup, because time is what's needed to find a multitude of wholesale product sources for selection to determine the best places to buy. Once your business is in this category, your

Sample Basket Cost

Item	Cost	Details
Basket	$2.75	$33.00/12 baskets or $3.00 each
Newspaper	.08	Based on a 50-page newspaper for 50 cents, 1 cent each page; 8 pages used in the bottom as filler
Sahara foam	.70	$13.95/case (20 foam bricks in a case)
Tissue paper	.04	$18.50/500 sheets (4 cents/sheet)
Bamboo skewers	.03	$1.25 for 100; 2 sticks used (1/3 each for 6 products)
Cinnamon spice drink	3.00	
Chocolate chip cookies	.25	
Whimsical diet book	3.18	
Tea bags	.99	
Shelf-stable cheese	1.28	
Preserves	.80	
Bow	.17	$2.00/50-yard roll (4 cents/yard); 13 feet (4 1/3 yards) used for bow
Cellophane	.12	$3.00 for a 30-inch-by-100-foot roll (3 cents/foot); approximately 4 feet/basket
Shred	.80	$25 for 10 pounds/sizzle shred ($2.50/pound or 16 cents/ounce); approximately 5 ounces/basket
Ting ting (5 pcs.)	.28	$5.50 for 100 (.055 cent each)
Star spray	.50	$6.00/12 (50 cents each)
Curling ribbon (2 yds.)	.01	$1.50/500 yards (.003 cent/yard)
Total goods	$14.98	
Multiply by 3	3	Increase multiplicant if desired
Total	$44.94	
Actual retail cost	$45.00	Always round off higher

profits will skyrocket, as this is one formula that aids long-term professionals in successful growth.

To properly price your wholesale products, freight charges associated with getting the items into your workspace must be evenly divided into the quantity ordered and individual cost. The foam bricks were purchased at a nearby floral distributor, and even though the distributor is 5 miles away from the home office, the travel cost is logged as a regular monthly business mileage expense. If the bricks were shipped by an outside carrier charging $5.00 for delivery, each brick would cost 95 cents rather than 70 cents ($13.95 + 5.00 = $18.95 / 20).

> *My first basket sold for $30, and I put $22 worth of products in it. That didn't even account for the enhancements or shrink-wrap. I'll never do that again.*

Keep a combination wholesale/retail cost sheet and product listing by the telephone. The sample Product List and Cost Sheet on the next page shows how to structure an alphabetized list of available products with basket costs. "Quantity in Stock" and "Wholesale Cost" represent available products and their cost, including freight. The first line is a sample of how to complete each row. "Quantity Sold" x "Wholesale Cost" = "Total Cost of Quantity Sold."

When a client calls saying he or she wants a $50 basket, you have a ready-made list in hand to ensure that you don't undercharge yourself when giving price information. Update the quantity list as each product is sold. This chart is kept either on computer or by using manual slashing for updating. Unless you've chosen a software program that automatically tallies the information, this list is easy to develop to show the inventory available for sale and the cost of products sold, which you'll need for end-of-year taxes.

In time, you might maintain a basic list of all-occasion baskets containing preselected products that your clients consistently order. For example, a thank-you gift basket might include crackers, cheese, sausage, nuts, biscotti, and bottled water that wholesale for $10 (including basket and supplies), with the retail cost charged to the customer at no less than $30. If this becomes a standard basket that you create, then a custom listing such as this can be kept by the telephone and offered to your customers as a specialty basket. You'll automatically know the costs, and you must also maintain an updated inventory list to ensure that each product within the specialty basket is available.

Product List and Cost Sheet

Products	Quantity in Stock	Quantity Sold	Wholesale Cost	Total Cost of Quantity Sold
Foods				
Biscotti - 4 oz.	24	8	$1.20	$9.60
Coffee - 6 oz. decaf.	12		0.99	
Coffee - 6 oz. mocha	12		0.99	
Cocoa - 6 oz.	12		0.75	
Cookies - choc. chip	18		0.75	
Cookies - shortbread	18		0.80	
Crackers - champagne	12		0.99	
Crackers - water	6		0.99	
Pancake mix - 8 oz.	6		1.30	
Popcorn - cheddar	12		1.30	
Popcorn - chocolate	12		1.50	
Gifts				
Baby bottle	6		0.90	
Baby rattle	6		0.49	
Business card holder	12		1.10	
Golf balls	24		0.75	
Golf tees	12		0.80	
Linen napkins	12		1.29	
Notepads	18		0.85	
Paperweight - pyramid	6		1.85	
Paperweight - square	6		1.85	
Stuffed animal - bear	6		2.50	
Stuffed animal - clown	12		2.30	
TOTALS				

Basket Cost Sheet *(based on triple markup)*

Wholesale	Retail	Wholesale	Retail
$10.00	$30.00	$26.00	$78.00
$12.00	$36.00	$28.00	$84.00
$14.00	$42.00	$30.00	$90.00
$16.00	$48.00	$32.00	$96.00
$18.00	$54.00	$34.00	$102.00
$20.00	$60.00	$36.00	$108.00
$22.00	$66.00	$38.00	$114.00
$24.00	$72.00	$40.00	$120.00

You're in business to succeed. Calculating all charges correctly will ensure fair rates for customers while ensuring your profitability.

Tracking Production Time

How long did it take you to make that sample basket? Professionals usually take no longer than fifteen minutes to make an average basket, and the time increases for styling larger or more intricate designs.

Knowing how long it takes to create a basket is an important factor in understanding what your time is worth versus what you currently make and how much you'd like to earn. Other considerations are:

- *Multiple baskets.* If asked to make fifty baskets, you'll have a better understanding of how long it will take to complete the order.
- *Outsourcing.* Retail stores needing gift basket expertise want your services, but is the price right for you according to what they need, what they will pay, and time parameters?
- *The value of your time.* As your business grows, what is your time worth?

Of course, the larger the basket, the more time that's factored into making it. But if you have mastered the techniques and mechanics, less time is used, thereby increasing your worth and available time to market your business.

Follow this example: Last month, Jane met with state transportation executives, which resulted in an order for five $100 baskets. She's calculated that her total wholesale cost is $166. Her labor charge is $34 per basket. This is derived by doubling the $33 wholesale cost for each basket ($66) and calculating the difference between $66 and the $100 retail charge. If one basket is completed in fifteen minutes, Jane will earn $2.27 per minute, or $136.20 an hour. However, if she takes thirty minutes to make each basket, her time drops to $1.13 a minute, or $67.80 an hour.

$34 labor divided by 15 minutes = $2.27/minute. $2.27 x 60 minutes = $136.20/hour.

$34 labor divided by 30 minutes = $1.13/minute. $1.13 x 60 minutes = $67.80/hour.

It's up to you to practice your basket-making abilities before securing orders. The per-minute charge may not seem like much, but as the clock ticks, which rate would you rather earn?

Learning techniques for making gift baskets, perfecting your style, and establishing prices brings you to a milestone in setting up your business. Let's move on to corporate clients, the second largest selling category after holiday sales.

Gift Basket Design Techniques Checklist

		Completed
1.	Make sure all needed products for basket creation are in-house before assembling your first basket.	_____
2.	Plan where each product will fit in a basket before securing it into place.	_____
3.	Make your bow before applying cellophane or shrink-wrap to the basket.	_____
4.	Experiment with your basket-making style to become comfortable with the techniques before receiving your first order. Time yourself to prepare a basket in the least time possible for the greatest earnings potential.	_____
5.	Check all products for bug-related problems as products arrive in the office and before placing them in a basket.	_____
6.	Find a lightweight cloth for covering sample baskets to minimize dust and flying debris.	_____
7.	Prepare a Product List and Cost Sheet on available products and markup price.	_____

Chapter Six

The Elusive Corporate Market

N o longer a corporate luxury, gift baskets have established themselves as an integral part of the world of business. They are a key component to opening the doors between companies and clients. Gift baskets are part of the multibillion-dollar corporate gift market, composed of gift certificates, engravables, travel, crystal, clocks, and other appreciable incentives that compete for corporate attention.

Why Corporations Need Gift Baskets

The corporate world buys gift baskets for every reason imaginable. Some of the more common uses include opening the doors of new business opportunities; maintaining goodwill at any time during a company's life; apologizing for mix-ups, blunders, and other errors; congratulating a client or prospect; expressing appreciation; sending condolences; and saying thanks during the holidays.

The U.S. Department of Commerce classifies a corporation's size by the number of people employed in a firm:

- Small—99 or fewer employees
- Midsize—100 to 499 employees
- Large—500 or more employees

Other businesses, as mentioned in Chapter 1, are also prime candidates to buy gift baskets. They include independent professionals (doctors, dentists, interior decorators/designers, veterinarians, consultants), nonprofit organizations (youth agencies, community groups, charities, blood banks), and institutions (hospitals, schools, nursing homes). These professionals and groups depend on the generosity of donations, volunteers, benefactors, and referrals, and they thank their sponsors by using baskets and elaborate gifts at benefits and black-tie events.

Who Makes the Decision to Buy?

Typically, people in managerial positions and those who assist them lead the list of gift basket buyers. Some of the more common positions are human resources personnel, sales and marketing executives, CEOs and vice-presidents, office managers, purchasing managers, and executive assistants by any name (administrative assistants, secretaries, clerks). Every potential corporate client needs your business name in his or her PDA or your card in his or her Rolodex or rotary file or on a notepad, magnetic sticker, or other desk accessory displaying your name as the only logical source for corporate baskets. (More information on the many types of advertising specialties appears in Chapter 7.)

Where and How to Find Corporate Clients

Clients are found in the most common places—they're where you live, work, play, and shop. Many gift basket designers start selling to the corporate sector by introducing their businesses to companies with which they already have a solid relationship. Such companies belong to the independent professionals who provide them with services, such as dentists, doctors, accountants, attorneys, cleaning services, and others whom they see periodically. Although not independent, you can add your banker and post office personnel to this lucrative group.

No longer will you visit a service professional, give him or her your money, and walk out the door. Right after the service ends and before you leave, it's time to casually mention how your gift baskets open new doors of opportunity. In time, you will also ask about organizations that each belongs to in order to gauge opportunities to make presentations to entire groups of service professionals that also need gift baskets to build their businesses.

My veterinarian is a longtime client, a relationship which commenced immediately after one of my pets was lifted from the examination table. The end of the pet's visit was my signal to start talking about gift baskets. I told the vet that my gifts had helped other business owners introduce their companies to prospects who, in turn, started doing business with them because of the door-opening gifts I designed. Within weeks, I received an order from the veterinarian to send a basket to relatives he had recently visited.

Independent professionals are stressed for time. They work for themselves and are often affiliated with health-care or other facilities, and that leaves them little time to shop for gifts.

Always carry your business cards and distribute them after your teeth are cleaned, taxes are completed, and will is drawn. If you are doing business with independent professionals and other service individuals, they should be doing business with you.

Potential clients are also people you read about and admire. Sometimes they're a victim of circumstances, the front-page news story or back-page advertiser. Here are some worthwhile places to start your search.

Your Town Newspaper

- Business section—for general businesses in all industries
- Real estate section—Realtors' names
- Living section—interior decorators, remodelers
- People page—promotions, new hires, good news
- Classified—ads containing human resources names
- Automobile section—car dealers, automotive services, car repairers and restorers
- Adopt-a-Pet section—veterinarians, animal shelters
- Health section—physicians, hospital staff names
- Travel section—agency names, cruise organizations, travel clubs

Not taking time to read the paper is like losing a sale every day. The Sunday paper takes about thirty minutes to review; the dailies, less time. Keep paper, pen, and scissors handy to write down names and clip articles of interest. Then you can create a tailored message to introduce yourself and how your gift baskets will benefit a company's image and future sales.

City, State, and Regional Magazines

- Feature articles
- Advertisements—spas, restaurants, theaters

Networking Events

- Chamber of commerce gatherings
- Charity balls and auctions
- Business over breakfast, group luncheons, and after-hours dinners
- Museum exhibits
- Annual conferences

Special Events

- Private company group meetings
- Nonprofit organization charity functions
- Holiday parties

Company Meetings, Gatherings, and Special Needs

- Weekly staff meetings
- Lunch-and-learn sessions in company cafeterias
- Corporate apartments for out-of-town executives and visitors

Specialty Newspapers and Industry Journals

These publications are found in business libraries across the country. Examine the papers your clients read to stay in touch with the industry's trends, insights, and current issues. These facts are key to understanding a prospect's reason to buy baskets.

Town and Regional Lifestyles

- Boating events
- Convention town—hotels, destination management companies
- Ski resorts
- Casinos and other gaming establishments
- Entertainment capitals—New York City; Hollywood; Chicago; New Orleans; Branson, Missouri; Nashville, Tennessee

Local Company Web Sites

Yahoo.com's search engine quickly points you in the direction of possible gift basket clients who have a Web presence.

One way to find local businesses on the Web is through Yahoo's home page. Look for the U.S. States' link under the Regional heading. Click on your state's link, then on your city's link to reveal potential clients on the Web.

Company Web sites tell you a lot about each organization—what it manufactures or the type of service, firm size, officers, and other key personnel—the kind of preliminary information you need to compose your contact strategy.

This is just the beginning. The source materials that benefit your entering this lucrative market depend on how well you develop your marketing plan to introduce your baskets to the business world.

Another way is to type your city or county name and state into any search engine's search box. Be sure to place the words in quotation marks (example: "Boise, ID" or "Boise, Idaho"). Every potential customer or competitor in your area that has a Web presence will be found using this technique.

Choosing the Best-Selling Themes and Products

Themes

Corporate baskets obviously center on business themes and events, but buying also revolves around everyday occasions. Popular themes include:

- Thank You
- Appreciation
- Condolences
- Apology
- Happy Birthday
- Happy Administrative Professionals Week
- Congratulations
- Happy Holidays
- Happy New Year
- Welcome
- Best Wishes/Good Luck

Products

Corporate-based products are almost the same as your choices for general gift baskets. The differences will depend on the client, receiver, and theme. Here's a look at some corporate favorites to add to the Buying Chart outlined in Chapter 4.

Foods

- Smoked salmon, pâté, and seafood spreads
- Flavored crackers
- Jellies, jams, and preserves
- Gourmet mustards
- Boxes of truffles
- Instant coffees, teas, cocoa, and cappuccino
- Bottled, nonalcoholic beverages
- Cookies of all types (chocolate chip, shortbread, biscotti, and assortments)
- Kosher and sugar-free snacks
- Flavored and chocolate-covered nuts, pretzels, and popcorn
- All-in-one pasta dinners—great for visiting executives at corporate apartments
- Access to a reputable fruit market and bagel shop for daily, fresh goods that can be included in custom baskets

Gifts and Other Nonperishables

- Linens—a great gift and a terrific over-the-rim basket liner
- Paperweights
- Golf products and accessories
- Self-stick notes
- Travel accessories
- Stress relievers
- Journals, personalized notepads, and stationery
- Access to a newsstand with daily newspapers and business and regional magazines

Gift basket differences for corporate and individual buyers are separated by characteristics, such as (1) appropriateness (Are the gifts suitable for a corporate client?), (2) frilliness (Is the product too feminine or too personal? If so, it doesn't fit the corporate image), and (3) theme (Does the product fit the occasion?).

> *I know a local basket business that just got a contract with a real estate developer. New tenants receive picture frames and hangers, work gloves, a tool set, and an inventory book to list what they own, all contained in a personalized metal bucket.*

Your search through catalogs and conversations with clients will give you other ideas for products that please corporate buyers. If you cannot find a requested product after searching extensively, offer the client alternatives that suit his or her needs. Keep regional foods and leisuretime activities in mind, as products that remind the receiver of a favorite travel destination are extremely popular in gift baskets throughout the country.

Approaching Them with Care: Techniques and Key Words That Sell

Once you have identified prospects and decided which baskets to offer, you're ready to take the first step: contacting the client. The best contact method is the one that you're most comfortable with, gets you the appointment, and increases your sales. Your contact options are:

1. Call Them Directly

Making a cold call is a frightening task that is easily calmed when you find something in common to discuss. If a company has recently been under public scrutiny, has experienced good fortune, or is attempting to heal wounds, your baskets pose the perfect solution as you discuss with the client how to keep a good momentum going or what helps to smooth over bad times.

If the thought of making a cold call still leaves you as breathless as a roller-coaster ride, use these strategies to warm up the call:

- Ask clients for referrals. Name recognition is the glue that bonds you to prospects, making them more comfortable to take your call. A prospect reasons that if Bill Jones recommended you, you're worth talking to.
- Show your baskets at business events. Here is where executives wind down after a day's work to meet colleagues and new contacts in a relaxed environment. Bring tasting samples to place among your baskets. However, don't put everything out at one time—hungry prospects will make a meal of your goods and keep walking. Collect business cards in an empty container for an on-site prize drawing, and tell passersby how important gift baskets are to secure business relationships.

Asking direct questions gets to the heart of a prospect's need: "How many events does your company sponsor that require baskets? When should I call to prepare your end-of-year gift basket order? What promotional gifts do you currently use as incentives?" These questions open the door to understanding how best to approach prospects when you place your follow-up calls. Within days of the event, mail your literature as a reminder of the past meeting. In a few more days, call to review the prospect's need for baskets based on your conversation, make an appointment, and ask what other departments or associates need your service. Your focused plan of action quickly turns a cold call into a hot sale.

2. Fax by the Rules

According to the Federal Communications Commission, Title 47 of the Code of Federal Regulations, "No person may use a telephone facsimile machine, computer, or other device to send an unsolicited advertisement to a telephone facsimile machine." This rule makes the fax machine an option only after you've established a relationship with the prospect or have made the cold call and received an OK to send a fax.

Your fax message must get right to the point. A letter sent by fax tells the prospect why he or she should be interested in your baskets. Make the next action easy for the prospect— the bottom of the letter should include a portion to be filled out by him or her, giving you information on what the prospect's pending or future basket needs are. From there the prospect can fax the information back to you, and the process of serving a new client can begin.

3.   Create Mail That's Opened, Not Trashed

Postal mail is more often thrown away before it's opened, and what's not trashed is often scanned while we're doing something more important.

Colored envelopes, mailing tubes, and the use of first-class stamps beckon prospects to open the mail with undivided attention. Once they open it, the inside must contain a message as intriguing as the wrapping. Tell prospects why your gift baskets are the key to their professional success. Back up your message with one or two pictures, a color flyer or brochure, a news story on your company (if available), your Web site address, and whatever else will convince prospects that they need your product. As with e-mail or fax contact, make the prospect's next action easy. Invite him or her to an upcoming open house or offer a complimentary appointment. Focus your message on getting the prospect to do business with you.

Postcards are also very effective. There's no mail to open, and the picture and message tell an immediate story. Chapter 7 gives you more information on using postcards.

4.   E-mail the Executive

E-mail is said to be one of the most effective ways to get a prospect's direct and immediate attention. As with faxing, you must receive permission from the e-mail addressee before sending a message. Unsolicited e-mail, also known as spam, is rude and labels you an intruder rather than a professional. When you obtain permission to use an executive's e-mail address, there's still a slight chance that his or her secretary will review the message, but there's a better chance that the executive will read it personally and respond.

Create a compelling subject line, or the e-mail will never be opened. Subjects that state,

"Thought you should know" or "I have what you want" will send your e-mail into the re-cycling bin. Use phrases such as "Gift Basket Info from Tuesday's Meeting" or "To (Prospect's Name), From (Your Name)." Try to keep the subject as concise as possible.

An e-mail message is written in the same concise manner as a letter or fax. Here's an example, which gives the recipient several response options:

Dear Mr. Mayberry,

Congratulations on your recent promotion, which I read about in the *Daily Record*. You probably have many people to thank, and I have the perfect solution.

At Moore Baskets, we create custom gift baskets for busy executives like you who seek quality and impeccable service. Your time is important. In just ten minutes, we'll show you a display of thank-you baskets at your office, and we'll bring a sample of our exclusive truffles. If you like what you see, you can place an order and then continue your day's work. We'll leave the truffles as a token of our appreciation.

Tell us, by e-mail, if Wednesday, April 6, at 3:00 P.M. is best for an appointment. Or you can call us at (800) 555–2323 to respond by phone, and we'll follow up with your assistant. Our Web site, www.moorebaskets.com, will introduce you to the award-winning baskets that executives have ordered for staff members and colleagues.

Again, congratulations, and let us show you why Moore is your business partner.

Sincerely,

Getting Past the Gatekeeper

The gatekeeper is a most formidable opponent, standing between you and the prospect. Armed with the ability to separate friends from solicitors, the gatekeeper takes the job se-riously and knows that he or she will have to answer for calls that shouldn't have gone through. Yet the gatekeeper—better known as the assistant—is not the enemy but your ally, the person who makes the decision to let you talk to the boss.

While the thought of speaking with the gatekeeper may scare you, preparing a tele-phone script will guide you through most of the gatekeeper's questions. A script arms you with techniques to convince the gatekeeper that you are the boss's best weapon for conducting better business. The following example shows you how to set up your script. Even though not all scenes will play out exactly in your experience, this will give you an idea of what to say.

Scene 1. It's your first call. Although you've had no prior contact with the prospect, your experience with his industry tells you that your baskets will open doors to new business for him. The gatekeeper answers. Introduce yourself and ask for her name if not already mentioned when answering the phone. "Hello, Jill, this is Jane Moore." Get right to the point. "A number of area construction companies have increased their businesses by giving our gift baskets to clients. If Mr. Smith is not using gift baskets now, we'd like to show him how business will grow using them. I'm hoping Mr. Smith has ten spare minutes next Tuesday at 11:00 A.M. for a quick meeting. How does that sound?" If his time is not free, ask if a better time is available. If told that an appointment is not appropriate at this time, ask if you can mail information or send a fax. In a few days, follow up with another call. When mailing, it's OK to send Jill a sample gift basket treat. She will definitely remember you when you call again.

What if there's no gatekeeper or the electronic kind is minding the office?

Scene 2. There is no gatekeeper. The executive himself answers the phone. No time to freeze and utter unintelligible words. You start by saying, "Mr. Smith? Good morning! This is Jane Moore of Moore Baskets. Yesterday's paper had a pretty big story about your competition. Now's probably a good time to remind your clients you're still the best in the business, and a gift basket will bring that point across. We have lots of basket options to show you. How does a quick, ten-minute display next Thursday morning sound?"

Scene 3. The gatekeeper you've reached is Mr. Smith's voice mail. You have two options:

1. Leave a message with such impact that he must call you back. "Mr. Smith, we're celebrating our grand opening and want to thank you with a special gift for convincing us to open our doors. We're just calling to verify your mailing address. Our number is (212) 555–2545; ask for Jane. Thank you, Mr. Smith. We're eager to send the gift. Hope to hear from you soon."
2. Keep calling until the real person answers the phone and then proceed with your message.

They've Responded! Now What?

Knowing what type of baskets the prospect requires before the meeting ensures that less time is wasted when you meet face-to-face. Preliminary questions like the following will help you prepare your presentation.

- Is the current need general, incentive-based, or for a special event?
- How many baskets are required and what size?
- What is the budget (price range per basket)?
- Are certain foods or products required, or is the prospect open to ideas?
- Will custom items be used, such as personalized ribbon or mugs?

Now you can set the time and place to meet. If you work full-time, you must allow for flexibility. Early morning or late afternoon appointments are possible but not always probable. If you really want to quit that full-time job to run a gift basket business, you will find yourself making many sacrifices, such as using vacation days and other time off, to succeed.

Tell the prospect in advance how long you expect the meeting to last. This limit lets you prepare an effective presentation within the allotted time. Also find out if the prospect is the person authorized to make the sale. Simply ask, "If I prepare the purchase order, are you the only person needed to approve the sale?" If you don't ask, you may be told, "I'll run this by my boss" at the end of the meeting, which can put your sale in limbo for several weeks. If more than one person must approve the sale, confirm that the approving parties will at least be in the office that day.

What should you bring to the appointment?

- Your gift baskets—three of different sizes, tailored to the prospect's need assessment, are usually enough. Too many baskets will confuse the client.
- Photographs of other basket alternatives, placed in a binder or other presentable folder.
- No more than two tasting samples of snack-based goods.
- A calculator.
- A clipboard, holding the purchase order to write the sale. Use two purchase orders

with carbon paper between them, or use carbonless paper, and give the client the duplicate copy.

> *I take three baskets according to what the company is looking for. I ask about its budget. I also take photos and my catalog, showing other baskets that might interest them. Usually I'll give prospects a box of truffles to thank them for their time.*

How do you intend to bring your baskets and literature to the meeting? One suggestion is to place your baskets in oversize bags. Some of these carryalls are long enough to hold two baskets each and make carrying your display into the meeting less awkward. Another suggestion is a tissue-lined inverted box top to carry your baskets. A rectangular box top that covers a case of duplicating paper has 3-inch sides and is a convenient, no-cost carryall sturdy enough for multiple sample baskets. Because the basket carryall will occupy your hands, place all literature in a briefcase with a strap to hang from your shoulder. Also insert into the briefcase a calculator, a clipboard for holding order forms, photographs, and business cards.

The Meeting: Getting Down to Business

A handshake and a smile begin your meeting. The ball is in your court, as the prospect waits to hear about your baskets. Begin by saying, "These baskets will convey appreciation, open the doors for new opportunities, or say thank you during the holidays." Add information on (1) what you've learned about the company or industry, (2) what the prospect has told you, and (3) whatever else shows the benefit your baskets bring to the company.

The following nine points address the most common situations that may occur at your meeting.

1. Watch the prospect's temperament. Is he or she laid-back and at ease (a relaxed thinker)? Quick and no-nonsense (a bit stressed, in a hurry-up mode)? Or money-driven—"What's the bottom line?" (budget conscious)? Adapt your presentation to that person's temperament. If you're too slow or too fast, the

client may not respond positively. Read the signals, meet his or her specifications, and you'll have a good chance to close the meeting with a sale.

> *Most corporate clients don't want to see a lot of baskets at the meeting. They're busy and don't have time to see one of everything. I usually take three, and one is out of their price range. To my surprise, some order the most expensive one.*

2. Don't just hear the prospect; listen "between the lines." Write notes while you talk; it shows you care about the prospect's needs and getting the order right the first time. Ask questions; this sometimes gets to the root of other concerns. Rephrase the prospect's questions and comments; it shows both that you're in agreement and that you understand what the prospect has said.

3. Offer the prospect a taste of the sample products. Pleasing the prospect's palate might be the key to making a quicker sale.

4. Be ready for both standard and unexpected questions, such as "Can I get a discount? When can you deliver the order? Can I change this product for another and pay the same price? Can all the gifts be a certain color? Can you make each gift basket a little different? Do you personalize ribbon?" If you're asked a question you can't answer on the spot, say, "Let me get back to you on that." It's not unprofessional, and it allows you to answer the question correctly the first time, without retraction. It also gives you another opportunity to call the client.

5. Ask for the sale. If you're both in agreement and the client has identified the style of baskets he or she wants, say, "It sounds like you're ready to write the order. May I?" Asking permission confirms the sale. Then write the order, inform the client about the necessary deposit (discussed later in this chapter), and spell out all the details on a form similar to the sample Purchase Order shown. Your own form will actually be filled in by hand during the order. You can make the order area (quantity, description, etc.) as long as you wish to accommodate four or more orders per client. Have the client review and sign the order, then give him or her a copy. Do not oversell—no anecdotes, giggling, or high fives. Thank the client verbally and with a handshake, pack your bags and boxes, and walk out the door. Now you can dance a jig, shout, raise your fist in victory, or do whatever else you do to celebrate.

Purchase Order

MOORE BASKETS

No.: <u>182</u>

P.O. Box 550, Pandora Station

Date: <u>1/10/04</u>

Pepperton, NY 13838

Phone (607) 555-8580

Fax (607) 555-8585

E-mail: mooreisbetter@moorebaskets.com

DELIVER TO:		ORDER FOR:
Name:	Peter Towns	ABC Software Design Company
Company:	Miller Associates	683 Mission Way, Suite 723
Address:	125 Hill Street	Passport, NY 13028
	Haworth, NY 13535	Contact: Sara Peters
Phone:	(607) 555-9000	Phone: (607) 555-8823
Fax:	(607) 555-9696	Fax: (607) 555-8824

Qty.	Description	Restrictions	Price Each	TOTAL
1	Executive Basket—ice bucket, 2 handkerchiefs, journal, popcorn, calendar, bottled beverage, champagne glass	Kosher ___ Sugar free ___ Fat free ___ Allergies ___ Other: ___	$50	$50
1	Secretary Basket (for Rita Sims)— pastel basket, assorted cookies, hot tea/coffee, cinnamon sticks	*Secretary— Chocolate Allergy*	$25	$25
			Delivery	$10

Greeting: Thanks for everything. Regards, Sara

Delivery date/time/instructions: Deliver on 1/15; leave at front desk in A.M.

This order may be canceled by phone or fax within one (1) business day, after which time the deposit is nonrefundable.

Deposit paid by:

Company check	_____	Order Subtotal	$75.00
Visa/MasterCard	_____	Tax	4.50
American Express	_____	Shipping/delivery	10.00
		Other costs	
		Total	$89.50
Credit card acct. no.:_____		Deposit	89.50
exp. _____		Bal. due on receipt	$0.00

Name on card: _____

Signature: _____

Approved: **Your representative is:**

_____   _____

Authorized signature   Print name

The contract must specify the container, contents, bow, price, tax, and other charges. It is wise to consider sending a photo of the chosen basket before delivery to show all approving personnel what they're getting. While you're at it, double-check the delivery date and the name of the receiver.

6. Don't always give in to get the sale. Know your bottom line and how low you can go before entering the meeting. If you cannot give a discount or make other allowances because the order is not large enough or for some other reason, stick to your decision. What's the point of making a profitless sale? You won't recoup the lost revenue in future orders; you will be seen as a pushover, easy to manipulate; and you'll feel cheated and won't be happy with the sale or yourself. Offering something of little cost to you yet conciliatory to the client, such as a larger bow or printed cellophane instead of plain, might be another way to cement the deal without losing money.

   My husband told me something long ago that I stick by. He said that some people like to play "executive Donkey Kong"—they roll a barrel (ask a question) to see if you jump (give in and say yes). You're in business to make money. Stick to your standards, and you'll profit with every sale.

7. Sometimes price really is the issue. Corporations are legally allowed up to $25 per gift as a business deduction. Keep this in mind as you select the baskets you'll present.

8. Some prospects ask if you can leave the sample baskets on site. The answer is up to you, but most professionals don't allow this as a rule. Your samples will be disbursed all around town, possibly for weeks, and you won't have a sale. Then you must run around to retrieve your baskets at a time convenient for the prospect. In some cases, you'll never get your baskets back. A better solution is to e-mail a photograph of the sample baskets to the prospect to aid his or her decision.

9. Tell clients how to contact you if they have questions. Your contract should contain phone and fax numbers, your e-mail address, and any other way clients can reach you.

Discounts, Deposits, and Collecting Payment

Discounts

Some gift basket professionals offer some type of discount for large corporate orders. Others have decided to never discount their baskets. If you decide to offer a discount, there must be enough of a cushion in your markup price to allow for it. If a client is buying twenty-five $25 baskets and your wholesale price is $8.33 per basket, you might decide that there's some flexibility to offer a 2 percent discount, especially if that helps the client agree to the sale. Let's look at the calculation:

Retail price:		
Twenty-five baskets @ $25.00	=	$625.00
2% discount	=	12.50
Client's price	=	$612.50
Wholesale price:		
Twenty-five baskets @ $8.33/each	=	$208.25
Summation:		
Retail price	=	$625.00
Less wholesale price	=	208.25
Profit before discount	=	416.75
Less client discount	=	12.50
Total gross profit	=	$404.25

Deposits

Once an order is placed, insure yourself against a client's canceling the order by requesting a deposit of at least half the total order amount. The example above shows that a $312.50 deposit on a $625.00 sale will cover your expenses. Not collecting a deposit leaves the client in the clear, with no obligation to keep the order without penalty.

The sticking point here is, What constitutes a large order? Think about this—how much money can you afford to lose if the client cancels? Most professionals collect either half or the full amount of the sale, no matter what the quantity or amount. This is a business where the professional sees no reason to lose any money.

Orders are documented on a purchase order with the client's signature and are finalized with a deposit check. Terms of the order should include an option for the client to cancel the order within one business day. After that the terms are binding, and if the client cancels the order after the term limit, the deposit is nonrefundable. This ensures that any products you have ordered or purchased that cannot be returned are covered by the deposit. After the purchase order is approved and the work completed, prepare a sales invoice showing the baskets purchased, total price, buyer's name, deposit received, and balance due (see sample Sales Invoice).

Collecting Payment

There was a time when gift basket professionals would allow clients to set up "net thirty" accounts, which gave the client thirty days from receipt of the gift to pay for the purchase. The economy, as well as the practice of some clients who've kept designers waiting months for payment, dictate that gift professionals now collect payment before the baskets are delivered or receive a check upon delivery at the client's office. This is one of the reasons why accepting credit cards is paramount in this industry.

When a corporate client places an order, whether in person or by telephone, payment terms are discussed, and the option of charging the order to a corporate card is addressed as an alternative to issuing a check. If you allow the corporate client to pay the whole or partial amount at a later date, you may be waiting for months while your own bills become due. As a business owner, you must be firm and address payment terms up front. If you lose the order because you would not provide the corporate client with a staggered payment option, then it is probably an order you would have regretted filling.

Keep your peace of mind by collecting the balance or entire payment before the order is shipped or delivered.

What to Do after the Sale

Saying thank you today entails more than simply uttering a phrase. Let your actions show appreciation.

Sales Invoice

From: MOORE BASKETS
          P.O. Box 550
          Pandora Station
          Pepperton, NY 13838
Phone: (607) 555-8580
Fax: (607) 555-8585
E-mail: mooreisbetter@moorebaskets.com

Sold to: ABC Software Design Company
          683 Mission Way, Suite 723
          Passport, NY 13028
          Attn: Sara Peters
Phone: (607) 555-8823
Fax: (607) 555-8824

Bill to: Same as above

Invoice no.   306
Invoice date: 1/10/04
Salesperson: J. Moore
Special orders: Deliver A.M. at
                   front desk

Order Date: 1/10/04
Shipping method: Courier
Shipping date: 1/15/04
Payment terms: On receipt

Quantity	Description	Price Each	Total
1	Executive Gift Basket for Peter Towns	$50.00	$50.00
1	Secretary's Basket for Rita Sims	25.00	25.00

Greeting: Thanks for everything. Regards, Sara
Delivered to: Miller Associates
                 125 Hill Street
                 Haworth, NY 13535

Thank you for your order!

Subtotal	$75.00
Tax	4.50
Shipping/Delivery Charge	10.00
Other Costs	
Total	$89.50
Deposit	89.50
Balance Due on Receipt	$0.00

- Start with a telephone call directly to the client. This is, again, a good time to ask if the person can recommend colleagues and clients who need baskets or to mention that you spoke with someone he or she recommended.
- If this was a substantial order, show your appreciation by treating the client and his or her spouse to a night's stay at a bed-and-breakfast or dinner at a posh restaurant. You and the bed-and-breakfast or restaurant can have an arrangement whereby if you supply X amount of baskets to the establishment, you'll receive coupons for your clients to stay there or dine complimentary, thus making the arrangement a winning combination for all. Remember, everyone likes receiving gifts and other tokens of appreciation that amount to more than a 10 percent coupon off the next purchase.
- Send the client clipped articles from newspapers and magazines about his or her industry. This demonstrates uncommon support and concern for the client's professional well-being. Include a note stating, "Thought this might be of interest to you. Regards."
- Mail monthly postcards and flyers, and e-mail on-line newsletters about your baskets.
- Send the client yearly birthday cards.
- Use contests to get the client's office staff involved and make them part of your external sales team. For example, a newsletter can invite secretaries to mail you the boss's business card, entering them in an Administrative Professionals Week drawing for a special basket.

Problems, Concerns, and Solutions

If you don't make an on-site sale, consider these questions: What's keeping you from making the sale? Are there underlying issues that the client isn't addressing? Is another appointment needed to show alternative baskets? Should you send literature by mail? Was the client "fishing"—seemingly interested in your baskets but shopping around to get the best price before ordering from a competitor? Or perhaps the need is three to six months away. If so, how will you secure the order now to guarantee you'll get the account?

Problems sometimes occur and are not always foreseeable, including these:

- *The prospect has no idea what he or she wants, even after the meeting.* In this case, review your notes with the prospect. Go over the information given about the theme, event, size, and price. Talk about other options. If that fails, tell the client that you'll investigate some other ideas and send information by e-mail, following up with a call a few days later. Keep trying.
- *You haven't brought anything that interests the prospect.* Again, you must review your notes and see where the miscommunication lies. Tell the prospect you'll call when new baskets are ready, and make an appointment to show your new creations. An alternative is to e-mail photographs of the newly created baskets.

  Before new prospects decide to buy your baskets, they might first test your talents by ordering a few one-only baskets. If you pass the test, you may just get the big accounts in future orders.

- The unknown is, unfortunately, part of the business. That's why you not only bring baskets that resemble a prospect's perceived needs but also bring photos of alternatives. That's the best you can do outside of making another appointment to show more baskets once the prospect has reviewed what you're offering at the first meeting. Learn from your experiences. If you've prepared your presentation to the best of your ability, you've done well.
- Ask questions about other possible clients. Do other departments in the organization use gift baskets? Which of the prospect's associates has a need for baskets? Ask if you can use the prospect's name as an introduction (a cold-call warming technique).
- *Sometimes prospects just won't buy.* There are buyers, browsers, and some who simply aren't interested. That's OK. The sooner you understand that not everyone will buy your baskets, the sooner you can move on to other, more receptive prospects.
- Keep a few of the nonbuying potential clients on your promotions list for up to two years. It is said that prospects see your name about seven times before they order. After two years, it's OK to delete them from your list.

What have you learned in your face-to-face meeting? Think about this as you drive back to your office. Which of your actions were you especially proud of?

What could you have done better? Overall, do you feel you conducted yourself professionally, doing everything possible to conclude the sale successfully?

Asking for Referral Business

The more people you meet and businesses that become clients, the more referral business you can find. Asking for referral business is a common sales generator, and every business owner asks colleagues and clients for leads. Referral business can be acquired in many ways:

- During a sit-down dinner with new or existing associates
- At a cocktail hour, as you go from group to group for conversations and to greet others
- At the end of a client meeting
- At leisure events where you meet new people (but only after you've spoken to the other person on topics of interest to him or her)
- Whenever you attend a personal or professional function

In Case of Error, Break Glass

With luck, you will experience few problems, but there are many errors that can occur between meeting a client and delivering the baskets. From miscommunication to delivery errors, anything is possible. Even if clients make a mistake, you must let them know that you do not hold them responsible. It's a tough side of the business, but one that becomes less of a problem through trial and error. What should you do when problems occur? First, you can apologize. Live with it, kiss and make up, and sell them more baskets. Second, use good judgment. If no one is at the receiving home or office, is it really OK to leave a basket on the porch or with a neighbor? A call on your cellular phone to the client helps make the determination easier. Third, if you're not sure of something, double-check before doing it. Again, the telephone can be a lifesaver when you're unsure what to do.

> *The person who orders from me requests that I bring the baskets to his office. Always check with the buyer and ask how he or she wants the delivery handled.*

Gift baskets express feelings that are difficult to put into words. Your product has the power to cement multimillion-dollar relationships in times of crisis or to reopen doors seemingly glued shut from neglect or miscommunication. Recognize the role your baskets play in corporate success, and your services will always be in demand.

The Elusive Corporate Market Checklist

Completed

1. Document the number of companies in your area you can approach for corporate orders.
   - Businesses of all size _____
   - Private practices _____
   - Public and private institutions and organizations _____

2. Decide what products (foods and gifts) you will add to your buying chart to specifically market to corporate clients. _____

3. Check newspapers, journals, and other reference materials for names of potential corporate clients. _____

4. Decide on your best approach for speaking with decision makers. Make introductory calls and appointments. _____

5. Ensure that all materials needed to conduct a corporate meeting are in place (tasting samples, flyers and other printed materials, products to assemble sample baskets, purchase order, etc.). _____

6. If you've made a sale:
   - Check purchase order and your notes to ensure that you've documented all necessary information. _____
   - Request a deposit check or credit card number for at least half the total order. _____
   - Call your contact immediately for any clarifications. _____
   - Collect the balance due before the order is delivered or shipped. _____

7. Evaluate the presentation.
   - Were you fully prepared to meet the client? _____
   - How successful was the meeting? _____
   - What would you have done differently? _____

8. Ask the client for names and phone numbers of other possible clients. _____

Chapter Seven
Advertising and Promotion

C alling all customers! When you open for business, you want the word spread far and wide through the most cost-effective means possible. What's the best way to get the most money back for the dollars spent on advertising and promotion? This section unveils the popular methods used to market gift baskets.

There are three terms to understand before continuing: *marketing, advertising,* and *promotion.* The term *marketing* is described in Chapter 1. Look at marketing as the root of a tree from which all branches grow. One branch is advertising, which is any paid method of communication used to tell customers about your company. Promotion, another branch, is mostly nonpaid methods of media and on-line communication.

Your budget will guide you to select the proper tools for effective marketing.

Advertising Specialties

Promotional catalogs and Web sites offer many advertising specialties to keep your company name visible all year long. A quick search through the Internet will uncover many companies that will personalize anything from pens to Post-it notes to duffel bags and ponchos. There are hundreds of items to consider, and each product usually has a minimum purchase requirement.

Some advertisement specialty companies display their goods at local business shows, where you can view the merchandise before ordering. Look for out-of-the-ordinary but affordable advertising tools like paper-clip-shaped key chains, pens with neck cords, and candy jars that sit on receptionists' desks filled with goodies while announcing your name.

Selectively Spreading the Good News

Word of Mouth

Can a business exist by word of mouth alone? Although this type of promotion generates some interest, it does not make the business a best-seller. Everyone has his or her own agenda. Clients work, rush home to fix dinner, tend to their children, and play with the dog. Do you really think that all they have to talk about are your gift baskets? The only effective word-of-mouth promotion is your own, and that's determined only after the marketing statistics are tallied to reveal how clients learned about your company. Word of mouth works even better when an incentive is attached, as discussed under the section "Fun with Contests" later in this chapter, and through creating other ingenious methods.

Postcards

This is a great form of advertising that should be seriously considered. Postcards sell gift baskets quickly and effectively, with professionals swearing by them, rather than at them, to develop a successful marketing campaign. When postcards show a picture on one side and tell the story in text on the other side, a client is more likely to call you immediately with an order, get more information or ask questions, keep the card for future reference, or pass it on to someone with an immediate need.

Postcards are less expensive to mail than letters and are well worth the cost. You'll find local and national postcard sources on the Internet by using search engines such as Yahoo.com and Google.com.

Postcards mailed to clients each month are a different theme and a different color. They are printed four on a page by a local office supply-store, which keeps the cost low while increasing my sales.

Today's technology allows you to make your own postcards that have a professional appearance rather than a homemade look. That's why some designers are printing their own postcards using Avery products, a color printer, and gift basket photographs that have been scanned into their computer. This is an affordable alternative when you don't need 500 postcards or another high minimum imposed by outside companies.

Newspapers and Magazines

Advertising in daily or weekly newspapers and magazines is an option that most gift basket professionals reject. These ads don't produce enough sales to justify the cost. The only print media to consider are specialty newspapers—those for women only or for a certain industry that constantly buys your baskets and needs a gentle reminder. Daily papers are discarded quickly, and so is the ad. A reader must have an immediate need for the ad to make an impact, but which of thousands reading the paper on that particular day have a need? Reaching people in this fashion becomes too broad. Your best option is to move on to other options.

Flyers and Newsletters

Because clients have little time for extra reading, flyers should be held to one page in length and newsletters to a minimum of two or maximum of four on a double-sided 11-by-17-inch sheet. A flyer focuses on one subject: a new gift basket theme or product line, new containers, or live operators where an answering machine once existed. Announce a Web page or upcoming television segment showing your baskets. Newsletters offer multiple stories that interest your core market; leisure and entertainment themes can be coupled with incentives to buy baskets now and later.

The sample newsletter shown was made using Microsoft Publisher, a user-friendly software package and one of the many desktop publishers on the market. Newsletters are distributed by mail with or without an envelope. Experience teaches that an envelope is a wise investment against postal ink, which smears onto the message, leaving an untidy mess that never gets read.

Flyers are also sent by mail or used as promotional literature on display tables at business and consumer events. Think twice before placing flyers on car windshields. This is not

Sample Newsletter

Volume 2, Issue 3

Summer 2004

Better Business Baskets

A Courtesy of Moore Baskets, Your Corporate Gift Basket Partner

www.MooreBaskets.com   *Call us Toll Free (800) 555-7487*

Broker Learns How to Increase Sales and Support

Suzie Scott quit. Once she saw the sales numbers, Scott knew it was time to stop ordering gift certificates as employee rewards and began looking for a better gift to increase productivity.

As vice president of sales for Mort Rickey, the nation's leading real estate broker, Scott realized that her staff needed more motivation to close sales that slipped away each month. After all, the real estate market was booming.

Each sales manager is responsible for over $10 million in assets. To stay ahead of upstart firms looking to slice into Mort Rickey's pie, Scott searched for alternative

ways to get her managers thinking out of the box.

"When I received a gift basket from Jane Moore, I knew her baskets were the answer," said Scott.

She called a staff meeting and laid out plans for a new sales campaign.

First, she'd have each manager visit past customers to renew old relationships.

Next, every region would be checked for unique purchasing opportunities and methods to sell new acquisitions to current clients.

Last, each sales manager would receive a basket of

Court more sales with Moore Baskets.

corporate gifts and personal items based on their sales performance and productivity.

"It's a win-win proposal for the entire force," said Scott, who ordered 1,000 gift baskets last month to distribute to the entire team. Ready to challenge your staff and boost productivity? Call us today.

Summer Baskets Make Your Sales Sizzle

Looking to increase your summer sales? We have something special for you.

On July 14 at 9:30 a.m., Moore Baskets will appear on The Corporate Network to feature a selection of baskets that are perfect for corporate

gift giving. You'll see a wide assortment of snacks and gifts wrapped in briefcases, ice buckets and tote bags.

If you love our basic baskets, you'll have a chance to see our newest collection of wicker and wood. It's a

collection that's destined to boost your sales. Mark your calendars, and call (800) 555-7487 to order.

Can't wait for the show? Visit our Web site at http://www. MooreBaskets.com for a preview. See you on TV.

an effective way to reach your market, plus city laws may prohibit this type of distribution due to littering statutes. How many times have you pulled paper from your windshield and let it fly in the wind?

On-line (Electronic) Newsletters

It is becoming standard practice for gift basket professionals to create on-line newsletters. The same information that populates the printed version can now be sent electronically to prospects and clients who have given permission to receive your news through their e-mail accounts. Most professionals add a newsletter subscription link onto their Web site's home page. On-line newsletters have long been distributed as all-text publications, but newsletters containing photographs of gift baskets and other graphics have become very popular. Like the printed version, these newsletters provide readers with quick information about new baskets, old standards, and the upcoming occasions for gift giving. Ideas for populating your on-line newsletter can be found by subscribing to other gift and nongift electronic newsletters.

Rotary-File Cards

If you plan on selling baskets to corporations, rotary-file (such as Rolodex) cards are your ally. Some executives leave companies with nothing but their card file in tow. Any cargo deemed that precious must always include your card.

Rotary-file cards are available in a high-gloss, hard plastic so they won't break, rip, or tear, or you can make your own card-stock version on a computer. Several mail-order stationery catalogs offer one-color, eight-on-a-page blank cards to create a custom message using your computer and printer. As mentioned in Chapter 3, print a small quantity until you are satisfied with the design, then print several hundred at a time and distribute them generously.

A Catalog of Your Own

Some companies have multipage color gift basket catalogs made before they open for business; others wait years down the road to decide on using a catalog; and still others don't have one because of the cost and depend on other, less expensive advertising mailers to do the job. A color catalog ranges from more than $500 to well over $2,000. If you truly want to show your baskets this way, first consider a glossy catalog sheet that will show up to nine gift baskets and smaller gifts on one side. This less expensive option has as much sales impact as a saddle-stitched catalog.

> *I'm eager to have a brochure made, but brochures are expensive and my flyers and postcards steadily sell the baskets. That seems to suggest that people want to see your work and don't care whether it's on a postcard or in a brochure.*

The bottom of the catalog sheet includes your business name, slogan (e.g., "Corporate Gift Basket Specialists"), address (if appropriate), and telephone number. Some professionals print text on the sheet's back side that describes the depicted photographs and price ranges, but others decide to leave the back side blank, opting to attach an additional descriptive sheet. This is done because when the glossy sheet is printed, the text and price ranges cannot be changed, whereas the additional sheet can be updated as necessary.

As with postcards, many companies specialize in creating color catalogs. Other than finding a printer, you must secure a photographer who takes commercial pictures. Some professionals have found Sears Portrait Studio and other mall-based photographers to be an adequate solution. Review other one-page catalog sheets to decide how to display your baskets, compare printing prices, and follow through to recoup the expense as quickly as possible.

Gift basket professionals are quickly turning their Web sites into on-line catalogs rather than printing an expensive product that will become obsolete within months. There's more on creating a Web site later in this chapter.

Doorknob Hangers

These hanging tags work well at homes in and around town and in real estate developments only after receiving the green light to leave a hanger on each door. Soliciting on the development's grounds without permission is prohibited; the practice leaves a poor impression and the inability to pursue the group for future sales. Introduce yourself the right way to get the account. Also check each town's soliciting laws, for you may be liable for picking up each discarded hanger or be fined for littering.

Doorknob hangers bring good sales from homeowners. Not all homes have a Rolodex, but doorknobs are inescapable.

Yellow Pages

Calling a Yellow Pages representative will net you one piece of advice: "Take out a full-page ad. You'll make the money back in no time." Since that advice is easier said than done, start sensibly by considering a small text message, then graduating to a display box if one is warranted by sales.

A text message display consists of the business name in bold and two lines of text beneath the name. Home-based businesses have the option of listing their city's name in the ad and not the home address to give the reader a general idea of the location. The next largest ad is a small boxed display. Ads are conveniently charged and paid through the monthly telephone bill.

Another plus about the Yellow Pages is that an ad can run in any telephone book. If most customers live in a certain area or if you want to attract new customers in an affluent community, this is easily accomplished with ads in specific books. Yellow Pages representatives keep detailed demographics on every region and will send data by mail for assessment. Expect to pay about $20 per month for bold name and a two-line listing and to pay much more for display ads. The price depends on each book's rates.

Professionals have found that separate listings under "Gift Baskets" and "Fruit Baskets" gain the best exposure. Prospects aren't really looking for fruit; they simply start their search there to determine what to buy.

Business Trade Shows

Real estate managers, temporary employment specialists, cruise directors—they and many more prospects attend business trade shows to meet other professionals and find new and upgraded tools to perform their jobs efficiently. Not relegated to just the chamber of commerce, any group can host a business trade show. Large superstores play host as well as women's groups, libraries, and copy centers. Whoever has a room to rent is turning the extra space into an event hall.

If you are considering a display, request the names and phone numbers of past exhibitors for an idea of what to expect in terms of participation, building access, atmosphere, and the like. Ask the hosts about display table size, draping, and whether competing gift basket companies will be attending. A display table should hold seven to ten baskets, individual corporate gifts, literature, and a drawing container for all to deposit their business cards. If you've decided to exhibit, it's up to you to entice the attendees to visit your table so that you can make the pitch to sell your baskets, remembering that any glowing review from exhibitors in previous shows is no guarantee that your experience will be as good.

> *Food samples and a raffle always bring more visitors who
> stay longer at my table. That way, I can ask them about their
> basket preferences. To make the presentation better, a black
> cloth is draped over different size boxes to vary the height of
> each basket on the table.*

Also ask the host for a list of all attendees as a condition of participation. The worst the host can do is say no. If you wait until the event is over, there's no reason for the host to fulfill your request.

Craft Shows

Craft shows have become less attractive as a place to display gift baskets. Individuals who visit these events aren't looking for the bundle of goods that we painstakingly create, and if they were to buy, the prospect expects a hefty discount.

Craft shows used to be a place to sell unwanted inventory—the product you buy, thinking it's a good gift basket candidate, but simply didn't sell. This is no longer the case.

If you find a craft show that you believe will be a good place to showcase and sell your baskets, by all means, take a chance. However, be aware that gift basket designers nationwide have consistently reported less-than-stellar results at these once favored venues.

Fun with Contests

Everyone loves a contest because there's a remote chance to win something, no matter how small. Contests can be held by your company or linked with another organization or event. Promotion starts through your newsletter, a public service announcement (PSA) on radio stations, exposure on free public access channels, your Web site, and more innovative ways. PSAs and public access channels allow you to promote the contest without a charge as long as entrants don't pay a fee to participate.

Contests are a great way to generate traffic on your Web site. A monthly contest, presented on one Web page, can also feature details about new gift baskets, products, promotions, and anything else that will keep them on your site and add to sales.

Contest themes are endless. They can be centered on grammar or high school students, AIDS or breast cancer awareness, a corporate promotion, or a current event. On the flip side, contests are a business builder for restaurants, movie theaters, and candy or craft stores. The person who guesses the correct amount of jelly beans in a jar or the date your business was "born," or who writes an essay on something he or she believes passionately in, is crowned the winner and awarded a gift basket. Newspaper photographers and television camera crews should be notified to attend the festivities. Contests are a valuable, inexpensive component of business.

Donations

Promotions bring opportunities to donate gorgeous baskets to charities, black-tie affairs, and ribbon-cutting events, enticing buyers and making an event more memorable. Donations expose your business to those in the best position to become clients. Show baskets that mix general products with high-end foods and small gifts to indicate the range of creativity offered. Donations also make good use of items flirting with expiration.

If I didn't monitor my donations, these groups would have me give away more than I sell. Now I choose groups and events carefully instead of randomly giving donations, such as working with a women's social club that receives 10 percent of all sales to fund its activities. It's a real moneymaker for me.

All business groups and organizations hold events and solicit donations, sending word about the star-studded event by mail and through news releases. Look for civic organizations, nonprofit groups, organizations for youth and senior citizens, and others listed in Chapter 1 under "Nonprofit Organizations," and "Institutions," where more detailed information on donations can be found.

Radio Promotions

Not all radio stations allow companies to barter for on-air promotions, but for those that do, it's a partnership made in heaven. Bartering is the exchange of goods for comparable value of other products or services. Although money is a prime motivator, at times giveaways are more valuable to a radio station. These help the station increase ratings and draw extra revenue from advertisers who buy airtime.

Radio stations look for gift basket giveaways all year long for holiday events, for college team finals, and as seasonal ratings boosters. Contact the morning show's producer for an interview. With each disc jockey change comes a new show producer, so about three to four producers, along with sales and marketing executives, look for new and innovative ways to market the station. Put your plan in order before calling the station:

1. Do your potential customers listen to the music or talk format featured on the station?

2. What baskets will convince the station to promote you in exchange for some free baskets?

3. How many baskets will you show and what themes? Treat the producer like a corporate account and show only three baskets in varying sizes. The themes are determined by season, upcoming holidays, or special occasions.

4. Do you have a backup plan if the station will not barter? The answer depends on how important this promotion is for your business. Are there other, less expensive options to reach the same results?

A backup plan also consists of events that the radio station plans each year. If the station gives away tickets or sponsors a cruise, you could donate a basket in either case and receive a backstage concert pass or free admission onto the cruise in return. In either case, you mingle with the people most likely to have an interest in your products.

Meeting New and Interesting People

Your region offers special opportunities to meet new people every week. There are events for singles, couples with and without children, seniors, executives, plumbers, carpenters, interior decorators, accountants, designers, and a host of organizations whose members meet socially and professionally. Aside from finding new clients, support and camaraderie are found through knowing like-minded people.

Joining groups is another way to meet new people. Attend a few meetings first as a nonmember, to ensure that the group is interesting and supportive. New recruits are expected to join one of several committees. Consider whether this activity will fit into your schedule and ask yourself:

1. Do the members buy from one another before going outside the group?
2. Because I am a nonmember, will members embrace me or treat me like an outsider?
3. It's important to support the organization, but how will the membership support me?

On a personal note, I sought membership in a newly formed women's golf group and volunteered to create and edit the newsletter. Every two months I received articles by fax written by each committee chairwoman, edited the submissions, and added graphics where needed. There was little camaraderie outside of meeting to have dinner, and I felt like an outsider, which was compounded by the fact that no one bought my baskets. The members either worked for large companies or had their own businesses, and being very successful at selling baskets to others, I decided it made no sense to continue publishing a newsletter that took time away from my prime business and that the group did not support. I thought this group would introduce me to new people who would increase my business. Instead, I did extra work with no trade-off value.

Keep up with events and group gatherings through newspaper listings, and carefully select groups to join. Things will never be perfectly balanced, but make sure you get some benefit for your work.

Selling on Consignment

Consignment selling is a good way to broaden sales opportunities around the state. It requires that you supply the consignee (the company selling your baskets) with goods for display that the consignee's current clientele may buy. In return, the consignee receives a percentage of the retail cost when the product is sold.

Locations to Consider

Consignment shops that have proved profitable for gift basket incorporations are flower shops, card stores, and various specialty shops. Consignment opportunities can be found in mall craft stores where only consignment merchandise is sold. Because the response rate in these mall shops is uncertain, it's best to get references from people currently consigning. On any Saturday count the number of people going into and buying from the store. Just because this setup exists doesn't mean it's a moneymaker. Choose your opportunities wisely and only after thorough investigation. If you're feeling that the store won't reap adequate sales, don't enter into an agreement. Be wise and save money, time, and energy by concentrating on alternative opportunities that make more dollars and sense.

Constructing a Consignment Agreement

As mentioned, a consignment is an agreement between you and a shop owner who agrees to display and sell your merchandise for a certain period. An agreement should include the parties entering into the agreement; a listing of the products to be sold in the consignee's establishment; the length of time the products will be held for sale and the terms for consignment termination; the consignee's obligation to insure the products against fire, vandalism, flood, or other casualties; and how payment will be settled between the two parties. An addendum, or additional sheet, is drawn up and signed by both parties, verifying each basket for sale and its contents. Visit your local library and ask the reference librarian to assist you in finding sample consignment agreements, which should then be reviewed by an attorney for completeness and accuracy before being signed by either party. Look for sample consignment agreements and other helpful forms on Web sites found through search engine listings.

The consignment percentage varies from region to region, with 10 to 35 percent being the typical range agreed to by both parties. The percentage amount brings up the eventual bottom-line question, How much can I afford to pay in consignment fees to profit from this type of agreement? The answer lies in your ability to create gift baskets that sell briskly in a fast-paced consignment environment of your choosing.

This once again brings wise-buying procedures to light. The more you use manufacturers and distributors that sell great products at a low cost, and also take advantage of show specials and sales notices, the higher the profits, whether selling baskets direct or through consignment. For example, if a basket costs $10.00 wholesale, a general markup is 3 times that price, which is $30.00. A 15 percent consignment agreement on $30.00 would give the consignee $4.50, leaving you with a $25.50 sale. Twenty percent ($6.00) is a $24.00 sale, and 25 percent ($7.50) equals $22.50. If there were no other way to display your baskets in a buying market, consignment might be a logical choice, even at 25 percent. The consignee might not appreciate your company label outside the basket, but a business and rotary-file card buried on the inside also alerts the buyer to who you are. Now the buyer has the option of coming directly to you for custom baskets, increasing monthly sales while decreasing the need for consignment in multiple shops.

> *The shops I consign with get 20 to 25 percent for each sale. It's well worth the money, since I don't pay for rent or employees. One drawback is that some customers damage the wrap, and the baskets have to be resealed on occasion.*

Some shops have never consigned before, so when approaching them, don't assume that the owner will understand consignment sales. Your initial offer is a low percentage, such as 10 to 15 percent. The owner is inclined to be excited about incorporating baskets for sale that add only to the store's atmosphere and profit margin and not to the existing inventory.

Experienced gift basket designers have come up with their own solution to consignment sales—they use their knowledge and buying savvy to create gift baskets that are priced low enough to make a profit and sell outright to stores. Consignment sales sometimes demand more time and money than it's worth. This sales option means that you never return to the store to replace damaged cellophane or expired items. Keep this in mind as you learn through experience.

Advertising on the Internet

Never in our wildest dreams did we think that the Internet would allow us to run a home-based business internationally without anyone knowing about the home base. We hear about how big the Internet is, how many people are signing on each day, and about the business potential, but is lots of money really changing hands?

In recent years gift basket professionals have found their Web sites courting many more sales from Web surfers looking for local, national, and international deliveries. As more households plug into the Web, the opportunities for individuals to find your business are increasing every year.

One thing that the Internet will never replace is the need for people to see and touch the products they buy. Still, the Internet lets clients view baskets from their desk at home or work and read company information. After you distribute printed literature by mail, your Web page is an excellent marketing tool, allowing a prospect to follow up by browsing for more information on your Web site as easily as the click of a mouse. E-mail linked to the Web site encourages requests for price estimates on multiple baskets and ordering by calling or faxing you or by sending the order through e-mail or shopping cart options.

Informing and Exciting Your Audience

Web sites should be visually appealing, informative, and exciting. They should give the viewer the same feeling of anticipation as waiting for dessert after a great meal. Browsing through gift basket and other Web sites will guide you to understand how to set up your own Web pages. Some sites take forever to load because there are too many pictures. Others offer only text, and that won't sell anything. Even sites that don't sell gift baskets include pictures. Change your site at least every month, just as you change an answering machine's greeting to announce special holiday baskets. Site visitors will welcome the change and be intrigued with the messages and offers. Change is crucial to a Web site's success.

When you decide to establish a presence on the Web, you must add your Web site information to everything associated with your business. That includes stationery, business and Rolodex cards, doorknob hangers, and advertising specialties. Your voice mail message should also mention your Web site. For example, the announcement should begin by saying, "Welcome to Moore Baskets, where Moore is better. Visit us on the Web at www.moorebaskets.com."

Postcards and similar advertising products that you create by computer or order through a specialty company announce your existence when mailing the cards to clients and prospects. Everyone from postal employees to office staff loves to read postcards.

Ingenious methods to promote your Web site have expanded, thanks to this technological phenomenon, but your work doesn't stop here. You must seek other methods to bring traffic to your site. First, your business plan identifies the type of companies and individuals you wish to service. You must find places on the Web where they visit and research ways to get their attention without leaving spam-type messages. For example, if the site has a message board and a visitor asks a question about gifts, you can answer that question (without blatant site advertising) and include your Web site address and the availability of your on-line newsletter under your name. Such a tactic, which is known as a signature file, might look similar to this:

Jane Moore
Make Moore of an Impression with Moore Baskets
www.moorebaskets.com
Subscribe to our on-line newsletter
www.moorebaskets.com/newsletter

A signature file can be created in most e-mail accounts and automatically appear at the end of your e-mailed messages. If your site includes helpful information about holidays and gift-related resources, your response can also mention this to the visitor.

Second, if you wish to promote your business to convention centers, hotels, and other corporations, this can be done in two ways. Send postcards to business sales executives announcing the site and its benefits, or use the business's e-mail feature to ask a question regarding the company and leave your Web site's address under your name. The responder may not visit your site, but he or she might click on the link in curiosity. Asking a question is a great way to get exposure without sending spam to announce your site.

Setting Up Your Web Site

Web site setup options have expanded over the years and mostly for the better. This fact does not make your choices easier, but there are ways to narrow the field.

First, you must find out if your preferred domain name is available for registration. A domain name is the address that individuals type in the browser address bar to find your Web site. For years, Network Solutions (www.netsol.com) was the only authorized site for domain name registration.

As of 2003, Network Solutions was no longer the only registrar. Register.com (www.register.com) and GoDaddy.com (www.godaddy.com) are two popular companies within an extensive list of firms that are also authorized to register names, many of which offer very low registration fees.

Visit several domain registration sites, choose one for name registration, and follow the instructions. It's also a good investment to research domain names with similar spellings. For example, if you register GiftBasketsbyCathy.com, consider registering GiftBasketsby Kathy.com and GiftBasketsbyKathi.com, if available. This is done so that competitive sites don't use a variable of your name, thus drawing customers away from your site. Your Web site's host (the company that provides space to let you set up shop on the Internet) will set up your site so that the additional names lead to the main site, usually for a small monthly charge in addition to the hosting fee.

Would you rather pay a monthly fee to an Internet service provider (ISP) to host your site, or would you rather pay no monthly fee, using the services of a free host? Understand the trade-offs before choosing the free option.

Check your current ISP's Web hosting rates, and compare them with other fee-based providers such as Earthlink and AOL. If you decide to set up shop with the company that provides your current Internet access, you can keep your e-mail address and receive additional mail addresses for your Web site (e.g., Jane Moore uses moore@earthlink.net and will gain moore@moorebaskets.com when setting up her site). The benefit is that if customers e-mail you now, the old address will still work if you stay with your ISP. Also, your stationery, business cards, and other advertising that bears the old e-mail address won't need updating. Your ISP will also allow use of your domain name (e.g., www.moore baskets.com) without any complications.

There aren't as many free Web site hosts on the Internet as there have been in past years, but some still exist. Use search engines to find companies in this category. Some free hosts place their domain name within your Web site name. For example, if Moore Baskets was hosted by Freeservers.com, the site's address would be www.moorebaskets.freeservers. com. Prospects won't remember this long string. If you don't want this type of address, you must register your domain name on your own and find a host that lets you use the name without any restrictions.

Another drawback to monitor is banner ads that some, if not all, free hosts place on hosted sites. These hosts may have the right to litter your site with banners of their choosing, and that includes some that you may find objectionable. Each free host provides on-site questions and answers about their services. Read the information and the contract very carefully before signing up for free hosting.

You must also decide what software to purchase to set up your site. Packages such as Microsoft FrontPage and Macromedia Dreamweaver are touted as easy to use, but nothing is easy if you don't understand computer technology. Register for an adult school software course, and ask gift basket designers on gift and nongift message boards about their experiences. You'll also receive lots of comments and suggestions from others who are knowledgeable about Web site software and setup.

Your software decision is also guided by your ISP's or free host's parameters. Before buying software, check to see if one package is better for the particular system than another.

Other costly Web site components, if not included in the host's package, are a shopping cart for Internet ordering and e-mail addresses over and above the allotted amount.

Does it seem overwhelming to set up a Web site? Then it may be time to recruit a computer-literate high school or college student who is looking to expand his or her resume through work experience. Ask friends and family for referrals. Web site setup is not quick and easy, but it is worth the business gained.

Success Profile
Flora M. Brown, owner
Gift Baskets by Flora
Anaheim, California

Flora Brown opened Gift Baskets by Flora a few years after moving to Anaheim, California, in 1989. A native of St. Louis, Missouri, her life's ambition was to become a teacher. She fulfills that dream by day as a professor of humanities at Fullerton Community College in Fullerton, and caters to gift basket clients during off-hours in her home-based shop.

Instinctively, Brown knew that her sideline business would be craft related because she often made felt bookmarks as gifts for coworkers. In 1992 she began searching for her part-time penchant at craft stores and weekend fairs. Then she received a book on careers from a friend. It ranked gift baskets as the number one business. "Why didn't I think of gift baskets?" she wondered. And soon her decision was made.

Brown's research led her to wholesale gift shows, magazines, and gift basket classes. She attended a gift basket convention days before beginning a new semester. Brown credits her lesson-planning background for giving her the skills to organize and to absorb information during the business's start-up stage. But even the best training can concede to stress. Overwhelmed by the options, she decided to give herself six months to research and to start her gift basket business.

Gift Baskets by Flora caters to busy professionals who have a high regard for quality gifts. Her clients include therapists, land developers, and attorneys. Brown never regrets choosing gift baskets as her sideline and views mistakes as a learning experience. She admits some ideas can't be implemented quickly because of job and family responsibilities, although she does write industry articles and teaches gift basket classes when time allows.

Brown started her Web site, GiftBasketsByFlora.com, in 1998. It consists of an inviting home page, several pages of gift basket photographs with descriptions, a monthly contest, and a biography page. It also offers gift basket seminars and industry links for designers who frequent the site. A year later, she was contacted by a supervisor at a major telecommunications firm who had visited her Web site while searching for gift baskets. A sale for forty $50 baskets was finalized two weeks after contact. Each basket contained a snack mix, cookies, cinnamon stirrers, truffles, coffee, biscotti, pear sparkler drink, a wall calendar, and mugs supplied by the client. "She chose my company because she was impressed with the designs I showed," says Brown. "She said that my site seemed very professional and that it was easy to navigate."

Brown doesn't believe that this client would have found her without an Internet presence. "The great thing about the Web site is that when people arrive on the Internet, they are actively looking for gifts. They are able to compare my company to as many others as they want. By the time they call, e-mail, or fax me, they're ready to buy."

Brown shares her ten tips for starting and maintaining a successful Web site:

1. Decide on your Web site's goals before setting it up. Do you want to just get clients to call you, or do you want clients to be able to shop and order on-line?
2. Hire an affordable Webmaster if you don't have the expertise or time to set up and maintain a quality site. But remember that you, not the Webmaster, are responsible for deciding the content and style of your site. You must stay in frequent contact with your Webmaster to make changes, corrections, and additions.
3. Make your site colorful, but not too busy; avoid more than two font styles per page.
4. Provide large, sharp photos of your products, with descriptions and prices of each design.
5. Use flashing and movement very sparingly—it takes away from the professional atmosphere you want to create.
6. Inspire confidence on your site by posting your background, training, and experience in the gift industry. You want to be seen as an expert.
7. Make it easy for clients to navigate your site.
8. Make your ordering process as simple as possible. If your site does not have a secure order page, clients should still be able to call to place the order.
9. Give your clients a reason to return to your site other than just to buy. For example, offer a monthly contest or provide gift tips.
10. Visit your competitor's sites and sites in noncompeting industries to see what additional ideas you should consider implementing without blatant copying.

Brown's work with motivating other gift basket designers in classes and seminars has led her to start another Web site, this one for the trade, www.giftbasketbusiness world.com. Visitors to this site will discover lucrative resources that will help them expand their businesses. A free newsletter and information on trade shows, vendors, new products, and more are available. Her advice to newcomers serves as words of wisdom and encouragement: "Stay committed to make your gift basket business work, so much so that you don't think of it as work."

Once your site is up and running, consider bringing more traffic to it through partnerships, which is explained in Chapter 11.

Mixing Photos, Text, and Tips

Visitors want instant gratification when viewing your site. They want to see gift basket photos, but not so many on a page that it takes an inordinate amount of time to load. Some professionals decide to show one gift basket on the home page, while others introduce visitors to the site with text only. Other pages within the site are used to display gift baskets, separated by themes, occasions, and corporate designs.

The text accompanying each basket explains the design and contents without being too wordy. As with print literature, you must let visitors know that product substitutions of equal or greater value will be added to any basket where the pictured product is not available.

Corporate gift tips, interesting holiday facts, an occasional contest, and a link to read or subscribe to your on-line newsletter are also worth considering on your Web site. These give the visitor additional reasons to return and are a great way to boost referrals and sales potential.

Pulling Photos from Other Sites

While it may be tempting to copy, borrow, or otherwise take gift basket photographs and text from established Web sites, it is a practice that is frowned upon in the industry. Using other people's pictures and words on your site is unethical. A true gift basket professional creates a Web site using his or her own property to showcase the creativity that customers can expect when a basket is delivered or shipped to its destination. You will not be able to re-create someone else's gift basket in the manner in which it is shown, so why use another person's picture on your site?

Gift basket designers often surf the Web to see what competitors are offering and the types of baskets created nationwide. This should be done periodically to stay aware of trends and changes, but you should refrain from attempting to pass off someone else's work as your own.

Preparing for Slow-Selling Seasons

March, July, August, and October can be slow sales months, due to the lack of key holidays, a greater number of people being away on vacations, and an increase in leisure activities that don't call for gift baskets. The marketing plan is key to organizing money-based activities during these dry spells, which can become as busy as any holiday season by taking advantage of the not-so-obvious opportunities:

1. Review your plan of action. Have you done all you can to increase business? Are there new business opportunities to research?
2. Are your work area and office in order? Do you need to reorganize?
3. Does the visitors and convention bureau have new listings of conventions and annual meetings coming to town?
4. Take time for a sales and expense analysis. Are your sales where they should be? Why or why not? What opportunities have you procrastinated about that shouldn't wait any longer?
5. Have you seen new competition, new businesses, or new homes? Opportunities to expand your client list and increase sales spring up quickly. Take a tour of your region, make notes, and enhance your action plan.

Marketing your business to corporations, offering incentives year-round, and knowing what conventions are coming to town will keep your sales as brisk as any holiday season.

Establishing a Toll-Free Number

How many customers call you from out of the area to place an order? How interested are you in attracting prospects in other states to buy from you and not the competition? The answers to these questions determine whether it's time to consider installing a toll-free number. There are good reasons why companies decide to go this route: (1) installation is easy and affordable, (2) the company with toll-free access is the first chosen by most customers, and (3) the line instantly allows out-of-area callers to respond to a message if the business is being promoted on television or radio.

All long-distance carriers offer toll-free service. If you're interested in a certain phone number, dial that number to see if it's in use. Then call carriers and ask about their service and rates, including questions on:

- What the cost per call is and whether it fluctuates during the day, evening, and weekend.
- Whether you must pay for wrong numbers, especially during the first months of service. This is important, as people will call thinking you are the number's previous owner.
- How long the service must be in effect before cancellation. You're not looking to cancel yet, but you want to know about all penalties.
- What the provider can do about harassing calls. Do you have to live with them, or can the provider trace such calls and initiate criminal proceedings? Do you have to pay for these calls too?
- What is the cost to block calls in a certain area? If you work in Montana, you may not want to allow Montana-based calls, for instance. However, the blocking cost may be more expensive than the less costly proposition of paying for every toll-free call, including calls from your next-door neighbor.

Installation is best coupled with promoting business on television, radio, the Internet, and in print ads. Using the number during the start-up stage may cause more headaches than you're ready to handle. Many calls will be for the company that previously had the number, and you will be busy documenting the right and wrong numbers when the bill comes in. The process is a bit unnerving, as it is one more procedure to do while attempting to concentrate on building a great gift basket business. However, once you've been established for a year, it's time to consider the toll-free option to expand and enhance your business.

Whether you choose to pay for advertising or promote through bartering and/or an Internet site, these are the best ways to saturate the marketplace with a distinct message of who you are, what you offer, and why your gift baskets are the best addition to Earth since air.

Advertising and Promotion Checklist

1. Request catalogs from companies specializing in promotional products or visit their Internet Web sites. Identify the items you can afford that will best promote your baskets. _____

2. Call radio station producers to discuss a barter arrangement of free advertising in exchange for promotional gift baskets. _____

3. Look for area business organizations in order to meet new people and possibly join groups. _____

4. Create contests and other inventive promotions to implement during nonholiday periods and slow sales months. _____

5. Approach noncompeting florists and other specialty shops to discuss selling baskets on consignment. Decide on the best consignment percentage range for your baskets. Prepare a consignment agreement. _____

6. Decide how to best set up your Web site.

   • Register your preferred domain name. _____

   • Call your current ISP and other hosts for Web-hosting rates. _____

   • Research whether to set up a Web site through a fee-based or no-fee host. _____

   • Investigate and select a Web site software package. _____

   • Find appropriate Internet software courses through adult schools. _____

   • Decide how your site will look (pictures, text, tips) and how many pages are required. _____

   • Consider using the services of a high school or college student to set up your site. _____

7. Subscribe to on-line gift and nongift newsletters and review the format and contents. Use their strengths to create your own text-based or graphic newsletter when your Web site is launched. _____

8. Call several toll-free carriers and calculate the cost of installing a toll-free number. _____

Chapter Eight

Delivery Methods

"How do you ship your products?" It's a common question asked by professionals at trade shows, at conferences, and on gift basket message boards. Everyone is looking for a magical answer, a no-hassle, low-cost method of finding shipping materials to use and the best shipper for pickup or physical delivery. Research is the key to finding the best solutions, and gift basket deliveries are no exception. At the same time, you must watch for marketplace changes that occur over time and cause adjustments in your shipping procedures. Changes include your favorite courier going out of business; the nearest shipper's location closing, with the next closest location 50 miles away; a new courier opening in town with better rates and exceptional service; and the box manufacturer no longer stocking the box sizes needed most.

The three most used delivery options are (1) transporting by personal vehicle, (2) a courier or delivery service for local and surrounding-town deliveries, and (3) shippers who mail box-packaged baskets anywhere in the world. It's not uncommon for gift basket professionals to consider making their own deliveries as they work through the logistics of finding reputable help. Let's start with delivery basics that steer you in the right direction.

Making Your Own Deliveries

The Benefits

The biggest benefit of delivery is meeting the recipient and seeing his or her reaction when handed the gift basket. The recipient now associates a caring face with a beautiful gift and feels a kind of "bond" through your smile and well wishes. It makes the person want to do business with you again. When delivering, that bond is 99 percent of gaining the next sale. Recipients enjoy the interaction between the delivery person (who just happens to be the owner) and want the same enthusiasm for the person they choose to receive the next basket. Personal deliveries enhance referral business, turning one sale into two, two into four, and so on.

Another benefit is the care a gift basket receives while in transit. Although it's hard to break the bond between "mother and child," this benefit slowly becomes a liability, as time will not allow you to supervise every basket's delivery. As business grows, you must prepare to let other modes of transportation take over. Investigate every delivery option, and narrow down the best methods that meet each need and keep your mind at ease.

Benefits are also found on the Internet through Mapquest (www.mapquest.com) or Yahoo's map feature (www.maps.yahoo.com). Both sites provide door-to-door directions for most destinations and city-to-city directions for every location. A home-based company that prides itself on giving superior service never asks a client for directions, and with Mapquest there's no need to chart your destination using cumbersome maps. Just enter the starting and destination points, click the button, wait for the directions to appear, and print when ready.

The Drawbacks

Most delivery disadvantages are easily conquered with a bit of ingenuity, foresight, and trust in your own judgment. The biggest drawback is time spent on the road and energy used negotiating traffic instead of deals. If a recipient is thirty minutes away, that time is increased by extra traffic, waiting for the recipient to come to the door or front desk, and every other situation that can and will occur. If delivering in a busy downtown section, where will you park? Will you pay to park? Will you get a ticket for double parking? What about the time spent away from work at the home base? Upon returning, you must refocus on the day's business, which takes—you guessed it—more time.

Mapquest and Yahoo maps, mentioned under "The Benefits," also present problems. While these on-line services help with navigation, the directions can sometimes be wrong or misleading, especially during construction of old or new roads.

If the client knows that you are the delivery person, there could be an unreasonable assumption that no delivery charge should be assessed or that the charge is lower because you are delivering. Such clients feel that they are already paying for a basket, so why should they pay another $10 to $15 when it's you and not a courier? The solution is simple: Clients usually don't ask, so you don't tell. If you are asked, say, "I might deliver in an emergency because my clients are very important." Your job is to provide superior baskets, knowing that clients don't have to understand anything about your business except the fact that you intend to be their only gift basket source.

To make deliveries more official while acting as your own courier, use a form like the sample Delivery Schedule Form. Attach it to a clipboard and have each receiver sign to confirm receipt. This is also a good form to give a contracted courier, as disputes may arise about a delivery and who received it.

The last major drawback is an accident that occurs while you're on the road. In Chapter 7 one advertising product not mentioned is a magnetic car sign. This type of removable sign is made from heavy plastic and adheres magnetically on the driver's door. Such signs are often used by plumbers and construction companies. In an accident, if you're a sole proprietor and use a magnetic car sign as an advertising billboard, you could be sued as an individual and a business, increasing the risk of losing personal and business property. Talk with your attorney about the problems that can develop by using a sign. Legal problems aside, accidents do happen, and the less you're on the road delivering baskets, the more likely the chance for a healthy business and a happy life.

The Basics for a Smooth Delivery

Though seemingly apparent, deliveries are made easier by preparing for any situation you can imagine and some you've never dreamed of happening. Where are you going—to a private house, a corporate office park, a construction site? Are your directions clear? What if there's a detour? Will you be able to get back on track without losing your way? How do you find out ahead of time if a road is blocked? Do you have the recipient's telephone number in case there's no answer at the door? What about the client's phone number? Is there a plan B if the recipient is not available? What if you're on a college campus that's as big as New York's Central Park—amid the buildings on the surrounding ten acres, can you find

Delivery Schedule Form
MOORE BASKETS
Delivery Schedule—3/18/04

Company/ Address	Recipient	Telephone/Floor/ Special Instructions	Received By: (print name)	Time

the destination? Or what if it's rush hour—how much time will it take now?

Smoother deliveries start with being prepared for anything. It is the difference between keeping delivery time to a minimum and adding hours to what should have been a thirty-minute trip. Jane Moore, our fictitious new gift basket professional who shared her business plan in Chapter 2, has a three-point system that might offer solutions to your delivery questions.

Point 1. When taking the order, find out if the client is familiar with the delivery environment. Is it an area of one-family homes or an apartment building? Are there dogs, cats, or pythons on guard? Is it OK to leave the basket with a secretary, at the office front desk, or with a neighbor if the recipient is in a residential area?

Point 2. Before leaving the office, get a detailed delivery route from Mapquest or Yahoo. If the route includes a long stretch of road or a major highway, call the local police department or highway transportation authority and ask about any construction, road closures, and detours along the way. Call the recipient to ensure that he or she will be there at the time of delivery. If not, and this was not expected, call the client to confirm or discuss an alternative plan. You can still keep the element of surprise by telling the recipient, if asked why you need to know his or her whereabouts, the gift giver's name without revealing the type of gift to be delivered. If delivering to the client, ask how he or she intends to pay for the delivery if payment will be made on-site (in this case, see point 3 for further instructions).

If you've done everything possible to make the delivery and still must return a second time to deliver, it is not uncommon to charge the client an additional delivery fee. This policy should be in writing on the purchase order and told to the client by phone when discussing delivery. This is, of course, up to you, and keep in mind that no matter how long you've done business with a courier, you will still be charged a fee for return trips. Someone must pay the cost.

Point 3. Before starting your journey, make sure the basket is well secured in the vehicle. Have directions, all other delivery information, and a cellular telephone by your side. If delivering to the client and that person will be charging the purchase, the charge should be finalized before leaving the office so that the client is handed a receipt along with the basket. If the person will be paying with cash, take enough combinations of bills and coins to give the correct change. Remember, as a retail merchant, you must be ready and able to give the customer the correct change. There are no excuses and no stopping passersby to ask for change; it's your responsibility.

Check with your car insurance company for business-use riders and any other coverage to consider. It's extremely important to protect yourself adequately.

Securing Baskets in the Car

Basket placement in a car or van depends on the vehicle's inner structure. If traveling alone, secure the basket in a box or bag on the passenger-side floor. If you have a van, the available space between the driver's and passenger's seats may provide a snug fit. The backseat floor provides safety and security from prying eyes if several stops will be made along the way. Many professionals also enlist the services of seat belts fastened around a basket placed on the seat. Consider the following low- and no-cost items that aid in making smoother deliveries.

Large Shopping Bags

Some baskets are small enough for containment in a large handled shopping bag. If the bag is a bit too large, insert tissue or newspaper evenly on both sides of the bag alongside the basket. Add a festive look to the bag by tying strands of curling ribbon on the handles and curling it with scissors. Your company label on the bag's front and back acts as a permanent billboard. When delivering to the client, decide if the paper inserts should stay or be removed upon arrival.

Boxes for Better Deliveries

Sometimes a basket is too large for a bag or another holder is needed to deliver multiple baskets. Top-open boxes in many sizes are handy to aid your travel and delivery. These free boxes can be collected from product deliveries you've received, boxes discarded by other companies, or boxes found while shopping in warehouse superstores. One example of a sturdy box is the type that holds ten reams of duplicating paper and has an inverted lid with 3-inch sides. You'll find that different sizes will accommodate any situation.

If the box has short sides like a box lid, line it with tissue paper that coordinates with the basket's colors. The box allows easy and appropriate transport into the home or to an office desk and makes the handling easier for both parties, while the tissue paper turns a generic container into a stylish carryall. Other soft materials, such as sheets or blankets, can fill box pockets if needed during transit, but don't use anything that adds excess lint to the cellophane, basket bag, or shrink-wrap. Company literature should sit in the box just beneath the basket.

A basket can be wrapped in regular gift-wrapping paper or tissue paper to hide the surprise, even when sitting in a tissue-lined box.

Take some baskets for a test drive to see what methods work best before delivering the first order.

Plant and Grocery Bag Stabilizers

Compartmental structures that are made to keep plants and supermarket shopping bags upright during transport are another product that gift basket professionals use to keep gift baskets stable during the twists and turns of vehicular travel. This equipment looks similar to a tic-tac-toe board and allows you to nestle your baskets inside the square compartments. It works well in trunks and in the storage areas of SUVs and usually collapses flat for easy storage when not in use. These types of stabilizers can be found in department stores, discounters, specialty stores, and outlets that cater to floral retailers.

Keeping Your Car in Good Condition

There aren't many worse things in life that you can think of when a car breaks down en route to a delivery. How grand life would be if the car fairy whisked our car away while we slept, changing the oil and checking the tires, then returned it just in time for us to drive away to make deliveries! Maintaining your car is a lifelong habit. Understandably, a car will break down for reasons beyond your control, but breaks in service are worse when coupled with a lack of commitment to attend to every area of business, including on-the-road safety.

Car maintenance can be monitored in your daily planner or PDA. When the car is serviced, document it in the planner. Cars should have regular LOF (lube, oil, filter) service every 3,000 to 5,000 miles or during the time specified in the owner's manual. In the planner's calendar section, indicate the car's mileage when the car was last serviced. This procedure can be eliminated if the mechanic places in the upper-left-hand corner of the front windshield a press-on service sticker that tells the month and odometer reading for your next service. That reminds you of the car's next checkup. Either way, you now have a quick, accessible record. Get into this habit and you'll have a smoother ride every delivery day.

Finding a Reliable Courier

The time will come when you can no longer deliver. Perhaps you've decided from the outset to use a delivery service. If a client orders one hundred baskets and your car is too small to make a one-trip delivery, you must seek outside help. Maybe you don't own a car, so there's no other choice but to use a local courier and a shipper for faraway destinations. What are the options to find a reliable delivery service?

The Yellow Pages and the Internet are your first steps in finding local couriers to ask about the three R's: rates, reputation, and reliability. Also check the business-to-business Yellow Pages for courier listings. Any ads that mention flower and gift deliveries are called first. Start by saying that you are looking for a courier to deliver gift baskets. Ask if the vans are properly equipped for delivering baskets, and find out how products are stabilized. Other questions to ask are:

- What areas have the lowest delivery charge, and what is the rate?
- What is the out-of-area charge? Name some cities for approximate rates.
- How much lead time is needed to request your services?
- Is rush service available, and is the rate higher?
- Do drivers use a delivery sheet that's signed by the recipient for receipt verification? (Whether theirs or yours is used, you need proof of delivery.)
- In the summer are the vans adequately air-conditioned, or will chocolates delivered 10 blocks away be a gooey mess within three minutes? (Chapter 5 addresses seasonal merchandise.)
- How are the drivers dressed—in casual, everyday clothes, uniforms, or at least a custom shirt that sets the driver apart from the person on the street? (Security is a must for individuals opening their door to a stranger.)

Request a rate sheet and additional information by e-mail or fax to ensure correct note taking and quotes. After tallying all data, choose the best courier for your needs and keep the others in mind for backup help.

The service must be reputable and insured against theft and liability. Accidents can happen, and you must be assured that your baskets are protected against damage. What if other gifts are being delivered and yours is stolen? How will it be replaced? The inconvenience is bad enough without adequate courier protection. The representative should have all information ready for faxing or sending by mail, including references from other companies using the service.

> *Florists in this area use two couriers who specialize in delivering floral arrangements and gifts. Their charges are very reasonable, since they want all the business they can get. At the same time, they're both good, since neither one wants to gain a bad reputation.*

You can consider paying a neighbor or a friend for deliveries, but what if he or she is involved in an accident? Since that person is technically working for you at the time, you will be responsible for the liability. Your best defense is to use a reliable, insured firm that secures your baskets from tumbling in the van en route to the receiver, delivering the product on time and with a smile.

Rates You Can Afford

Courier rates average about $10 per delivery in a local area and sometimes more. It is an accepted cost of doing business, a rate that is passed on to the consumer after other calculations are also factored. Later, we'll discuss how to determine the rate you charge. For now concentrate on making your baskets the rage of the community, and the delivery rate won't matter.

Choosing a Shipping Service

Four modes of transportation influence your choice of shipper: express delivery (one-day service), two-day, three-day, and ground shipping (the slowest but most popular service).

The United States Postal Service (USPS) and United Parcel Service (UPS) usually offer the most economical rates. This is verified (or disputed) by creating a chart like the sample Shipping Rate Chart and calling shippers to compare rates, prices, and number of days for delivery. When making calls, use eight pounds as the estimated box weight. The shipper will also ask for the box's starting and destination zip codes. Since these are estimates, give the home-base zip code and the point (zip code) farthest from you where a box might be mailed. That will give the best price estimate before actual shipping.

Shipping rates can also be determined through the USPS (www.usps.com) and UPS (www.ups.com) Web sites.

Another important question is what each company's shipping requirements are for packing gift baskets. This answer helps to select the proper materials for safe shipping, most of which are discussed later in this chapter. Then use the service that's best for overall delivery or one that's requested by the client. Consider other shippers as alternates if problems like slow deliveries, broken baskets, or torn boxes begin occurring when using another company. Always have a plan B ready if your first choice doesn't work.

Federal Express, Airborne, and DHL also ship, but the large, eight-pound, odd-shaped boxes that gift baskets are packaged in are expensive to ship through these carriers. There will be occasions when clients will specifically ask for them, and if the clients are paying, by all means use that carrier. Keep in mind that USPS and UPS also ship overnight at a lower cost than other shippers.

I bookmarked all of the shipping carriers' Web sites and visit
them on-line when I need to compare rates fast.

Your Location or Theirs?

Shipping fees are always lower if you take the package to the shipper versus having the shipper pick up from the home base.

A UPS representative informed me that the weekly shipping charge depends on your weekly shipping costs, as shown in the following chart:

Your Package Cost Per Week	UPS Weekly Pickup Charge
$0–$14.99	$16.00
$15.00–$59.99	$11.00
$60.00+	$7.00

Shipping Rate Chart

Based on an 8-lb., 18-by-21-by-16-inch box mailed from zip code 01000 (ME) to zip code 90000 (CA).

Shipper/ Closest Location/ Toll-Free Number	Cost			Regular Ground	# of Days for Ground Delivery	Weekly Pickup Rate
	One-Day	Two-Day	Three-Day			

If you have no deliveries to pick up in any week, you are charged a flat rate of $16. If you mail six boxes in one week and each costs $5.00 to ship, you will be billed $30.00 for shipping plus $11.00 for the weekly pickup. There are two-sided YES and NO signs available to hang in a window or on the porch so the driver can see from a distance if you have a pickup. Do not set up the service for a week, cancel it, set it up again, cancel, and so on. Having the shipper come to your home is beneficial when you start shipping multiple packages every week. That's when the rate becomes worth the cost, and the price is easily transferred to the client by calculating an adequate shipping charge.

The decision may also depend on where you're located in relation to the closest shipping station. If the shipper is just 5 miles away, you may decide to take packages directly there or possibly contract a courier to do it for you. However, if the closest shipping destination is 30 miles away, the weekly charge may be worth the cost when business increases and you find yourself with less time and energy to travel long distances each day for anything except a presentation.

Protecting the Cargo

How is a product packaged when you receive a mail-order shipment? The materials used by gift basket professionals are the same as other companies use—boxes, bubble wrap, and peanut or paper fillers.

Boxes

Three different-size boxes will work for most if not all of your shipments. The three sizes are established by determining the three average gift basket sizes you create and adding about 2 inches more around the height and width of the basket so that wrapping can be added before placing the basket in the box.

Box manufacturers are found in your local Yellow Pages under "Packaging Materials" and on the Internet under the same heading as in the Yellow Pages. Boxes are also available at retail office-supply stores, where they are bought individually or in bundles of three.

Once you start shipping, monitor the number of boxes purchased each month. Boxes are used quickly, especially during holiday months, so don't be caught short. Order or buy again when about five boxes of one size remain. The closer a box manufacturer is located, the quicker the order is received. If you run out of a certain size box and need one quickly, you should have an alternative source for replacement boxes until the ordered shipment arrives.

Boxes can be customized to display a company name. Manufacturers offer this imprinting at an extra charge. For now use generic boxes, as they will be discarded for the basket contained inside.

Bubble Wrap

Years ago a television commercial featured a gorilla tossing a suitcase around a cage to prove the case's durability in rough handling. Bubble wrap provides baskets with the same protection against mishaps that will occur while the package is in transit. Once the basket is ready for shipping, about 3 feet of bubble wrap should be wrapped around the entire basket and taped in place.

Bubble wrap is available through most mail-order box manufacturers and at retail office-supply stores. Compare prices carefully, as the wrap seems sometimes to be less expensive at the retail level.

> *Before closing the bubble wrap, I place tissue or brown paper*
> *wads between each bow loop so it ships well without the bow*
> *arriving flat.*

Peanuts or Newspaper

After wrapping the basket in bubble wrap and placing the basket inside the shipping box, you can fill the openings between the basket and the box with foam peanuts or newspaper, printed or unprinted. Each filler works the same as a cushion to protect the basket, so the one chosen is a matter of preference.

Foam peanuts are purchased from box manufacturers and other corrugated product sources, but the most inexpensive way to find peanuts is to reuse the ones received in delivered merchandise and to ask area merchants to save the peanuts from their packages, making arrangements to pick these up weekly. The newspaper used to fill the basket cavity also works as a box filler. Wad and insert it in the open spaces. Most designers use newspaper to pack their baskets. Peanuts are often messy, covering the floor of the recipient's home or office and clinging to their skin or clothes when unwrapping the basket.

> *Saving the packaging materials I receive for reuse has saved me from buying shipping materials costing hundreds of dollars each year.*

Shipping Tape

Clear box tape comes in varying lengths, with 2 and 3 inches being the most popular widths. The 2-inch tape is the easiest to find in retail office-supply stores and through box manufacturers. Some tapes come prepackaged with a tape gun, while others come in packs of six or twelve. Tape prices vary widely according to manufacturer, size, and gauge, so compare options and don't be fooled by a low price—you may be buying an inferior tape without the strength needed to hold the box and contents securely.

As with custom boxes, mail-order companies offer shipping tape customized with your company name repeated throughout the roll. The tape can also be printed with your toll-free number or Web site address. The price is, of course, higher than that of the all-purpose tape but less than ordering a custom box. Using customized shipping tape may be an affordable investment to advertise your business while gift baskets travel nationwide.

Outside Labeling

Shipping labels placed on box corners announcing THIS END UP are a good investment. Since gift baskets are tall, make shippers aware of the correct box position when they are placing boxes on trucks and planes. Not every shipper complies with a label's instructions, but if you pack the box as securely as possible, the basket will still get to its destination looking as fresh as the day it was made.

Proper Attire for the Traveling Basket

When you are delivering by courier, each recipient's name should be clearly marked on every basket, using a general or customized gift tag for easy identification. The name is printed by computer or in printed handwriting, as the courier must understand the text for proper delivery. Many professionals have had at least one delivery nightmare caused by basket switching, late arrivals, or a basket's complete disappearance from the planet. The courier is your partner and depends on clear information to take a basket from point A to point B. Prepare a delivery schedule to give the courier everything needed to complete the day's mission.

As already mentioned, for nationwide shipping, boxes should be at least 2 inches larger on each side of the basket to allow for packing materials and extra cushioning. After cellophane, basket bag, or shrink-wrap closure, bubble-wrap the entire basket for all-around protection. The box should be taped shut on the bottom and newspaper placed on the box bottom for added basket protection. Place the bubble-wrapped basket in the center of the box. Add peanuts or newspaper in all pockets between the box and the basket. Always add your advertising literature in the box with the gift. Add more filler between the wrapped basket and the top lid. Close the flaps and seal the box with shipping tape. Affix labels on the outside showing which end is up, and put the mailing label on top.

Now shake the box. Does the basket move? It's essential that the basket does not move for more than the obvious reasons. Although the mailing label tells who you are and where the package is going, if the contents are not packed securely, shippers have the right to open the box for inspection before delivery if they believe that the product is dangerous. In today's security-conscious environment, a bottle of jam that explodes and leaks through the box is viewed as being as hazardous as any other dangerous cargo. Spend a few dollars shipping a test basket to a relative or to yourself. Unpack and view the contents. If all is in order, pat yourself on the back. Your next order is ready for shipping.

Charging Your Customers Appropriately

How far will you travel to deliver a basket? A 5-mile round-trip delivery at the current 36-cent deduction for business use of your car costs only $1.80, but turn that trip into 40 miles round-trip and the cost becomes $14.40, not counting the wear and tear on your car or time away from the home base. When you arrive at the destination, will you pay to park? Must you tip the person who helps unload multiple baskets at a country club or other destination? These costs are prime reasons why more professionals are enlisting the service of local couriers.

> *Not only is my delivery charge determined by area and basket weight, but I also incorporate some of the shipping charge into the total basket cost. The client is none the wiser, while the delivery price stays fair and reasonable.*

What is the total cost to ship a basket? A clear picture is gained from accounting for every cost, from the amount of tape used to close the box's openings to the courier who delivers to the ultimate shipper. Use this example as a guide:

Box =	18" (L) x 12" (W) x 14" (D) =	$1.80
Bubble wrap =	$25 for 100 feet = 25 cents/foot x 3 feet/basket =	.75
Peanuts =	Free, but must travel to get them. Based on round-trip travel, 10 miles round-trip = 10 x .36/mile = $3.60 for peanuts. If these peanuts are used in 10 baskets, $3.60/10 =	.36
Newspaper =	An average charge for all shipments =	.15
Tape =	One tape roll = $3.00, which closes about 15 boxes. $3.00/15 =	.20
Labels =	Recipient address and THIS END UP labels =	.10
		$3.36

Rounded up, $3.50 is the minimum cost incurred to pack a basket before adding the shipping charge. If UPS or USPS charges $6.00 to mail the box, the total cost is $9.50, but you cannot forget about (1) the travel cost if you or a courier drives to the shipper or (2) the weekly fees if you use UPS pickup. You can see that it is not unreasonable to charge $12 to $15 for shipping. Examples are also gained by asking colleagues about their charging methods, documenting competitors' charges, reviewing charges on gift basket Internet sites, and investigating other methods used by mail-order catalogs, where $20 charges and above are what customers pay every day without question.

Your shipping charge should never decrease, whether the basket is delivered by you, a courier, or the shipper. If you allow your prices to fluctuate, your business is the ultimate loser in an industry where gift basket professionals intend to win.

Delivery Methods Checklist

Completed

1. Start documenting your car's service to keep the vehicle in good working order. Test-drive your car with baskets inside to assess the best methods of transport. _____

2. Call and ask courier services for rates, general and rush availability, and other relevant information. _____

3. Call shippers and prepare two cost comparisons.

    Check delivery rates. _____

    Check pricing to pick up from your location versus taking the package to them. _____

4. Determine which three box sizes are to be used most often to ship baskets.

    Call box manufacturers and request catalogs. _____

    Search for box suppliers on the Internet. _____

    Visit retail office-supply stores to investigate the cost of boxes and other shipping material. _____

    After cost comparison, order boxes, bubble wrap, and shipping tape. _____

5. If needed, arrange for area companies to save peanuts and other packaging materials from delivered packages for a weekly pickup. _____

6. Calculate the cost of all products used to ship baskets to determine the customer shipping charge. _____

Chapter Nine

Checks, Balances, and Payments

We sometimes look at accounting for our sales and expenses as a drawback to business, a tedious function that takes us away from making the gift baskets we love to create. Yet we have entered into this business to make money, and recordkeeping reveals whether we are living up to the challenge of making a profit while providing a service. Tallying our monthly activities is a crucial part of owning a business, and finding the accounting tools that match our individual style of keeping the books makes the task more pleasurable.

The word *payments* in the chapter heading not only deals with how you will collect monies owed from customers but also represents the idea of withdrawing cash for personal expenses, if at all possible. That too is discussed here.

The main accounting and recordkeeping documents needed, whether manually written or computer generated, are a sales journal, expense spreadsheet, inventory list, accounts payable and receivable, customer database, balance sheet, income statement, and cash-flow projection.

Reliable Recording Systems

Manual Recordkeeping

So you don't own a computer. You're neither alone nor relegated to chiseling records onto clay tablets. There are many manual systems available that keep your business on track while making recordkeeping something to look forward to. These systems consist of multicolumn ledgers that are either kept in individual books or combined in one integrated system working together to keep the business orderly.

Recordkeeping manuals are needed for (1) sales, returns, and discounts; (2) expenses; (3) accounts payable; (4) accounts receivable; and (5) inventory. Another group of records, the customer database, is appropriate for a rotary-file type of setup rather than a ledger. Now comes the decision of how many columns to use in each ledger, keeping in mind that it's better to have a few extra columns than to underestimate. For example, the sales journal will need at least six columns (the date and transaction description don't count as columns), including one each for the type of sale (cash/check, credit card), a discount column, and a column for returns. That's four columns plus two extra ones to anticipate other transactions or documentation, such as a column listing the type of basket sold or the client's check number.

Next, look at the manual recordkeeping systems available at retail office-supply stores and through companies that sell systems by mail order. Such companies include NEBS (800–225–6380 or www.nebs.com) and McBee Systems (800–526–1272 or www.mcbeesystems.com). Each system is similar in format, but one may have advantages over the others that make it more attractive than the rest. Companies selling recordkeeping systems often exhibit at regional business trade shows. The representative will be happy to show you every detail and point out the system's advantages. Tell the rep about your specific gift basket business needs and decide if this system should be given consideration.

Let's pause for a positive thought on getting started with documenting those first sales and expenses. I urge you to consider taking a recordkeeping course at a local adult school if you don't understand bookkeeping basics. A few weeks of instruction can make a world of difference, turning procrastination into a can-do attitude. When you've purchased the system of choice and have the monthly receipts in front of you, use a pencil to enter all numbers just like accountants do all over the world. It's OK if you make a mistake; erase it and reenter the correct number. Also use a calculator with a paper tape to keep calculation errors to a minimum.

Some pages may end up being used for trial and error. Since recordkeeping is new to you, after the initial setup you may want to rearrange the journal for better efficiency. Change the structure now, before you're into the sixth month of business and wish you had changed it earlier.

Computer Systems and Software

Once upon a time owning a computer was an option only the largest corporations could claim. Today computer prices and payment options make ownership easy and affordable.

The right computer system to buy in any market is either the fastest system available or the one just below it. Any other computer will not keep you updated enough to withstand the needs of today's memory-hungry software packages and computer downloads. Find support through retailers, computer magazines, and professional contacts versed in this technology to understand basic memory and upgrade requirements.

Software, as mentioned toward the end of Chapter 3, is available to record sales, maintain inventory, and manage expenses. The computer will also store your business plan, help you brainstorm new sales techniques, and allow you to network with other professionals through Internet access. Some software offers a complete package that includes word processing, spreadsheet, database, and Internet access. This type of product bundling saves money you'd normally spend on separate software programs.

Records You Need for Business and Taxes

The Sales Journal

A client's order generates a sales invoice, which documents the purchase and completes the sale. This transaction is listed in the sales journal, which includes all information on sales, discounts, returns, and adjustments. Gift baskets are a custom product that nets few returns, since the gift is immediately given or sent to the recipient. However, there may be adjustments from time to time for customer satisfaction, such as switching one product for another or duplicating a basket due to a lost delivery.

Expense Spreadsheets

On the flip side of recording sales, the expense spreadsheet is one of the most important documents to create. Here's where you see how the money is being spent. Sometimes funds move through your hands so quickly that there's not much left after paying bills and buying equipment.

The sample Expense Analysis Spreadsheet on the next page was created using a basic computer spreadsheet program. There is no rule that says all recordkeeping documents must be kept on a certain type of ledger or computer program, but the law does say that these records must be maintained; thus, do so clearly and accurately. Once you set up your spreadsheet, it's just a matter of filling in the information each month and calculating the side and bottom totals.

Inventory List

Keeping up with inventory is of prime importance but can be as puzzling as recordkeeping software options. To keep accurate count, and as discussed in Chapter 3, inventory should be taken out of all shipping boxes and stored on easily viewed shelves or in storage containers. This way, every product motivates you to sell it instead of playing hide-and-seek, increasing the possibility of incurring spoilage or forgetting about purchased products.

A count of all inventory should be taken at least once a year, between January and March, though you may decide to take count twice a year. If you've ever worked in a store at inventory time, you have some idea of what's involved, but just in case you've never had the pleasure of tallying hundreds of mismatched infant socks, here's your introduction.

> *My inventory is done in June, so I can decide what to buy in*
> *the fall, and in January, to prepare for tax time.*

Inventory is best taken by two people, though it can be done by one. Before starting, you should have an alphabetized list of all products for sale. Anything you've forgotten to place on the list will be added at the bottom. Each product is recorded on its own line so there are no quantity mix-ups.

Start with the top shelf or container. One person calls out the product name while the other places a "tick" mark on the line. (For example, see right.)

Move from left to right until all products are counted. Group ticks in sets of five, shown by four short lines and one longer line diagonally across the four previous marks (ꟷꟷꟷꟷ). When the inventory is complete, add each count for a total quantity of all listed inventory.

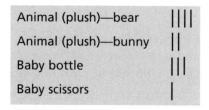

Expense Analysis Spreadsheet
Moore Baskets
For the Period Ending May 31, 2004

DESCRIPTION	JAN	FEB	MAR	APR	MAY	TOTALS
Postage:						
Post office						
National shipper						
Shipping supplies:						
Boxes						
Tape						
Bubble wrap						
Advertising						
Subscriptions						
Telephone:						
Office						
Fax						
Cellular phone						
Internet access service						
Office equipment:						
Telephone						
Five-tier steel shelves						
Office supplies:						
Stationery						
Envelopes (9-by-12)						
Duplicating paper (10 reams)						
Travel:						
Tolls/parking						
Meals						
Gas						
Bank:						
Merchant account fees						
Service charges						
Credit card interest charges						
Exhibits/trade shows						
Education						
Computer software						
Photocopies						
Gift basket photography:						
Film						
Developing						
Basket products:						
Baskets						
Food/snacks						
Enhancements						
TOTALS						

The inventory's value is a combination of each item's cost plus an evenly divided freight charge added to each item. Here's an example of how to distribute freight costs:

Cost of shipping ($12.40) divided by 36 (total number of products shipped) equals 35 cents (rounded figure). The new cost of the gels ($2.30 + $.35 = $2.65), lotions ($2.30 + $.35 = $2.65), and powders ($2.50 + $.35 = $2.85) is updated for each inventoried item.

12 bath gels @ $2.30	=	$27.60
12 body lotions @ $2.30	=	27.60
12 body powders @ $2.50	=	30.00
Subtotal		85.20
Shipping		12.40
Total cost		$97.60

Some professionals create their own inventory tracking system using a spreadsheet format to document each product, quantity available, wholesale price, and quantity sold to date. Others use one of several retail management software programs advertised in gift trade magazines. When you read about new software, call the manufacturer or visit its Web site to request a demonstration program (possibly for a fee) to see if the software adequately controls your business and inventory.

Some use software packages like Mind Your Own Business (MYOB) and Quick Books. MYOB has been customized by one gift basket business to update inventory each time a gift basket is sold by decreasing each product by one when used in a basket. This same software documents the date products are purchased, giving the professional a built-in shelf-life tracking system. Remember, however, that what works for one gift basket business may not be a suitable program for another. To keep from wasting precious capital on software, read the product box carefully and call the manufacturers for demonstration disks to investigate further before deciding on a program.

Accounts Payable and Receivable

Manual records must be kept separately for accounts payable vendors (also known as the cash disbursements journal) and accounts receivable clients, obviously, since one owes you and you owe the other. Each record should include room for extended payments and the amount of interest charged by the vendor or interest you charge to a slow-paying client. These two records play an important part on the balance sheet. Loan officers want to see how much debt is incurred, as well as your methods of collecting payments from clients. A minimum of four columns is needed for these transactions: total due, payments, interest, and balance due.

Customer Database

When was the last time Ms. Smith placed an order? Is Mr. Jones's birthday next month? These and other questions are quickly answered when you employ a customer database as part of your recordkeeping documents. It is a detailed record of basic customer information: name, address, and telephone number; business information; title, company, address, phone, fax, e-mail, and other necessary data; previous orders; children's names, birthdays, likes, and dislikes. All of this links you with customers and their preferences and yearly gift basket needs.

A database is set up either as a manual rotary-file system or on computer. High-rolling executives set a good example by treating a rotary card file like a personal prize wheel; they spin the knob to find the right name and number to contact for referrals, new business, and ongoing business relationships. Rolodex files, for instance, are available in many sizes, from early basic design to the futuristic look of bubble-domed pedestals. Even the basic model is made with a wider frame to hold 4-by-6- or 5-by-8-inch cards that document lots of data instead of squeezing everything on a small card. Computer software for these file cards also exists.

Manual customer databases are still common. Some professionals prefer a manual system for instant accessibility or in case the computer fails to work properly, thereby severely limiting access to important client information. Computer-based systems, such as ACT! and Goldmine, are extremely popular in the gift basket industry. Both software systems are user friendly and easily track names, addresses, birthdays, and many more details on thousands of clients.

Keeping Everything in Order

Get a Receipt!

It's amazing that the usual receipts for purchasing groceries, a movie ticket, or a pair of shoes are taken for granted, while business receipts for paying cash at the gas pump or buying stamps are the ones we forget to request. Every receipt that documents business spending must be retained to prove to the IRS and ourselves that money was expended. Receipts give a clear picture that answers the bottom-line question, How's business?

Make a conscious effort to get a receipt for every business transaction. When approaching a toll booth, go to the toll collector for a receipt unless each lane has a button dispenser. How many times do you say, "It's just 50 cents" before realizing how quickly the cost adds up in dollars? Maintaining receipts also shows you where expenses can be cut when the monthly transactions are logged on the expense spreadsheet. If a company says that its service will save you money, the calculations are easily checked by reviewing the spreadsheet's totals.

A flat pouch or envelope eagerly awaits the day's receipts. It should travel with you everywhere you go. You'll find various types of receipt holders in office-supply stores. No matter what you decide to buy, get a receipt!

Make a habit of asking for receipts to satisfy the IRS's need for proof of business activity and your need to add up the costs of maintaining a profitable business.

Monthly Reconciling

By now you know that there's much more to a home-based gift basket business than simply creating baskets. You document sales on invoices, collect receipts, and order products. Each month the receipts are transferred to ledgers or entered on computer spreadsheets.

A more experienced person can be retained to complete the paperwork if you choose. Some professionals hire a bookkeeper who records everything once a month. While it is good to delegate certain responsibilities and concentrate on your stronger talents, a basic knowledge of bookkeeping is extremely important, for several reasons:

- If you cannot afford a bookkeeper or find suitable help, you must complete your own records.
- If the bookkeeper relocates, you must do the work until another person is retained.
- Leaving the records solely for the bookkeeper's eyes opens the door to embezzlement, a silent and costly theft that occurs when you least expect it.

Balance Sheet Preparation

A balance sheet is prepared at the end of each month. It shows an overall picture of business worth at a given time during the year by documenting your assets (cash, inventory, or equipment), liabilities (whom you owe and how much), and your net worth (the difference between the assets and the liabilities). This is an important document to maintain not just for your own knowledge but as part of the financial package that convinces outside investors and banks of business soundness for possible investment and loan retention.

The sample Balance Sheet shows how the asset accounts are documented, including depreciation. Any office equipment, such as a computer and printer, can be depreciated over five years. This business purchased a computer, printer, and fax in January 2004 totaling $2,600. Over five years (sixty months), depreciation each month is $43.33. The depreciation amount shown is $43.33 x 5 ($216.65), rounded to $217, the nearest whole number.

The owner's equity section, located below "liabilities" on the balance sheet, examines how to document a cash withdrawal to reflect a drawdown from the capital account during the month.

Income Statement

How much money did you keep last month? The income statement answers this question by detailing the month's total revenue and expenses, which calculates net income (profit) or loss. The sample Income Statement is the short version of the larger sales totals and expense spreadsheet. Here many entries are condensed into a few lines of financial text.

On the sample statement, sales discounts reflects the reduced amount for a multiple corporate sale, while interest earned is bank revenue from current accounts. The operating expenses are divided into selling and general and administrative expenses. The few categories shown below don't necessarily have to be extracted on your own format. This company wants the expenses shown for comparison reasons. Your income statement can show one large total for each expense category.

Balance Sheet
Moore Baskets
May 31, 2004

Assets

Cash		$3,268
Accounts receivable		650
Inventory		3,830
Office equipment	$2,600	
Less accumulated depreciation	217	2,383
Total assets		**$10,131**

Liabilities

Accounts payable		$410
Loan payable		128

Owner's Equity

Jane Moore, capital, May 1, 2004	$8,153	
Net income—May	1,603	
Subtotal	9,756	
Less withdrawals	163	
Jane Moore, capital, May 31, 2004		9,593
Total liabilities and owner's equity		**$10,131**

Notes:

Office equipment =

computer—$1,500

printer—$700

fax—$400

Income Statement

Moore Baskets

For the Month Ended May 31, 2004

Revenue

Sales		$2,025
Less sales discounts		62
Interest earned		21
Total revenue		$2,108

Operating Expenses

Selling Expenses:		
Cost of goods sold	$208	
Advertising	40	
Delivery service	32	
Total selling expenses		280
General and Administrative Expenses:		
Telephone	48	
Postage	32	
Depreciation expense: office equipment	43	
Other expenses	102	
Total general and administrative expenses		225
Total operating expenses		**505**
Net income		**$1,603**

Cash-Flow Projection

The cash-flow projection, as shown in Chapter 2 for the start-up gift basket business, is used to anticipate how cash will be earned and spent within a specific period. This helps the delicate balancing act of planning sales before paying bills so a negative cash balance is less likely to happen.

It may seem odd to estimate figures in this fashion, but remember that this is a projection. Bakers estimate how many loaves of bread they can sell daily so they don't discard too much bread at day's end. To do a sample projection, let's estimate April's cash flow. The month's main event is Administrative Professionals Week. By now you know the area companies and can estimate a minimum amount of sales for that event. Can you make at least twenty sales at an average of $25 each ($500 total)? Your anticipated marketing methods should help answer the question. Sales hint: To get twenty sales, target your sales message for the office manager. If the office manager gets the company to order a minimum of ten baskets, he or she gets a free $20 basket; twenty minimum equals a free $35 basket; and so on. Present this incentive to every office manager at each company.

20 $25 baskets	=	$ 500
40 $35 baskets	=	1,400
		$1,900 sales in April

Other than Administrative Professionals Week, can you sell a minimum of two baskets per day at $35 each? You have a multitude of monthly occasions and regional people giving gifts every day. Two each day equals ten per week, or forty per month, plus a minimum of twenty sales for Administrative Professionals Week. That totals sixty baskets sold in April.

Remember, this is a minimum projection. Next year you'll use the actual sales for new projections. This is a great tool for setting initial sales goals and then attempting to surpass the projected revenue.

Update the cash-flow projection as needed throughout the year. It can even be set up with percentages, as in how much is sold and the higher or lower percentage than the projected amounts. Challenge yourself to succeed by setting attainable goals and going the distance to exceed the potential.

Analyzing Your Progress

The two documents that measure your success and financial strength are the balance sheet and the income statement. The balance sheet shows your monthly equity, while the income statement shows monthly net income or loss. From that you can find where problems lie and can implement solutions that increase business and decrease expenses. Even if you use a computer to create and store the records, keep hard copies of all financial data in a tabbed three-ring binder.

Consulting with an Accountant

Your accountant can guide you through understanding tax consequences to your business throughout the year. A certain amount of profit creates a liability to pay self-employment taxes, and an accountant keeps you aware of these details to pay the tax on time without being assessed IRS late penalties.

Since most personal and business taxes are due on April 15, tax consulting is best done twice a year—in July/August and in November—unless there are special situations where you must meet the accountant more frequently.

Take your spreadsheets to the meeting so that your accountant can review the setup and provide proper guidance. Also ask if your method of recordkeeping is appropriate, if the accountant can lend any suggestions to make extracting numbers and information easier, and if he or she recommends a certain recordkeeping system (manual or computer-based) for product-based clients.

Opening a Business Checking Account

A checking account with your business name printed in the top left-hand corner is a major component in establishing a business. Separate checking accounts must be maintained for personal and business use, as account mingling is not an acceptable business practice.

Before opening the account, compare business checking fees at several area banks. (Also find out which ones offer merchant credit card accounts; more on that later.) Some banks offer low or no fees, while others have fees so high that they can wipe out your savings in a few months. Take a look at the sample breakdown of fees giving pro and con data to assess area banks' fee structures. Typical business checking fees are (1) per-check charges, which will range up to 15 cents for every check you write; (2) per-deposit charges, usually the same rate as per-check charges; and (3) monthly service charges, which some banks charge if your average balance falls below a certain amount—such fees are usually between $10 and $25 per month. There may be advantages to opening your account with some banks, such as free use of a safe deposit box, notary public availability, or no-fee traveler's or cashier's checks.

Do not start your checks with number 001. Choose a higher, odd number such as 128 or 564. These higher numbers imply that your checking account is long established and

Bank Fee Comparison

Description	National Business Bank	United States Bank	City Society Bank	United Trust Bank	Midland Savings	Prospect Heights Bank
Monthly maintenance fee	$10	$8	$3	$15	$10	Below
Per check paid	.15	.15	.10	.15	.15	—
Per deposit	.10	.15	.10	1.00	.35	—
Per check deposited	.15	.10	.10	.12	.10	—
Earnings credit	5%	4%	Below	Below	5%	—

Notes:

National Business Bank
Based on account balance, the account earns 5 percent credit. The higher your balance, the less of an $8.00/month fee you will have. Bring incorporation papers or trade name authorization to prove the business.

City Society Bank
For earnings credit, each $100 is multiplied by .00438, which equals two monthly credit earnings.

United Trust Bank
Earnings credit is based on 88 percent of average account balance times ninety-day T-bill rate (7.47 as of 2/10/04).

Prospect Heights Bank
A sole proprietorship account is handled like a regular checking account. If the account has $500 or more, there is no maintenance fee. $250–$499 = $3; $0–$249 = $5. If a corporation, $4,999 and below balance = $15 maintenance charge.

that you have been in operation for at least six months. It's logical that a new account is established with an opening deposit, and it's also logical that higher-numbered checks can bounce like lower-numbered ones can; however, in this fast-paced world of high finance, some companies frown on taking the first check from a new business.

Designer checks are cute and pretty for your personal account, but don't use them in business. Safety blue, green, and yellow are "in"; crayon-drawn scenes and ducks swimming in a pond are "out."

Three-on-a-page checks contained in a large binder are the standard business style, though some banks offer styles that mirror a personal account. These checks are more expensive than the personal kind; five hundred checks can cost between $70 and $90, and the first batch usually must be made by the bank's designee, not the check discounters.

As with personal checking, maintaining your business account takes time every month to reconcile the ending balance and correct any errors made in that period. Ignorance leads to insufficient funds and a bad reputation. Then you must settle the account with creditors, who have the right to stop doing business with you. This, in addition to bounced-check fees from your bank and the creditor, who has the right to charge an added fee to the balance for a bounced check, is avoidable by simply taking the time to properly reconcile the account.

Bringing the Proper Papers

To open a business checking account, you will need to provide the selected bank with a copy of the business documentation issued by the state when you applied for a business license. If your business is incorporated, the bank will need a copy of the incorporation papers. In either case, bring the original documents as well so the bank is assured of their authenticity.

The bank may also require personal identification, so bring your driver's license or another valid photo identification (a photograph is usually not needed if you have an established relationship with the bank).

Accepting Checks and Credit Cards

Checks

The acceptance of checks is more difficult today than ever before. Technology has brought us products that make business easier, but it has also introduced a barrage of counterfeit checks through computer-generated forms on specialty paper. While the majority of your clients will be upstanding and not present a bad check, here are some guidelines for accepting checks.

When handed a check, take a good look at it. The rules of etiquette do not apply here; take your eyes off the client and scan the check. Look at the name and address—are they the same as the information you were given when the order was placed? What bank is the check drawn on—is it local or out of state? Is the check correctly completed? Is it signed by the client? Does it include a phone number?

Before depositing the check, you are allowed to call the issuing bank to ensure that there are available funds to cash the check, but understand that there are enough funds only at the time you are calling. Checks can take up to three weeks to be returned, and if that happens, you'll not only be out of the sales amount but also be charged at least $10 for processing the returned check. Many retailers have instituted a policy of charging $20 or more for returned checks, and it would not be out of line for gift basket professionals to do the same. This policy should be stated on your sales invoice and Web site. If the invoice form you use does not specify this policy, invest in a custom stamp to mark each invoice.

Credit Cards

We live in a credit-based society where businesses that do not offer customers the option of payment by at least one major credit card are guilty of doing their customers a disservice.

Regardless of whether you believe you can afford the costs, you must offer a credit card option to your customers. The initial perception about accepting credit cards is that the cost is astronomical. As with any other product or service, the companies and banks that offer merchant status must be sought, price comparisons made, and one chosen to process the sales. Your investigation will reveal the best price available for your needs. If you sit back and complain about the pending costs, the lost sales will leave you with one alternative—closing the business for good.

Your business plan is where you begin to list the costs associated with accepting credit card purchases. In most cases, it will not take that long to begin selling baskets that pay for the fees, which you'll find are not as excessive as you thought. Credit card purchases are also more reliable than checks: It takes ten seconds for a credit card number entered into an electronic terminal to be accepted or denied, whereas some checks are mailed back marked "insufficient funds" three weeks after the goods were delivered.

> *Lots of companies offer credit card processing, and the rates vary. I spoke with five service providers before deciding on a company to do business with. Although my bank would have given me quicker access to the funds, I signed with another company, which offered lower rates.*

Remember that you are a retailer who happens to be home-based. All retailers adjust their prices to incorporate a small fee to charge each customer for credit card sales, no matter what form of payment is used. Gas stations are a perfect example. They used to charge one price for cash and a higher charge for credit purchases. Some may still do this, and although most gas stations now use the one-price option, the cash price still incorporates a small fee for all credit transactions. Your prices must also reflect a fixed merchant charge, which is why we triple our wholesale costs and round up odd figures. Let's move on to explore the costs of opening and maintaining a merchant credit card account.

Installing a Merchant Credit Card Account

Many banks offer merchant credit card accounts, which means that you have the ability to process all or a combination of Visa, MasterCard, American Express, and Discover Card transactions when customers place orders using a credit card. The bank where you've established a business checking account probably offers this service. The actual bank does not offer merchant accounts; rather, an outside company does the recordkeeping in conjunction with the bank for its customers.

If such accounts are not offered by an area bank, you'll have to obtain a merchant account from a nonbank source, such as Costco (800–220–6000 or www.costco.com), or inquire directly at credit card Web sites such as Visa (www.visa.com), MasterCard (www.mastercard.com), Discover/Novus (800–347–2000 or www.novusnet.com), and American Express (800–528–5200 or www.americanexpress.com). Ask other merchants or colleagues

Sales Checklist

Face-to-Face Sale

Cash

1. Calculate tax and write purchase receipt. _____

2. Receive payment for basket from customer and give back correct change. _____

3. Put basket in bag, along with company literature. _____

4. Ask customer if she or he has entered the show drawing. If not, ask if she or he would like to. _____

5. Ask customer if she or he wants to be placed on the mailing list. If she or he does, write the information. _____

6. Thank the customer for her or his purchase. _____

Check

1. Calculate tax and add to purchase price. _____

2. Inform the customer of the total check amount. Write a purchase receipt. _____

3. Review the check, ensuring that the correct date, company name, written and numerical amounts, and signature are complete. _____

4. Ask the customer for additional identification for verification purposes. (Note: In many states, credit card numbers cannot be written on the check; it is against the law.) _____

5. Continue with step 3 under "Cash." _____

Charge

1. Calculate tax and add to purchase price. _____

2. Inform the customer of the total order amount. _____

3. Verify that the expiration date on the credit card is correct. _____

4. Imprint the credit card with a manual imprinter; complete the credit purchase receipt. _____

5. Have the customer sign the credit receipt.   _____

6. Ask the customer for additional identification for verification
   purposes only.   _____

7. Continue with step 3 under "Cash."   _____

Phone Order
Customer Service

1. Ask customer for her or his name, address, and home and work
   telephone numbers.   _____

2. Verify the name and address for basket shipping or delivery.   _____

3. Obtain credit card number, expiration date, and name on the
   credit card.   _____

4. Ask the customer if she or he wishes to place another order at
   this time. If she or he does, take the order. If she or he doesn't,
   inform her or him of the total amount.   _____

5. Thank the customer for her or his purchase.   _____

6. Call the merchant account bureau for customer name and address
   verification, if needed.   _____

Package Shipping

1. Mail the customer a postcard to verify the order and thank her
   or him for the purchase.   _____

2. Call the shipper for pickup, or deliver to the shipper.   _____

3. Put completed basket inside box with proper protection.
   Add company literature.   _____

4. Seal box and add FRAGILE and THIS END UP labels.   _____

who accept credit cards about the merchant accounts installed in their businesses. The answers may provide favorable solutions.

> *I believe my merchant application was approved quickly because I attached my marketing plan and cash-flow projections for the first five years. The Small Business Administration helped me free of charge to put the package together. It was a big help, and my sales show a big increase because customers can charge their purchases.*

Credit cards are easily processed through a small electronic terminal installed to your telephone line. Transactions are entered into the terminal. The merchant account representative in charge of your service will install the terminal and answer any questions.

When processing an order, make sure to have the client's full name, address, and telephone number in case you must verify the cardholder's identity with the bank. Ask American Express cardholders to read you the four numbers imprinted above and to the right of the card number. This ensures that the card is in the client's possession and also acts as security against an invalid card if you must call American Express for verification. Developing a step-by-step procedure for each type of transaction, as shown on the sample Sales Checklist, helps ensure that no process is skipped, from documenting the sale to thanking the customer.

Merchant account monthly fees can range from $18.00 to $27.00, which includes a terminal fee of about $10.00 and a monthly service fee of around $8.00. Looking at these fees, I think you'll agree that $240 a year is an affordable investment to capture credit card sales. Visa and MasterCard fees for each processed transaction cost at least 2.25 percent of each sale; your cost may be higher or lower depending on the bank or processor. American Express transactions are about 3.5 percent. How are these costs reflected in the checking account linked with merchant account capabilities? A $50.00 gift basket charged to Visa or MasterCard will net you a $48.87 sale ($50.00 x 2.25% = $1.13 transaction fee). Charged to American Express, the sale becomes $48.25 ($50.00 x 3.5% = $1.75). After completing the transaction through your merchant terminal, the monies are credited to your checking account (usually within two days), minus the transaction fee. Be sure to write the correct amount to be credited to your account in the check register.

There are many steps to accounting for revenue and expenses and to opening new accounts for business transactions, but they're all part of the procedures to making your gift basket business the best it can be.

Withdrawing Money for Personal Use

Anyone who decides to start a business knows that he or she will invest a significant portion of time and money in the venture. Choosing to withdraw money too early in the start-up stage can result in undercapitalization, which is one of the top reasons cited for business failure within the first five years. Professionals in this industry understand that a gift basket business must secure corporate accounts that order monthly, have access to the region's movers and shakers at social gatherings, and take advantage of every means possible to build and promote business every day, without fail, to begin earning revenues substantial enough to draw down funds to pay personal bills and other expenses.

> *I tell all newcomers to this business to keep their day job. There's no "take home pay" for a few years because you're buying inventory and reinvesting the profits. I haven't withdrawn money from my business yet, and this is my third year.*

At the end of your second year, you might decide to experiment with a plan to withdraw 10 percent of your gross revenue (monies earned before you subtract expenses) for savings. This money can be parked in your business savings account until it grows enough for you to place it in an investment, such as an IRA or money market fund. Discuss the possibilities with your accountant, who can provide insights on the best ways to save a piece of your homemade pie.

Your name and reputation will take years to build. For some it takes less time than others, but it does take years. If you're in this for the long run, your work will pay off handsomely.

Checks, Balances, and Payments Checklist

Completed

1. Decide which recordkeeping system you will use.

   Manual: Purchase recordkeeping ledgers.   _____

   Computer: Purchase computer, printer, disks, and software.   _____

   Begin creating the recordkeeping system and update it as needed. _____

2. Always ask for business-related cash receipts.   _____

3. Call or visit area banks (starting with your personal checking account bank) to compile a business checking account rate comparison. Once that step is completed, open an account.   _____

4. Ask the same banks if they offer merchant accounts, and document their rates.   _____

5. Call other merchant account companies, if needed, for rates and terms of account.   _____

6. Visit merchant account service providers on the Internet and call nonbank sources for additional information.   _____

7. At the end of each month, prepare:

   Balance sheet   _____

   Income statement   _____

   Meet with accountant to review recordkeeping and for general advisement.   _____

8. Create a Sales Checklist to ensure that payments are processed correctly and the sale is fully documented.   _____

Chapter Ten

Competition

There are competitors and there are others who sell gift baskets. Contrary to popular belief, not everyone who sells baskets can make a good-looking, salable product. Some self-proclaimed gift basket makers (not professionals) place items in a basket, shrink-wrap the arrangement, and pray that the products don't shift downward into the basket, leaving the shrink-wrap loose and wobbly. Would you consider a person who does this type of work a competitor? Of course not—just as you shouldn't consider many other places where gift baskets are sold to be your competition.

Will the Real Competition Please Stand Up?

Competition is separated by how vigorously the opposition targets the market you want to serve. Direct competition is the companies who are after your target market, your customers, your accounts. They service similar markets, catering to those who don't have time to shop, are exhausted from going to malls for an extensive gift search, and are simply tired of the same old gift styles. Like you, direct competition gives customers many options to create a custom basket, is meticulous with details, and will ship baskets anywhere in the world. Such enterprises are most likely home-based, Internet, and mail-order companies. Some retailers are also waking up to the fact that they have to provide more in-store services than offered in past years. Providing exceptional customer service is a big part of business the competition thrives on. Sounds like your company, doesn't it?

Meet your direct competition:

- Larger card stores that carry exclusive lines of figurines and other collectibles, china, loose and boxed candy, and a selection of premade gift baskets created from store merchandise and other products
- Flower shops that have incorporated gift baskets into their product line
- Companies that make gift certificates, crystal, electronics, bath and body products, and other items that corporations consider buying to thank their employees for increased productivity or during the holiday season
- Mail-order catalog companies (Harry & David, Balducci's, Godiva, etc.)
- Pharmacies that deliver more than prescriptions
- Other home-based gift basket professionals
- Anyone who brings gift baskets and other competitive gifts to the customer via television, radio, the Internet, or catalog

Indirect competition caters to customers who are content with using conventional buying methods. These customers always shop outside the home, pounding the pavement to compare products and prices. Some people enjoy the thrill of the hunt, mingling with others who walk through indoor and strip malls, happily owning up to the day's challenge of finding something new and different. Customer service at the indirect competition is hit or miss; sometimes these competitors give it, and sometimes they don't. It all depends on the workers' day-to-day moods.

Some of the indirect competition's market has the ability to become part of your core customers. They can be cajoled into changing, but it will take time. This fledgling customer base might see you at a function or on a television show they happen to be watching, or they might work at a company where a gift basket just happens to be delivered. To make the ultimate sacrifice called change, they will need hand-holding. With that breakthrough first call, you'll have to walk them through the initial order, persuading them every step of the way that the basket will be more magnificent than anything they've seen before. It's difficult for people to change their style after shopping the same way for so long. Old habits are hard to break, and when it happens, the first gift basket becomes a bond of lifetime sales and trust between you and the new client.

Some of the indirect competition's customers adore premade gift baskets. Their world is made simpler when the place that changes a flat tire is also a place that sells gift baskets to go.

Say hello to the indirect competition:

- Retail office-supply stores. These sell baskets and gifts for the holidays. By New Year's they're begging you to buy the leftovers.
- Department stores. The markup due to overall operating costs is astronomical.
- Smaller card stores. These can be contained in a space so small that the business can barely accommodate cards, let alone other merchandise.
- Supermarkets. With labor problems, daily food spoilage, and illegally opened products found in each aisle, supermarket fruit baskets won't put a dent in your business.
- Warehouses/superstores. They sell baskets for holidays and special occasions. Club members make a habit of coming here each week for the same products and will buy an occasional generically made basket on impulse.
- Pharmacies (nondelivering). Here a person must enter the store to see what's available. If no prescription is needed, no one knows (unless promoted on window signs) that gift baskets are inside.
- Mall cart gift baskets. When the three-month lease is up, they're out.
- Gas stations (yes, some sell gift baskets). No competition, trust me.

One of the best features about the indirect competition is that these companies hold income-producing opportunities for your business. In most cases, none of them employ people who are uniquely skilled at creating quality gift baskets. Most if not all of them receive gift baskets through a practice called outsourcing. That means they have their baskets delivered by an outside contractor through a blanket purchase order for the larger chains or by a local professional who picks up store merchandise, makes baskets at his or her own facility, and brings back ready-made baskets for the smaller stores to sell.

Keep watch on ways to change the indirect competition's market into your customers (which includes a competitor's use of your outsourcing services), but for now you have the direct competition to monitor. Continue to seek customers who believe in and faithfully use your service, and be vigilant to change the minds of those who aren't used to the gift basket professional's standard of excellence.

Spying on the Competition

New competition spurts up around town as quickly as new grass, especially in areas where there are few competitors and plenty of room for new business. Some competitors will be home-based, and you'll find out about them through ads, cars with magnetic signs, deliveries you see being made, gossip, new Web sites, and in other ways.

Why did the competition set up camp in your territory? What do these businesses have that you don't? Are they going after groups you have overlooked, or are they after your direct market? Answers to these questions are found by looking for their Web site or by posing as a customer and calling the competition directly (as will be done to you from time to time). If you have a pretty distinguishable voice, have a friend or family member call. Afterward, reward that person with an incentive (a small gift of thanks) for his or her assistance.

Whoever makes the call should first ask for a catalog. If the competitor has nothing to send, that's one clue that it's either new to the business or hasn't taken the time to prepare marketing materials. If the competitor sends a full-color, multipage catalog, it means one of two things: (1) the enterprise has spent a tremendous amount of capital and expects to be in business for the long haul, or (2) it ordered the catalog without much forethought, is now heavily in debt, and is in business for the long, uphill battle to attempt to recover the money spent on the catalog. There could be other reasons, but as history shows, the only ones with a full-color catalog are companies that are long established as stores selling more than just gift baskets and specialty stores in major cities with specific clientele that order frequently. The rest of the home-based professionals use postcards and one-page glossy flyers, newsletters, and Web sites, saving the rest of their capital for inventory, promotions, and other kinds of revenue-raising opportunities.

If the competition places ads in the local media, (1) clip the ad, noting the newspaper and date published; (2) watch other papers for possible advertisements; and (3) read the ad to find the main reason why customers may respond (what is the company offering, or is it simply saying, "We're in business; call us"?). It's pretty easy to investigate the retail competition, whether direct or indirect. In a store setting walk in and start browsing. Look for unique products, themes, and creativity used to make the baskets. Of course you cannot stand in place and document every product and wrapping technique that interests you. Walk out of the store, take out a pad and pencil, and write down everything you remember, or take out a handheld tape recorder and document what you saw. Did you forget something? Walk back into the store and look around again. If approached, you instantly become a customer, asking questions about the product selections. Be as discreet as possible. Gift sellers can usually tell who's a customer and who's simply trying to get information.

As for the home-based, call and ask questions after studying the catalog. At the same time, it's a bit tricky to maintain your camouflage as a customer without revealing your hand by asking intricate questions only a competitor would ask. No matter who's making the call, questions phrased in the following manner will help you get the answers needed to learn what the competition provides:

- *Price.* "I often need a few $25 birthday gifts. Do you make those? What can I get in a typical basket?" Then later, "Can I charge my purchase?"
- *Product selection.* "It's hard for me to make a decision, especially if I can't see the basket over the phone. Where can I see your baskets? Do you have a Web site?"
- *Shipping.* "I have a friend in [a faraway state] whose birthday is tomorrow. How fast can you get a $50 basket to her, and what is the total cost?"
- *Discounts.* "My boss needs thirty baskets. He wants to spend about $30 apiece. Do you have a discount on an order that size?"
- *Last-minute orders.* "I'm in a lot of trouble. I forgot my boyfriend's birthday. Can you make a basket for him with lots of balloons and deliver it to his job—today?"

I can always tell when the competition calls me, and there are plenty of gift basket professionals in my area. They are the only ones who ask me what I'm using in holiday baskets and for other occasions. I'm thinking about capitalizing on it by teaching a class so they can start paying me for my answers. Obviously, they need help!

Because you may be the new competition to another established gift basket business, how would you answer these questions? Is this the type of service you are willing to provide?

Competitive Advantages

Competitors can be aggressive but also respectful of one another's business. There is no need for "bad blood" between companies that offer similar products or services, although one unkind word or deliberately set rumor can start a feud that continues for generations.

The advantages of being in the same industry as neighboring companies bring about opportunities that were once thought impossible. Here are four examples of how competitors help one another thrive.

Superstore Discount Products

The superstores are a very important component of our industry. While these stores may sell occasional gift baskets and grab a minuscule percentage of the overall business, they also provide foods, snacks, gifts, and ribbon at a low cost that are perfect for including in your baskets, especially when a product is needed quickly. As pointed out earlier, superstores are actually an industry ally, providing a fresh stock of products, often at a better price than some of the industry wholesalers.

> *I'm able to make quick-selling baskets with products that I don't need to stock, because the closest superstore always has a good supply on hand. It sells mini cheesecakes and pound cakes, truffles, chocolate chip cookies, office supplies, and gift items, all usually between $1.00 and $2.00 each. The manufacturers' shipping prices alone keep me from ordering all of my products directly from them. I'm sold on buying from the superstore.*

Although these stores provide a great assortment of products, don't count on any item being there on a long-term basis. Superstores purchase products by the pallet or truckload, and if they cannot get a bargain on the next buy, chances are you won't see the item there when it's most needed, and sometimes you'll never see it again. Count on this scenario for the products you enjoy using most often.

Business Overload

Competitors are like neighbors: They can coexist without getting in one another's way while enjoying the mutual space and individual privacy. Such is the case with a company that is completing a large order that may not have the time or employees to fulfill smaller orders placed simultaneously. If no rivalry has ensued between two competitors, a client's request to recommend another firm's services may grant the competing company a chance to gain a transferred sale, especially if the busier company believes that this overload situation has happened by chance and the client will not defect for good.

Such work is common in the Orange County, California, region, where the Gift Basket Professionals Network brings competitive businesses together in an atmosphere of camaraderie and industry news sharing in a social setting. Each company knows the other's work style and ethics enough to be confident that the transferred client will be treated well.

Sometimes a competitor is unable to service a client because of temporary illness, vacation, or not having the products the client wants. Hence, another reason why a competitor will refer a client to you or vice versa.

Closing Business Benefits

Gift basket professionals who do not properly prepare for a long-term business soon find themselves without enough clients to justify staying open. In such cases, the decision to cease operation is painful but a move that must be made before losses are insurmountable. The closing business must sell its inventory, which includes a client list of proven gift basket lovers. This is an opportunity to purchase an existing business, in part or whole, to increase clientele and revenues. The advantage here is that the seller may notify you first about the available inventory. Past politeness can net you good deals on products used often and on slightly used equipment you may be looking to purchase at bargain prices.

Other opportunities to expand a business through buying another firm's inventory are explored in Chapter 12.

Co-op Buying Alternatives

Chapter 4 introduced several ways to buy wholesale products for resale, which included the option of buying through a co-op. If two or more companies, whether home-based or storefront, buy the same products for their individual clients, why not purchase those products from the manufacturer in one large shipment and save money on the products' prices and shipping?

Co-op buying is a process that is undertaken only between companies that trust each other enough to enter into this multiple-purchasing agreement and present timely payment for the shipment. There may or may not have been past attempts to begin a co-op in your region, but the first thing to do is to extend an olive branch to businesses that may be ordering products from the same manufacturers you're using. Ask if they are interested in forming a buying co-op, explain the advantages, and mention names of other companies that are willing to join.

All co-op parties should sign an agreement of intent to provide on-time payment for such buying or face expulsion from the co-op and legal consequences for leaving the remaining parties to pay for the cost difference. The agreement should also specify who is responsible for gathering the order from all parties and placing the order with the manufacturers (the same person each time or responsibility through rotation), where the products will be shipped (whose location will store the boxes), and the time allotted to each party for picking up the merchandise from the central location (up to three days, two weeks, etc.).

Competitors that work together on agreeable issues foster goodwill, referred business, and the knowledge that competing companies can work together for everyone's well-being.

Compiling Your Competitors List

The sample Competitors List will help you document your competitors' locations, what they sell, and their marketing methods, and provide for general remarks and interesting facts, such as whom they serve.

Watching the competition is similar to a game of chess: You can anticipate another player's moves by noting subtle hints. You know from experience whether the competitor

Competitors List

Competition	Years in Bus.	Location					Miles Away	No. of Staff	Baskets Only?	Web Site?	Advertising					Remarks
		Home-Based	Free-standing	Mall							Catalog	Paper	Mag.	Other	
				Indoor	Strip										
Direct															
Indirect															

will succeed according to area demographics and marketing materials used. If it's a store, the location and how customers are treated tell the story. Your own customers won't defect if you have been providing them with terrific baskets, great service, and monthly reminders. Ensure customer satisfaction by occasionally asking your customers to critique your products and services, as outlined in the next section, and by sending a survey, as in the example in Chapter 1.

Arrange the competitors' data in the best format for you. The "Remarks" column may include information on the use of a live operator or answering machine, catalog comments (graphics, products, styles, etc.), or in-store discoveries. Use check marks, the words *yes* and *no,* and other details to complete the chart. Under Advertising, "Other" includes Yellow Pages ads and use of rotary-file cards, doorknob hangers, and other promotional products.

If you are persistent in serving your market efficiently while gradually expanding your client base, you'll be shouting, "Checkmate!" all the way to the bank.

Rating Your Own Service

You may believe that your customer service deserves high marks, but what are your customers thinking? Are they pleased with the baskets you create and the service you provide? As you enter this business, compare it with the following areas to see how you rate.

Basket Variety

Do you maintain an adequate quantity and variety of baskets and containers? Are the products sturdy—sitting flat "on all fours" if the basket has legs? General and unusual baskets and a variety of containers keep your creations interesting enough to add the dazzle that makes clients buy only from you. Continue to amaze them using baskets no one else can find.

Customer Service

Do you consistently deliver baskets on time? Is your arrival at the client's office for the appointment so precise that the client can set his or her watch according to your punctuality?

Are clients' calls returned within the hour of the initial call? Do you send birthday cards, industry articles, and other tokens of appreciation to thank clients for their patronage? Do you sometimes deliver more than promised, prompting a call from an enthusiastic client who is amazed by your foresight? Do clients write or call you about their satisfaction? When a customer takes the time to call and rave about a basket and the recipient's response, enjoy the moment, then continue finding new ways to make the service even better.

Shipping Rates

Are your shipping and delivery rates competitive with those of similar businesses? If complaints are lodged, have you assessed the rate and compared shipping prices and delivery options to ensure that your charges are within reason? Do you assess shipping charges on a yearly basis? Nothing stays constant. Always monitor competitors' prices, shippers' rates, and your own cost management.

Product Selection

Do you attend trade shows to see the latest entries in delicious foods, beverages, and gifts? Have you considered an open-house event, inviting your customers to give their opinions as they sample products you've selected at shows to place in baskets for their clients, friends, and families? Do you maintain product freshness, ensuring that no sold basket includes stale products? Have you sent periodic customer surveys asking what products your clients enjoy and which items they'd like to see offered? You'll quickly get to know which products sell and which ones don't. Occasional surveys also help clear up some of the mysteries of why one product sells quickly and another is seldom ordered.

Web Site Maintenance

Do you periodically change the text and gift basket photos, or do customers see Valentine's Day specials when it's time for Mother's Day baskets? Have you posted shipping rates, return and exchange terms, and guarantee policies? Do you publish an electronic newsletter at least monthly to keep customers aware of how your gifts and baskets enhance their personal and professional lives? Visit other Web sites, whether gift basket related or nongift companies, for ideas on how to keep your Web storefront interesting, informative, and sales producing. If your Web site seems abandoned, your customers and prospects will not return.

Repeat Customers

Have at least 50 percent of your customers ordered from you two or more times? Are roughly one-third of new calls the result of referrals? If not, investigate where the problem lies, whether it's because of competition, marketing, not catering enough to clients' needs, or simply failing to ask for business leads and referrals. Have you asked previous clients why they have stopped ordering and assessed what to do to retain those accounts?

You will see from most of these questions that ensuring the quality of each product used and keeping in touch with your customers, whether through open-house events, surveys, direct phone calls, electronic newsletters, or Web site updates, is the only way to keep customers' business and grow through a rich source of referral clients.

When and When Not to Compete

By now you understand the difference between direct competition and indirect competition, but those who don't are as perplexed as is indicated in the words spoken by this next designer. Instead of concentrating on her business and the real competition, she ended up focusing on a nonexistent problem after visiting a local superstore:

> I just came from [superstore name] and am so upset! It's loaded with gift baskets filled with biscotti, napkins, tea and coffee, stationery, pens and pencils, a dish towel, pasta utensils, and sauce, all in a pasta bowl. It's selling for $15.99. How can I compete with that price?

There is no competing with Costco, BJ's, or other discount superstores; thrift shops; odds-and-ends stores; or outlets that buy products in volume and sell at discounted prices to anyone who walks in or is a paid member of the club. The superstore is a wholesaler selling to many individuals who buy on impulse and to businesses that buy gift baskets for re-sale in their own store. Ask yourself:

- Do all of my customers belong to a warehouse club?
- Do my customers like the premade, take-what-they-give-you basket?
- Which superstore delivers to homes and offices and ships across the country?
- How many discount stores make an in-office presentation and take orders on-site?
- Which indirect competitor has my personality, my flair for creativity, my commitment to service?
- Do my customers enjoy using their anything-but-free time to go to the store, choose baskets, load them on a flat truck, stand in line to pay for them, roll their exposed-to-the-weather purchases outside to the car, load them inside the vehicle, drive home or to the office, unload them—well, you get the point.

> *A new client called to order a basket to apologize for a mishap that he had caused his best client. He was really upset and knew from my past work that I could express his sentiments perfectly through specific gifts, foods, and custom styling. I assured him the work would be done correctly, made the gift, and delivered it the next day. He called me early the following morning (before I could call him) to say the client was giving him another chance. Can the super-store do that?*

You can't and don't have to compete with warehouse gift basket prices. The fact is that you provide a multitude of conveniences that a warehouse's customers don't receive: (1) time savings; (2) custom-created baskets delivered to the same location, all with a different theme and color (if requested); (3) one-stop shopping by phone; (4) prompt delivery and shipping services; and (5) familiarity with one person who consistently treats the client like royalty and does the job right the first time. These five points are the central qualities that today's home-based gift basket professional perfects to maintain a successfully competitive business.

Another industry person answered the distraught professional by saying:

> *The mass marketers will always be able to price their products for less. Don't try to match their price. Follow your marketing plan, create the best baskets possible, give top-notch service, and your clients will always come to you first. Remember, not everyone shops at the superstore.*

The only time these stores become your direct competition is during the holidays, when they send mail-order catalogs to their members. Other than that, you've had eleven months to woo their customers your way. With any success you'll be the one with the flatbed truck, rolling your custom gift baskets into the client's office.

Competition Checklist

	Completed
1. Visit direct and indirect competitors to view baskets and take notes.	_____
2. Read newspapers and magazines for other competitors' names and addresses.	_____
3. Call nonstore gift basket competitors and ask questions about:	
Price	_____
Product selection	_____
Shipping	_____
Basket discounts	_____
Last-minute orders	_____
Web site availability	_____
Request their catalogs and other print information.	_____
4. Make a list of all competitors and document findings.	_____
5. Periodically review your products and services to ensure that what you provide is the best of both for your customers.	_____

Chapter Eleven

Keeping Customers
for Life

"Once a customer, always a customer." Those words should be not a mere slogan but a faithful commitment guaranteeing a business's unwaning standard of reliability, from first call to basket delivery and after-sale service.

The motivation that makes a client call to order a basket parallels opening a door: Your mission is to consistently amaze the client with great baskets and service so that the idea of closing the door is not an option. Businesses find it much harder to open new doors than to keep serving an existing client. Although you strive to find new accounts, you must also focus on working with proven buyers who refer you to more prospects. They in turn refer you to others, and so on.

When a new client places the first order, it's easy for gift basket professionals to feel like they've just climbed Mt. Everest. The temptation to turn one's back on current buyers to only attract more new clients is strong. I must warn you that just the opposite is the true goal. While you should continue to make new contacts whenever possible, the job of coaxing that new client to buy again and bring his or her friends and family along is the real objective, and it's just beginning.

You can never contact a client or past buyer too often, especially when you send the appropriate greeting in a format the customer appreciates and enjoys. Here are a few ideas.

Traditional Tactics

Birthday Cards

When was the last time a store you frequent sent you a birthday card? Cards are a quick, effective way to stay in touch with everyone who has made a purchase. When contacting the client to verify the basket's receipt, end the conversation by asking the client for his or her birth month (as well as asking for referral customers). The gift basket delivery has the client in an upbeat mood, so he or she probably will tell you without reservation.

Another way to get this information is through a follow-up thank-you card. Add a self-addressed, stamped postcard asking the client to indicate his or her birth month. The postcard should be predesigned with a twelve-month listing that has a line next to each month for the client to check the answer and return the card promptly.

All you need is the client's birth month, not day of birth. If you happen to get the date, that's fine. Some people are very proprietary about personal information but do not feel violated by revealing the birth month. Send the card at the beginning of the month. That way, it sits on the client's desk or in the person's home as an all-month reminder that he or she is a very important person to your company. Send a card that stands out in the crowd and invites others to pick it up in admiration. Interesting cards inspire office conversations, and new prospects might visit your Web site or call to request a catalog or place an order.

> *My computer software program tells me at the beginning of the month which clients are to receive birthday cards. It's like having a personal assistant who never lets me down.*

Candy Jars

Multiple gift basket orders call for a small token of appreciation for clients and their assistants. Candy jars personalized with your company name sit on clients' desks reminding them of your company all year long.

Fill these treasures with anything but the same old hard candies. Look for gold wrappers, nougat- and nut-filled candies, individually wrapped truffles, or fortune cookies. Before filling the box or jar, place a handwritten note on the bottom, with the words "The first refill is on us," along with your company's name and phone number. This is a simple yet effective way to show your thanks and coax future contact.

Holiday Gifts and Cards

With luck, you'll be very busy at year's end preparing holiday gift baskets for the hundreds of clients served throughout the year. If you plan to give holiday gifts and cards to special clients, save your end-of-year energy for those needing last-minute baskets and multiple orders, and plan to send your gifts during the first week of the New Year.

A New Year's basket stands out as a grand way to begin the year. Before sending the basket, call your clients' offices to check their schedules. The first full week after New Year's Day is when everyone returns to a normal schedule. Reserve your basket for that week's arrival.

Send a New Year's card instead of a Christmas card. The logic here is that clients display Christmas cards in offices and on home mantels until the last day of the year, then they either discard them or save them as part of next season's decorations, without caring who sent the old cards. If you send a New Year's card, it will stay on the client's desk for about three months as a constant reminder of your business. You might also consider sending a Thanksgiving Day card, which stands out similarly to one for the new year.

If you still plan to send holiday gifts and cards, do so if it fits into your marketing plan. However, the New Year's option goes further to increase sales, reminding clients of your endless loyalty to their personal and professional success.

Family Matters

New Additions

The birth of a child also calls for a congratulations card, and if the client has been very generous, a small gift is appropriate to send and is well worth the modest cost. Reserve giving a gift until the mother and child arrive home, as there is plenty for the family to transport from the hospital.

If you are familiar with the expectant mother's or father's work environment, contact a coworker to find out the staff's plans for a gift or departmental baby shower. Such an event allows your basket to be seen by staff members who need gifts for personal family members, corporate use, and outside affiliations. Don't wait to be called; ask and you will get the sale.

Business Travel Gifts

Because of safety concerns, many companies have reduced employees' travel schedules. But some employees, especially those in sales and marketing, still travel often to meet face-to-face with clients. Children long to see a traveling parent, counting the days until the home arrival. Increase sales by informing these executives about your gift baskets for children, which include games and snacks to ease the child's wait. Executives are also parents who sometimes feel guilty about leaving children behind while they go do the work that puts food on the table. These baskets are best delivered the same day the parent leaves. That way, the child is assured of the parent's love, and the parent becomes a hero at the same time.

Professional Contact

Promotions and New Positions

What do you do when you read that one of your corporate clients was just promoted or has accepted a new position at another firm? Surprise the client with your well wishes by hand delivering (if close) or shipping a desktop item like a paperweight, a small inscribed box, or a jar filled with candy. A client is always amazed when someone outside the office and family says congratulations. Enclose a note with thank-you-basket suggestions to give associates who helped the client move up the ladder.

Industry Clippings

All workers want to get ahead in their chosen field or advance into another industry, and clients take special notice of anyone who acts as a partner in advancing their career. Informal conversations during and after the sale draw you into a client's journey to achieve professional success.

While reading the paper for your own business needs, watch for articles on other industries that may be of interest to clients. Always have a highlighter pen and scissors with you when reading. There's always something to highlight or clip, and if you wait, you'll never find the article again. Do the work the first time so the opportunity is not missed. Handwrite or type an envelope with the client's name and address, and enclose the article with a note saying, "Thought this might be of interest to you." It's OK to use a business card, but these words are usually too much to fit properly on a card. Use 5-by-8-inch stationery, notepaper, or a card specially made with preprinted text, available from local stationery shops and some mail-order catalogs. If a client has approved of e-mail contact, articles can also be linked electronically.

This idea also works for prospective clients whom you want to stay in touch with and feel are candidates to buy baskets in the future.

Monitor the effects of sending these notes. How much business is generated by contacting a client this way? Do clients call or e-mail to thank you or send a note of thanks in return? When calling clients to check their basket needs for an upcoming event, they should be receptive and take your call because of the support you provide by sending business-building articles. Monitor what's sent because you must determine when to stop sending these clippings to a client who has not ordered in the past eighteen months to two years. Is this person still a buying candidate? If so, the envelope and stamp are worth the effort. In times when you must cut costs, this practice, if done all year for roughly fifty clients, can add up and may be worth assessing whom to send clips to and whom to stop contacting. The same can be said for postcards, flyers, and printed newsletters (e-mailed newsletters should still be sent if possible). If, after a specified time, it seems a client will not order, you can decide to limit the number of contacts made to the person or simply stop the courtesy.

Clients have rewarded me with many sales and referrals just because I send them a clipping every chance I get. They even tell me about my competitors!

Combining Contests with Newsletters

Clients look forward to receiving mailed or electronic newsletters that not only inform them of what's new and exciting with your gift baskets but also provide them with chances to win prizes through fun and easy contests and unique buying options. Chapter 7 introduced the concept of both types of newsletters to stay in touch with clients, keeping them up to date on holidays and special giving events. Why not also add a contest and other opportunities to win baskets? These additions ensure that recipients are reading your news while building the chance to make sales with every mailing.

Assistants and secretaries are often responsible for ordering office baskets. When the boss authorizes an order, the total amount sold over time can qualify the secretary to receive a personal basket of snacks or relaxation products. Another contest can include the search for a misspelled word in the newsletter. The first person to find the word and call or e-mail with the answer is the winner, receiving a worthwhile gift. Professionals also find that adding a contest on the Web site motivates clients to return often.

There are many more ways to incorporate contests. Review the literature sent to you from other companies and devise ways to keep clients reading and returning on-line.

Teaming Up with Sales-Producing Partners

Regional companies often seek new ways to market their products and services. Many use gift baskets to thank customers for their patronage while enticing prospects to remember them. Your investigation will uncover many companies that service the same clientele who also want to increase their share of business over the competition. You can introduce your company to some of the more common businesses that depend on the public to patronize their establishment.

Sharing customers is a part of the growth factor of business, but for growth to occur, a business must be seen everywhere that prospects relax and have fun, attend social events, and travel, whether to work or for weekend getaways. This is where lifelong customers add to steady business growth. Keeping customers for life means incorporating a degree of excellence in product variety, communications (on-line and printed materials), and customer service skills, coupled with a flair for being in places where customers associate themselves with living the good life. Let's review some of the many places where customers go on their time away from the office.

Hotels

The turnover of customers in and out of hotels means big business for gift baskets. As mentioned in Chapter 10, many businesses don't have the expertise needed to create baskets for their customers and outsource the work to another, more experienced company. Although a hotel might have an expert in its catering department, not all hotels have capable staff, and so they look outside for assistance. That's where you answer the call.

Hotels have a multitude of gift basket needs that can keep you busily creating all year long: welcoming special guests, congratulating wedding parties, welcoming convention visitors, banquet hall receptions, conference room meetings, hotel staff celebrations, and concierge needs to service hotel visitors. Sales and marketing executives, catering managers, and the concierge desk are prime candidates to call you for gift baskets. Although they may know four months before the visit that a guest is arriving from out of town, a last-minute call the day of arrival is quite normal.

Structure your message to focus on their immediate need for the right gift, with that gift being your baskets. Another message is your extensive line of baskets for any occasion and your ability to customize, with personalized ribbon in the hotel's name, baskets for an incoming convention, or state-made products. Introduce yourself to sales and marketing executives through a letter, by either mail or hand delivery. Stress that you will need only ten to fifteen minutes for a presentation that will show the increased sales possible through a mutual relationship. Approach the concierge desk host with business and rotary-file cards and a small basket of goods for his or her enjoyment. Ask about visitors' gift basket requests (how often the need is, popular requests, price range) and offer a synopsis of what you provide along with the usual prompt delivery.

Hotels are one prospect that deserve plenty of coaxing to get the lucrative account. The sales possibilities have determined that these clients are worth going after and waiting for.

Bed-and-Breakfasts

The bed-and-breakfast industry is giving hotels serious competition. The strength of bed-and-breakfasts is a special environment that caters to the client's personal needs versus some hotels that register guests, provide a key, and give no further attention to guests until checkout time. Bed-and-breakfasts start with a welcome service that includes a basket of muffins and fresh fruit in each guest's room. The basket can be adapted for anything from a Valentine's Day weekend to a first wedding night to a weekend celebration.

Do your homework before making contact. Baskets that enhance the cozy environment make the best presentation. For example, take a container resembling a cottage and fill it with crackers, cheese, stationery, bottled water, and dried fruit—a perfect welcome for these guests. Investigate bed-and-breakfast trends by consulting the Internet or by reading bed-and-breakfast trade magazines.

After your research contact bed-and-breakfast owners or managers by phone or introductory letter. Identify interest and need before showing any items that may be of use. If you show the baskets prematurely, the owners may decide to try making their own creations, leaving you out of the loop and them with plenty of new ideas.

Housekeeping and Cleaning Services

People from all walks of life, whether a family on the go or an executive couple pressed for time, are starting to enlist the help of cleaning services more than ever before. Such services were once reserved for corporate offices and the megawealthy. Today housekeeping companies are also catering to individuals who are busy with social or family activities and have no time to properly clean their own homes.

Enter the part-time housekeeper, whose employer works with Welcome Wagon groups and real estate firms to find prospects who are new to the area or those recommended through current clients. The cleaning companies not only introduce themselves with gift baskets in tow but also present the same gift to employees when they are hired, as an incentive to stay with the company, and in appreciation for a special job well done.

Housekeeping and cleaning firms require the same type of quick, efficient service that they provide to their customers, which is what makes partnering with them a perfect match. You'll find local prospects in the Yellow Pages and through community Welcome Wagon and real estate affiliations that you secure over time.

Live Theater

When a play is set to open, anyone from the production company to the cast, theater owner, or hotel where guests stay will look to welcome the leading actors and others associated with the theater. Your first contact is the theater's marketing director, whose job it is to seat as many patrons in the theater each night as possible.

Whether they're upcoming talents or accomplished actors, the major players will be welcomed with fanfare that should include your gift baskets. No ordinary basket will get this account, so prepare to create a one-of-a-kind masterpiece. What plays have been performed at this theater in the past year? Put together a basket with past show accents to underscore what can be done for the present cast. The use of enhancements and old playbills works wonders to get not only the sale but the theater account. Look for these items to create a sample basket:

- Musical notes
- Stars
- A playbill cover glued on foil-wrapped cardboard
- Colors of black, white, and yellow
- Low-fat but delicious snacks (actors are always watching their weight)
- State or city memorabilia
- Boa feathers or other frilly stage attire
- Foot lotion

Please the production company and the show stars, and you've made a client for life.

Restaurants

To increase business, many restaurants now offer their facilities as a banquet hall or an alternative to traditional conference centers by serving as hosts of chamber of commerce and other business-related gatherings. Restaurant owners and managers order thank-you gift baskets and also refer services to inquiring customers.

Some restaurants sell advertising space in a softcover booklet that offers services to weddings, parties, and others renting space. While these booklets have not been successful for gift basket professionals to gain new customers, approaching the owners to purchase your baskets outright to thank patrons is the best option to obtain quick sales for an immediate need.

Web Site Partnerships

If you plan to make a home for your business on the Web, part of your plan should include asking prospects and clients if they have Web access, and if so, which sites they visit most. This information will give you ideas on how to increase your Web presence through partnerships with other sites.

Finding noncompeting Web sites to partner with to introduce and sell your gift baskets is not an easy task because the Internet is an environment where sales methods that are popular today seem to lose their luster within a month. However, there are ways to find complementary partners. Do your customers visit sites on beauty, health, games, or gardening? Your research might reveal common interests that clients share.

Partnerships start with a commonality between two sites that sell related products (e.g., furniture and wood-care polishes) or two that are totally different (e.g., books and kitchenware). In both cases, the two sites may share the same customers. A relationship between noncompeting sites can be as simple as trading links, where each site installs a link to find the other site through a banner or keyword or words.

The banner is a visual picture that, when clicked on, transports the visitor to the other site. A word link does the same thing but without a picture, such as www.giftbasket business.com. There is usually no money exchanged for complementary links. Each site simply decides to increase its Web presence through the other.

E-mail the Webmaster of a site that you believe is a favorite of people who buy gift baskets. Introduce yourself and your company, compliment the owner on his or her site, explain the bond between your sites, and ask if the person would be interested in exchanging links. If the site owner is not interested, find another site that may be more open to a trade. There should be no exclusivity here. For example, if you trade links with one beauty site, that doesn't mean you shouldn't partner with others selling beauty products. The more ways that Internet visitors can find you, the better. If you find that, after a certain period of time, a link doesn't net you any customers, just delete the link.

One tool that tracks how visitors find your site is available through site statistics that most ISPs provide to the sites they host. Other tracking devices are available through a free counter installed on the bottom of your site's home page. Counters provided by sites such as Bravenet (www.bravenet.com) and Sitemeter (www.sitemeter.com) supply information about individuals who visit your site. This includes the search engine used, keywords typed (such as *gift baskets*), and how long visitors stay.

There are other, more complicated and paid programs that sites use to link to one another, but for now it's better to concentrate on ISP tools and free services to increase your Web presence and customer base.

All of these ideas focus on one main point: You must remind clients of your presence, of your worth in their personal and professional lives, and of your commitment to being part of everything they do. Once clients have purchased your baskets in happy times, they will always remember you at the job under stress, for belated sentiments, and to bring comfort in times of grief. Keep the door of opportunity open by becoming a client's only choice for all-occasion gift baskets.

Keeping Customers for Life Checklist

Completed

1. List the best options to thank customers for buying your baskets. _____

2. Ask each customer for his or her birth month, then send an appropriate and timely greeting. _____

3. List additional and productive ways to stay in contact with clients during nonselling times. _____

4. Create an informative print or electronic newsletter, incorporating news and an interactive contest. _____

5. Update your Web site once a month or as often as possible. _____

6. Call complementary companies to offer suggestions on gaining sales and exposure from the same customer base. _____

Chapter Twelve
Growth Opportunities

A t times working solo is enough for your business to grow. But sometimes the help of others is needed to take advantage of maximum opportunities and sustain growth. Following are several possibilities for making your home-based gift basket business as grand as you please. Remember, any option is limited only by your imagination.

Growing from Part-Time to Full-Time

If you start a gift basket business while working at a full-time job, you won't be alone in the quest to wake on that eventful day when the only work to be done is your own. If you commit the strategies found in this book into daily deeds, it's certain that great day will come sooner than you think. It's OK to work at the other job to earn the salary that pays your living expenses. While developing the business, you'll gradually generate enough cash to pay personal bills and draw money from the increasing equity while keeping a decent amount of invested capital on hand. The outside work will eventually disappear, never to be seen again.

How do you know when it's time to leave the dreaded day job? It's a matter of knowing your personal monthly budget, factoring in 10 to 20 percent above that amount per month for emergencies, assessing how much of a drawdown you can live on versus making a salary, and having a steady flow of gift basket clients who increase sales every month. In Chapter 9 we discussed the minimum amount of sales one might generate in April by selling Administrative Professionals Week baskets and everyday designs. Are you able to pay your bills on that minimum amount of sales ($1,900) less your monthly business expenses? You might think this figure is adequate, but remember that this is an estimate. Your revenue will not be consistent each week. Your goal is to earn triple the personal monthly budget and increase sales each month as you grow.

Jane Moore, the budding entrepreneur, plans to leave her real estate employer in two years. She's slowly building her clientele and sales, getting good promotional exposure (through charity work and trade shows), and aligning herself with top regional organizations. The real estate employer is not doing well and has decreased Jane's work schedule and salary by switching to a four-day workweek. Sounds like the employer needs some of Jane's baskets to entice prospects—but that's another story.

The best way to track personal expenses is by keeping a personal expense log. Jane's log, as shown in Chapter 2's Sample Business Plan, lists all personal expenses documented in her business plan, which shows not only where money is spent but also whether money is overspent in one area. If this seems like a lot of work, remember that your employer expects plenty of work from you every day. If you want to leave that job, give this task the priority it deserves.

Resist the trap of thinking, "All I need is one big account." Cash cows are a temporary quick fix. Having several well-paying corporate clients and a cadre of individual buyers holds a better outlook. If that one big client goes out of business or has a string of bad luck, the buying stops, and back you go to full-time employment. Spread the odds of wealth by serving several big clients and many individuals.

Recruiting Help

One sign of growth occurs when you can no longer cover every aspect of business without leaving some details undone. Your desk might be perpetually unorganized or maybe the filing's piled to the sky. Then it gets serious: You forget to answer clients' calls or a delivery is late because the paperwork is lost somewhere on that messy desk. Your first reaction might be to take a vacation, but that won't solve the problem. Recruiting temporary, in-house help and an outside representative to attend sales functions you can't afford to miss is a smart solution.

Part-Time Support

Temporary help is used by one-person operations as often as by Fortune 500 companies. These personnel work every day, evening shifts, or a certain number of days per week. The worker needs a regular work schedule to devote certain days and hours specifically to you. Otherwise, having the help come in on an as-needed basis may put you back in the same unorganized situation.

Decide what help you need most. If it's filing, your system must be in a universal filing format so that you, the worker, and future helpers can follow the same system. What about general office cleaning (that shred can certainly pile up on the floor)? How about making sales calls, taking orders, returning calls, or running errands? Don't just give the person the work you like least; think about what needs to be put in order now. Then create a list of assignments that the part-timer will be trained to perform. This list will give you a good indication of how much support you need and approximately how many hours the person will work according to the time it now takes you to complete those assignments.

One major hurdle that must be faced is the ability to delegate task responsibility to allow the part-time person to perform the assigned work effectively. Over the years you'll learn to juggle multiple tasks while controlling every aspect of business. But there will come a time to recruit capable personnel whom you will train and then supervise to ensure that tasks are performed to correct standards. Remember, no one is your exact clone, and the helper will not do every aspect of the job exactly as you did. Try not to be overcritical; such an attitude will only hinder the person's performance and interrupt the business growth you envision. The worker may bring not only extra help but a wealth of experience and alternative methods of streamlining current procedures; listening to new ideas and critiquing through feedback will create an open relationship of mutual understanding and respect to help your business grow effectively.

Recruiting the right talent takes patience as you search for people who thrive in a creative retail environment. Start by asking family and friends to recommend people they know. Hiring someone whose character and dependability have been vouched for by friends softens the blow of adding an employee and also decreases the anxiety brought on by allowing a new person into the home workspace. If no one is found through close contact, widen the search through college postings (targeting mature-minded juniors and seniors), notices sent to parents through the administrative offices at local high schools (the same adults who volunteer here are great workers), notices to adults who take craft classes at community schools (a letter sent to the community school's office gets their attention), and postings at professional women's association meetings and on craft store bulletin boards. Never lose sight that safety is your first priority, so you must check credentials and weigh recommendations carefully before you hire anyone.

Your need for assistance encompasses many areas. Among other traits, the person who will assist you must be able to follow directions, have self-motivation and an eagerness to learn, be prompt, and, if creating gift baskets, work well under time constraints. The worker must know all the job duties, be told the length of the assignment, and be shown the work environment. Other questions you must address before hiring a worker are (1) Is there enough space in the workroom for a person to work adequately and safely? (2) Are there rules of conduct that must be set within the environment? and (3) Is the home structured in a way that is appropriate for a person to enter the workplace (concealed bedroom, personal items put away, etc.)?

Recruiting outside help also means additional paperwork to ensure compliance with all city, state, and federal employment laws. Once a person has been hired and working hours are established, recordkeeping starts with documentation ensuring that the worker is legally allowed to work. (*Note:* For workers under eighteen years old, each state has guidelines as to the number of hours and how late a minor can work per day.) You are required to photocopy two forms of the worker's identification, which includes but is not limited to a Social Security card and a driver's license. Your state's department of labor has pamphlets and other reference materials on employment guidelines that will help you ensure that you are in compliance with generally accepted hiring practices. One such publication is an employer handbook, which details employer recordkeeping, wage reporting, and tax payment; unemployment compensation; and Social Security taxes and remittance. This handbook also recommends numerous publications and sources for needed forms, is usually provided free of charge, and is an invaluable resource to streamlining this new duty. Be sure as well to check with your local department of labor and division of taxation for a schedule of periodic workshops that demystify new employer requirements.

A working environment is a productive place of business, no matter where the work is done. Provide the home area with an atmosphere of professionalism, safety, and team spirit and you'll be able to complete the necessary tasks.

Hiring a Rep

Trained, experienced representatives know what to say to get a prospect's attention and successfully close the sale. If you need to turn sales calls over to a trained expert, here is what to consider when hiring a rep:

- *What you need*—a professional individual or small firm with experience in selling gift baskets and similar products (you don't need a trainee just starting in the business).
- *What you pay*—a commission that keeps the person eager to work with you while paying an affordable fee.
- *Where to find help*—classified ads in newspapers and trade magazines, business meetings, and suggestions from friends, family, and colleagues.
- *What is needed between you and the rep*—an agreement that states what is expected of the rep (the scope of representation, e.g., exactly what the person does and how the person represents you), commission paid and when (weekly, monthly, etc.), the length of the agreement (six months, one year), a noncompete clause (the person cannot set up shop within a certain area with the information he or she has learned), and when either party can terminate the agreement.
- *How to form an agreement*—ask manufacturers and other professional companies about their rep agreements to get an idea of what is expected and the range of commission. Also contact an attorney for guidance. Library books and Internet Web sites found through search engine investigations also show samples and give construction tips.
- *Materials a rep needs from you*—a portfolio of promotional materials and professionally taken photographs, authorization to write sales and collect payment on your behalf, and training for proper representation.

> *My rep's commission is whatever he charges over and above*
> *the basket's cost. This guarantees that the price remains fair*
> *for all customers.*

Buying a Business in Whole or Pieces

The best-laid plans don't always work well for entrepreneurs in any industry. If a market is not properly studied, the wrong products are purchased, or promotional materials are consistently mailed late, one will find oneself with no sales and in massive debt. A yearning to get back to the serenity of the paycheck-producing corporate life soon sets in. When this happens, there's lots of inventory to sell and clients to refer to a more successful gift basket business.

Buying an Existing Business

If you are interested in buying another gift basket business, its worth depends on the inventory's market value, the client list potential (getting another company's client list doesn't mean you automatically get the account), and gross sales and profits over the past years. There is much more to consider, including whether this addition can be combined effectively in the home-based environment and whether the seller intends to open another gift basket business in the same area. Your own study, combined with an accountant's and attorney's advice, ensures the best decision and deal before signing on the dotted line.

Buying in Pieces

Most closing businesses want to dispose of their assets in one bundle, but for a gift basket business, that's more of a pipe dream than the norm. Few are willing to take the entire business for the price, except a liquidator paying 20 cents on the dollar. The longer it takes a former gift basket maker to sell, the more willing the person is to sell it piecemeal. When you hear about a closing business, first assess the types of products that interest you, especially at a discount. Call the seller and ask if he or she is selling by the piece. If not, ask for a list of the complete inventory by mail or e-mail. Even if you don't want to buy the entire business, you will have a listing of all goods. When the person decides to sell in pieces, you'll know what's available and how much to offer according to prevailing wholesale costs and the condition of the merchandise.

If the seller does not have an inventory list to mail, be wary. No one can sell a business without an inventoried list of products and equipment and their condition. If a list is in the process of being developed, give the seller your name, address, and phone number or e-mail address to receive it when available.

The big question is, What are used products and equipment worth? The answer evolves by deciding what you're willing to spend on products and equipment available through a former designer. Gift basket equipment is a buyer's market every day of the year. The seller wants top dollar, but you can buy merchandise elsewhere at a fixed cost with the knowledge that everything provided is fresh, unused, and returnable if damaged or defective. Once a liquidating business sells, there are no refunds and no recourse, so the question becomes, How bad does a seller want to sell his or her products? How low is the person willing to go?

If you are within driving distance of the closing business, call and make an appointment to view the merchandise. Any in-basket products being sold as a complete basket for resale would be a questionable buy. You don't know how long ago the package was made or whether the products are resalable once the gift is separated. Will the seller's labels come off the products? Will they tear? You can't resell that.

An offer of about 30 to 50 percent off the prevailing prices is a fair deal, especially in a buyer's market. Of course, 50 percent may not be reasonable to the seller, who probably paid full price for everything, but what's a seller to do? With a ready-and-willing buyer waiting to take products off the seller's hands for cash, the right decision is to sell.

Cash is the ultimate motivator, and you can make some great deals when speaking the language of money. Get a receipt for all purchases. Make sure you need everything you buy, and don't overspend as if you're using play money. Check all expiration dates on edible products, and don't buy foods without these dates—if a client becomes ill, you'll be the one sued.

Showing Baskets on Television

The countdown begins. "Thirty seconds." One last-minute check and all is ready. "Fifteen seconds." Loud voices become muffled whispers, then a dead silence. "Five, four...." There is no turning back. Then you, flanked by a dozen baskets, are the star on prime-time television!

If you're ready to increase sales by showing gift baskets to an audience of hundreds or even millions, then television is the place for you. This promotional tactic is free of charge, except for tolls, gas, and parking fees incurred getting to the station. To properly prepare for this monumental event, the home office setup and telephone equipment must be ready to sustain the impact of nationwide exposure.

Installing a toll-free line will increase the number of potential callers. Television exposure with a local number generates some calls, but not as many as the toll-free option guarantees. The telephone system used must be capable of storing many requests from interested callers. How long a message can a caller leave? How much total time can the machine record before it disconnects other callers? If your machine can't do the job, hire a phone sitter or an answering service.

Do you have materials to send callers, or will the television appearance encourage viewers to visit your Web site? If you prefer hearing from viewers and want to send materials by mail, prestuff your literature (catalog or flyer, order form, testimonials, and rotary-file cards) in envelopes for instant mailing. This mailing list will also help you build a database of prospects to contact periodically.

Daily and weekend morning shows love interesting how-to displays and enthusiastic guests who add to their ratings through a tuned-in audience. These shows' producers (not the on-air hosts) book each guest. Their names are found in the end-of-show credits; videotape the names to make sure you spell a producer's name and title correctly. If no names appear, call the station and ask for the producer's name, address, phone number, and the best method to reach the person. Whatever you mail has to make immediate impact. Like news editors, these producers receive hundreds of daily requests from others looking for the same on-air exposure. Send a letter about six weeks before an event. Your main point is that their audience wants to see gorgeous baskets. Also focus on the specialty (such as unique containers, state-made products, stress-free items).

The thought of appearing on television introduces a new word: *fear.* Are you afraid of failing, or is it succeeding that shakes you? The world's most noted orators still feel their hearts race before speaking. It's a normal reaction that can be controlled through practice and training. With preparation and confidence, the odds of conquering this fear are in your favor.

What to Expect When You Arrive

First you'll meet the producer's assistant or another person who greets guests. You'll be taken to the greenroom, a room with sofas, chairs, and a television with the channel firmly locked on the station's current program, where other same-day guests also wait. Some greenrooms have snacks and beverages. You should have only water before airtime.

The producer's assistant will prepare you for the interview's flow. Makeup is usually applied about forty-five minutes before showtime; smaller studios don't provide makeup, so ask in advance if you need to prepare yourself. Upper-body clothing (blouse or jacket) should be a nonwhite color. White doesn't reflect well on camera.

Your segment will be at most six minutes long (the average is three minutes) and can be taped or a live broadcast. The time may seem quick, but when you are on camera, the segment seems to take forever. Come ready to speedily walk the audience through each basket's features. Is it two weeks before July 4? What ideas do you have for a family picnic or an intimate evening under the stars? Be expressive and sell your baskets to an audience eager for something other than the same old ideas. Bring a sample product for the host to taste on the air. If the host loves it, your telephone will jump with sales and catalog requests.

Postshow Sales and Savvy

At the end of the segment, ask the producer or assistant for a videotaped copy. Reviewing the tape helps you enhance your next visit. Critique your segment—what could have been done better? After the show ask the assistant when you should call to appear again to show baskets for the next occasion. Mark the date in your daily planner or PDA (which should accompany you), and bring business cards to distribute to studio employees and visitors.

Send the assistant and the producer separate notes of appreciation, mentioning how well you were treated and stating your wishes for a long relationship that increases their ratings. Remember not to use the words *thank you,* as they may be mistaken for favoritism, though you may thank the assistant for his or her preshow guidance. Do not send a gift with the note, as this is also not permitted according to the station's rules. Document the number of telephone calls and sales received and share the statistics with the producer, who should know this information to monitor viewers' reactions and to have reasons why you should return.

Continue to stay in touch with them. This appearance will also serve as a springboard to appearances on other television shows, because you now have the on-air experience that complements industry expertise.

Preparing a Media Kit

A media kit is a selection of your best materials organized in a folder for distribution to the media, corporations, and other interested parties that have the potential to give you written or visual media coverage or multiple gift basket sales. It starts with a folder (also known as a presentation folder) customized with your company name and logo on the front, or this can be a generic, glossy folder of any color available at most office-supply stores. Choose a glossy black or silver folder if color does not matter. Inside the folder are two pockets and a small die-cut slit to insert a business card. The left side should hold gift basket photographs, information on your services, and copies of clients' recommendations; the right side, your cover letter, biography, press clippings, and list of your top corporate clients. (See sample Partial Corporate Client List.) *Note:* Kits should not be distributed to everyone. Your materials are costly and cannot be handed out frivolously. Each person or group should be qualified to receive a kit through your probing questions, or you'll be sending your expensive materials to everyone from neighbors to competing firms.

A biography (also called a backgrounder) is a one-page information sheet about your company, listing the principal owner(s), the date business commenced, a synopsis of the type of baskets made and the market served, awards, and other points of interest or achievement. Because you're just starting your business, you may think that there's not much to list on your biography, but the sample biography shows how Jane Moore structured hers to get the attention of people she wants to become clients. A biography is like a business résumé; it features the best of what you do and plan to do without wild exaggeration, for you may be asked to prove what is written. As business grows, you will increase your credentials and may decide to have two biographies: a one-page outline sent to the press with a news release (as discussed later), and a multipage biography, mailed in the media kit and to those interested in your complete history, to determine if your services are right for them. Important facts to list in the biography are donations made to charitable organizations, special baskets created with state-made products, and awards and commendations from nonreligious groups.

MOORE BASKETS

PARTIAL CORPORATE CLIENT LIST*

Worldwide Cable Network
Orangetown, New York

Electrocall Public Utilities
Whitehouse Station, New Jersey

Big Productions Theater and Restaurant
New York, New York

Sahara Travel and Tours
Edgewater Park, New Jersey

*As of March 31, 2004.

P.O. Box 550, Pandora Station, Pepperton, NY 13838
Telephone: (607) 555–8580 • Fax: (607) 555–8585

MOORE BASKETS

BIOGRAPHY

Owner: Jane Moore

Inception Date: October 1, 2003

Company Focus: Gift baskets and corporate gifts created using a unique blend of creative, all-occasion themes for corporations, organizations, and individuals.

Awards: Best Display Award, Tristate Chamber of Commerce Business After Hours Event, February 2004. Chosen from a field of 45 displays.

Media Publicity: "Gift Baskets Wrap Up the Holidays," *Daily Times*, Food Section, 12/20/03.

Community Involvement: Periodic workshops conducted at Bryant High School, Laurelton, NY, to mentor students on entrepreneurship and goal setting.

Provided the Pepperton Public Library with gift baskets for its summer reading campaign, resulting in 289 new members.

P.O. Box 550, Pandora Station, Pepperton, NY 13838
Telephone: (607) 555–8580 • Fax: (607) 555–8585

Using colored paper to identify each media kit page is acceptable. This ensures that the reader doesn't overlook any materials. Labels size 4 by 2 inches or larger with your company name, mailing and Web site addresses, and telephone and fax numbers should be placed on the front of the media kit folders to identify your materials at a glance. These labels can also double as identifiers on large bags when you are making deliveries.

You might also consider placing your biography and other newsworthy information in an area on your Web site. Doing so will make finding your background materials easier for editors who need additional details that aren't included in your release, are on deadline and can't contact you, or are looking for local companies with an Internet presence and happen to find your site.

Such Web site areas, known as press rooms, usually include your photograph, how and when you started the business, the types of baskets you specialize in and clients you serve, organizations and charities with which you are affiliated, links to past news stories featuring you, and little-known facts about your company that interest editors and other news writers.

As with the gift basket portion of your site, organize the press room so that viewers can quickly find information they seek. Look at on-line press rooms on gift and nongift Web sites for ideas on how to create your own. You'll also find articles on press room setup through Internet search engines.

Getting Attention with News Releases

Stories written with a good angle are the ones that get attention and are printed in newspapers, magazines, and industry trade papers. It's great to see your name in print and almost like money in the bank, because someone will call you for more information or a potential client will ask for a catalog or, if the timing is right, order without seeing a basket. What are the elements of a well-crafted news release?

News releases (also called press releases) are best submitted on plain white paper. Using letterhead makes your release indistinguishable from the hordes of other releases submitted that day. Type your business name, address, phone and fax numbers, and Web address at the top. Come down about five lines. At the left margin type FOR IMMEDIATE RELEASE, and type your name and contact phone numbers on the line below as in the sample News Release Shell.

News Release Shell

MOORE BASKETS

P.O. Box 550, Pandora Station

Pepperton, NY 13838

www.moorebaskets.com

Telephone: (607) 555–8580 • Fax (607) 555–8585

FOR IMMEDIATE RELEASE

Photograph available on request

Contact Jane Moore, day/evening (607) 555–8580

<u>Trashy Talk on Wednesday</u>

Pepperton, NY (June 14, 2004) —

# # #

Next comes the headline, a crucial tool to grab the reader's attention. Editors receive hundreds of news releases daily, so when they read the headline, they will either continue reading or throw it away. A title like "Trashy Talk on Wednesday" (a junk-food discussion) will get more attention than "Gift Basket Talk This Wednesday." The point is to keep an editor reading, even if the subject's not exactly what it seems at first.

Next comes the body of the release. Type the name of your city and state, followed by the date, placed in parentheses. The date should be two days later than mailed. For example, if you mail the release on June 12, your release date should be June 14. This date forwarding ensures the media that the news is current. You'll start the information on the same line after the date. The first two paragraphs must answer the six basic questions of news reporting: who, what, when, where, why, and how. Who is making news? What is happening? When will it take place? Where will it be held? Why is this needed? How will it be done? Every question won't be answered in this exact fashion, but this gives you an idea of how to mold the story.

Limit all news releases to one page and end it with "# # #" or "-30-" to signal the end of the story. Double-check all spellings, as releases must be written flawlessly. Your first news release may or may not be printed, but continue to practice good writing skills. Printed news is a fantastic way to increase sales through inexpensive means, add to your media kit, and stay in touch with news sources that are interested in your business.

Many editors allow news releases to be sent to them by e-mail. Visit your local newspaper's Web site to see if the targeted editor has made his or her e-mail address available. If so, you can send your release through electronic means. Consider sending the same release to regional newspapers if editors' e-mail addresses are on-line.

If you plan to send press releases on a regular basis (monthly, quarterly, etc.), place the editors' e-mail addresses in your e-mail program's address book. However, don't send additional releases without checking each newspaper's Web site to make sure each editor is still employed there and in the same position.

Track your results. How many of your stories are being printed in the press? Do the results increase your sales? Make a chart to track which media sources are receiving the releases. Once you've controlled these data by chart, it's easy to tell which source the public is attracted to most.

More than one editor at a paper can receive a story, but do not send them identical releases at the same time. If the topic is stress-related baskets, send a release to the health editor. If the topic is Mother's or Father's Day baskets, send the release to the food editor. What about car care baskets for automobile sales or housewarming baskets for a first-home buyer? Your release goes to the editor interested in a story that has a different angle from that usually covered.

Don't send a picture unless requested. The phrase "Photograph available on request" should be typed on the line between FOR IMMEDIATE RELEASE and your name. If editors are interested, they will call you. Don't say a photograph is available if it's not. When an editor says he or she wants a photo, it should be mailed or dropped off immediately.

A one-page biography should be sent with the news release if you're contacting a media source for the first time. If your release was e-mailed, add a link to your Web site's press area or other place where your biography is on-line. This is done so that the source gets to know who you are. The biography shows that you are a bona fide business and not a fake company looking for free press.

Should you call editors to see if they received the release or want more information? Gift basket professionals' opinions vary. Some say that you should call to verify receipt; others say don't call them, they'll call you. In most cases, you should not call, and here's why:

- If editors need more information, they will call you. That is why your telephone number is listed on the release. Call an editor and you'll probably do so during a deadline, turning the person against printing any future news about you.
- If the story won't be printed, you will know—it simply won't show up in the paper. To call and ask how the story could have been written better is to ask an editor to be a teacher: another wrong move. Teach yourself through self-study or enroll in a class. Don't turn the press against you by asking to explain their actions before you've had a chance to develop a relationship.
- If the story will be printed, asking when it will appear is like saying, "I don't get the paper, so tell me which issue to watch for, and send me a copy, OK?" Subscribe or get the paper from a newsstand and watch for your news—which, if printed, will show up within days in dailies and within three to four months in monthlies.

The only time to consider calling the editor is to contact him or her with an interesting fact that you (purposely) left out of the press release. It must be news that encourages the editor to print your story. Public relations specialists are experts at contacting the media in this way, which increases the chance of having their clients' story featured. As you are your own public relations expert, this is an acceptable reason to make contact with the editor.

There will be times when you send news releases and neither hear from an editor nor see the story printed. Don't be discouraged; editors collect news for story ideas. I once sent my local newspaper news about my business for a year and saw one small clipping and nothing else. Still, I felt this was a good start. Researching how to write better news releases, I continued trying to get coverage. One day I received a call from the paper's business editor, who was writing a story for Labor Day on the city's changing business population. Meeting for lunch, we talked about the gift industry, its challenges, and financing strategies. The story made the front page, with my daughter and me creating gift baskets in full color. Riding around the city early that Sunday morning, we were thrilled to see our faces beaming through every vending machine and home deliveries waiting to be taken off porches. The months of effort to develop well-written news releases had paid off and continue to do so today.

Follow the aforementioned examples, research news release writing, and continue sending releases to newspapers, trade publications, regional and national magazines, television stations, and other media that will give your company the promotion it deserves.

Working with Department Stores

Chapter 10 introduced you to outsourcing, wherein one company contracts another to provide goods or services it cannot produce in-house. Many retailers don't have in-store talent to create customized and everyday gift baskets from store products. Linking your company with these indirect competitors is another method of growing your business.

There are four key contacts in department stores. One is the special events manager, who needs occasional assistance in making custom gift baskets during holidays and special events. Two others are the store's gourmet food manager and its infant department manager, both selling lots of individual goods but perhaps needing help to bundle everyday and holiday baskets. Another prime contact is the sales and marketing executive, who may not specifically help you with outsourcing but does need occasional gift baskets for clients and can be a link between you and other store managers.

Face-to-face contact is best to meet these executives, as calls and mail are sidetracked by the executives' focus on sales floor management, unless they are specifically looking for your mail, are waiting for a return call, or will speak to you because of a higher-level store executive's recommendation. Visiting the store will give you insights into how to tailor your message before speaking with these persons. Look around the store to see whether gift baskets are sold, whether the store sells small items to bundle, or whether a clearance area has items that will sell better in baskets. It's easier to take notes about products while standing in a large department store, as customers aren't approached as often as they are in smaller stores.

After reviewing your notes and determining a strategy, call the special events manager and get right to the point. Tell the person who you are, give brief information about your company, and describe how your gift basket services will help sell more products in the targeted areas. Start with gourmet, as no store wants spoiled items and all such departments need new ideas to sell the products quickly.

Mention an upcoming special occasion (about two to three months away), and state that you'd like to send a proposal for your services. Have an idea of the lump-sum fee you will charge for the event. Think in terms of four-hour sessions. How much is four hours of your time worth—$40 an hour, $50 an hour, or more? After settling on a rate, multiply it by four hours and increase the amount to the nearest whole number; for example, $40 an hour for a four-hour event is $160, rounded up to $200 for the event. Then calculate the cost of all products you will bring to the event and again round the amount up to the next whole number. One-sum fees versus hourly charges work to your advantage in this environment. Keep in mind that the larger stores usually offer such an event free of charge to their customers, and management expects sales to cover the cost.

Stores usually have special events on Saturdays and Sundays, from 1:00 to 6:00 P.M., so plan to work within these times. This is a great opportunity to develop a long and rewarding relationship with stores because of the high staff turnover and your specific expertise. The more reliable you are and the more you increase their overall sales projections, the more they'll come to need your services. During the event keep a tally of the items wrapped and the retail price, which prove how successful the event was so that management can include it as a regular engagement. At the conclusion ask the contact when you should call to plan the next event. Keep the momentum going while the event is fresh. If you don't get a definite answer, tell the contact you'll call two months before the next holiday, as a courtesy.

Also bring business cards to place inside the wrapped baskets; doing so will draw sales to your business from those needing future gift baskets and wrapping services. Keep your cards out of sight from store executives. In their eyes (and rightfully so), you are here to sell their products, not promote yourself. Even so, keep the cards in your pocket, include them in the baskets, and distribute your cards to individuals who request one.

Postevent Contact

The event is over. Lots of people came to you for basket wrapping, and the time went quickly. Follow up the event with a note of appreciation to your store contact, sending a copy of your letter to the person's manager and any high-level executives who came by to watch the event unfold.

Your letter should mention the types of items wrapped, the total retail sales, and any customers' opinions that will benefit both of you next time. As is the case with television appearances, you now have a track record to increase your sales through the experience of a retail environment. This additional exposure should also be listed on your biography, which is expanding quickly because you dare to go after the rewards of starting a home-based gift basket business.

You Can Do It!

You deserve to reap the personal and financial rewards of owning your own business. Every tip, idea, strategy, and solution in this book comes from years of hands-on experience through the ups and downs of developing a successful business and finding loyal customers who keep coming back to buy. Yes, you will make mistakes—but what can be accomplished in this life without the wisdom of errors? Use this book as a guide, follow your instincts, and begin to live your entrepreneurial dream today for a brighter tomorrow.

Growth Opportunities Checklist

Completed

1. Use a separate book to log personal expenses, tracking the money needed to turn part-time gift baskets into a full-time venture. _____

2. Find part-time help by asking trusted acquaintances and posting ads. _____

3. Investigate hiring a sales representative by asking manufacturers and professional companies:

   How they select reps _____

   What sales percentages they pay _____

   How contracts are designed _____

4. Consider buying another gift basket business in total or by the piece as opportunities arise. _____

5. Contact television shows featuring multiple guests to explore an on-air appearance. _____

6. Prepare a media kit and mail it, as needed, to media contacts and producers. _____

7. Create a press area within your Web site for access to your biography and other press news. _____

8. Create a news release chart for regular mailings to media sources and other groups that will expand your sales. Mail and e-mail releases when appropriate. _____

9. Speak with specialty shop and department store buyers about their need to sell in-store gift baskets. _____

Appendix

Gift Basket Product Ideas

Finding foods and snacks for baskets is easier than remembering the gifts that also create a memorable theme. This gift list incorporates some of the most thoughtful, high-quality, affordable products available. Use and expand the list with items found in your local area that keep you busy and profiting.

Home

Theme/event: Wedding, hostess, welcome

Container: Ice bucket, watering can, colander, teapot, birdhouse/birdcage, nonstick pan, wok, teacup and saucer, silver-plated tray, cutting board, mini dish drainer

Recipe book

Notepad

Candles

Candleholders

Linen napkins

Cookbook

Potpourri

Place mats

Oven mitt

Coasters

Apron

Kitchen utensils

Soaps

Fireplace matches

Egg timer

Room freshener

Concealed safe (a book, head of lettuce, something undetectable)

Cutting board

Champagne glasses

Dish towels

Paper plates and cups

Pinecones

Picture frame

Coupon holder

Disposable camera

Gardening

Container: Flowerpot, watering can, birdbath

Flower and vegetable seeds

Tools

Knee pads/mats

Gloves

Stakes

Permanent marker (to write on stakes)

Water bottle with spray nozzle

Office

Theme/event: Corporate, executive, promotion, Bosses' Day and Administrative Professionals Week, businessman/woman, college graduate, at-home business, thank you

Container: Briefcase, desk organizer, mug (regular or oversize), cork or writing board

Notepads

Mousepad

Travel log

Paperweight

Picture frame

Appointment book/daily planner

Business card case

Writing instruments

Cubed pad

Mileage log

Portable shoe shiner

Portable lint brush

Men

Theme/event: Father's Day, birthday

Container: Upturned hat or cap, ice bucket, cooler, toolbox

Anything sports-related

Mug

Drawer fresheners

Handkerchiefs

Car freshener

Deck of cards

Soaps, lotions, gels, powders

Women

Theme/event: Mother's Day, birthday, thinking of you

Container: Hatbox, tote bag

Candles (floating, for bath)

Soaps, lotions, gels, powders

Appointment book

Mug

Potpourri

Drawer fresheners

Puzzle books

Notecards

Stationery

Rubber stamps and ink pads in various colors

Children

Theme/event: Birthday, miss you
Container: Child's chair, toy stroller,
    wagon, miniwheelbarrow, pail
Stuffed animals
Bat and ball
Sunglasses
Blow bubbles
Sun visor
Rubber stamps and pad
Stickers
Crayons
Coloring books
Games
Puzzles
Safety scissors

Infants

Theme/event: Baby shower
Container: Diaper bag, doll crib
Bottle
Scissors
Hangers
Bibs
Socks
Kimono
Rattles
Bank

Bath/Pampering

Container: Hatbox
Sachets
Bubble bath
Sponge
Loofah
Candles (floating)
Moisturizing soaps, gels, and lotions
    (some unscented)
Bath pillow
Cassette tape or CD with soothing
    music

Get Well

Container: Inverted umbrella (rainy
    day), doctor's bag, first-aid box
Games
Puzzles
Teddy bear dressed as a doctor or
    nurse
Books (recipient's preference)
Magazines

Bereavement

Container: Silver-plated tray,
    hand-painted bowl
Book of poems
Candles
Soaps in unique shapes and favored
    fragrances

Sports

Container: Golf bucket, inverted cap or
    football helmet, cooler
Golf tees
Golf balls
Scorecard
Visor
Spikes
Games
Puzzles
Dominoes
Football items
Baseball items
Fishing equipment

State-Based Gifts for Visitors

Container: Tote bag with tissue
Postcards
Writing tools with state name
Pen
Key chain
Stationery with state name
State magazines

Car Care

Container: Pail
Sponges
Car wax
Air fresheners
Reusable garbage bag
Magazine/map holder
Mileage log
Area maps
Flashlight (with batteries)
Tire pressure gauge

All-Occasion

Container: Top hat, mini wooden crate,
    upturned umbrella, tote bag, lunch
    bag, pail
Wrapping: Cellophane, shrink-wrap,
    tulle

Associations

Gift Basket Professionals Network
Telephone: (714) 254–7891
Web site: www.giftbasketbusiness.org
Founded in 1993, GBPN counts as its members gift basket designers, home-based business owners, retail store owners, gift consultants, writers, seminar presenters, wholesalers, and affiliates. Membership includes a membership directory, industry information, wholesale directory, newsletters, and monthly meetings.

National Specialty Gift Association
Telephone: (813) 671–4757
Web site: www.nsgaonline.com
NSGA works with gift basket retailers and wholesalers to strengthen the industry as a whole. It offers many benefits, including a private Internet chat board, merchant account discount, vendor discounts, and access to a lending library.

Gift Trade Shows

Gift shows are held across the country. While this listing highlights the major shows, trade shows are held in other states. Check show calendar updates found periodically in gift industry magazines. Proper identification is required to attend each show.

Arizona

OASIS Gift Show
Location: Phoenix Civic Plaza
225 East Adams Street
Phoenix, AZ 85004
Producer: OASIS
Telephone: (602) 952–2050
Toll-free: (800) 424–9519
Fax: (602) 952–2244
Web site: www.oasis.org

California

California Gift Show
Location: Los Angeles Convention
 Center
1201 South Figueroa Street
Los Angeles, CA 90015
Producer: DMG World Media
Toll-free: (800) 395–3901
Web site: www.californiagiftshow.com

San Francisco International Gift Fair
Location: Moscone Convention Center
747 Howard Street
San Francisco, CA 94103
Producer: George Little Management
Telephone: (914) 421–3200

Toll-free: (800) 272–SHOW

Fax: (914) 948–6180

Web site: www.glmshows.com

District of Columbia

Washington Gift Show

Location: Dulles Expo and Conference
Center

4320 Chantilly Shopping Center

Chantilly, VA 20151

Producer: George Little Management

Telephone: (914) 421–3200

Toll-free: (800) 272–SHOW

Fax: (914) 948–6180

Web site: www.glmshows.com

Florida

Orlando Gift Show

Location: Orange County Convention
Center

9800 International Drive

Orlando, FL 32819

Producer: Urban Expositions

Telephone: (678) 285–3976

Toll-free: (800) 318–2238

Fax: (678) 285–7469

Web site: www.urban-expo.com

Georgia

Atlanta Market Center

Location: Americasmart Atlanta

240 Peachtree Street, NW

Atlanta, GA 30303

Producer: AMC Trade Shows

Telephone: (404) 220–3000

Toll-free: (800) ATL–MART

Fax: (404) 220–2450

Web site: www.americasmart.com

Gift Fair in Atlanta

Location: Georgia World Congress
Center

285 Andrew Young International
Boulevard

Atlanta, GA 30313

Producer: Urban Expositions

Telephone: (678) 285–3976

Toll-free: (800) 318–2238

Fax: (678) 285–7469

Web site: www.urban-expo.com

Illinois

Chicago Gift Show

Location: McCormick Place North

2301 South Lake Shore Drive

Chicago, IL 60616

Producer: Merchandise Mart Properties

Toll-free: (800) 677–6278

Web site: www.mmart.com/mmart/

New York

New York International Gift Fair
Location: Jacob K. Javits Convention
    Center
655 West Thirty-fourth Street
New York, NY 10001
Producer: George Little Management
Telephone: (914) 421–3200
Toll-free: (800) 272–SHOW
Fax: (914) 948–6180
Web site: www.glmshows.com

Pennsylvania

Philadelphia Gift Show
Location: Fort Washington Expo Center
1100 Virginia Drive
Fort Washington, PA 19034
Producer: Urban Expositions
Telephone: (678) 285–3976
Toll-free: (800) 318–2238
Fax: (678) 285–7469
Web site: www.urban-expo.com

Texas

Dallas Gift Show
Location: Dallas Market Center
2100 Stemmons Freeway
Dallas, TX 75207
Producer: Dallas Gift Show
Telephone: (214) 655–6100

Toll-free: (800) DAL–MKTS
Fax: (214) 655–6238
Web site: www.dallasmarketcenter.com

Gift Basket Trade Shows

Jubilee
Producer: Festivities Publications, Inc.
815 Haines Street
Jacksonville, FL 32206
Toll-free: (800) 729–6338

Gourmet Trade Shows

California

Winter NASFT Fancy Food Show
Location: Moscone Convention Center
747 Howard Street
San Francisco, CA 94103
Producer: National Association for the
    Specialty Food Trade (NASFT)
Telephone: (212) 482–6440
Fax: (212) 482–6459
Web site: www.fancyfoodshows.com

Illinois

Spring NASFT Fancy Food Show
Location: McCormick Place
2301 South Lake Shore Drive

Chicago, IL 60616
Producer: National Association for the
Specialty Food Trade (NASFT)
Telephone: (212) 482–6440
Fax: (212) 482–6459
Web site: www.fancyfoodshows.com

New York

Summer NASFT Fancy Food Show
Location: Jacob K. Javits Convention
Center
655 West Thirty-fourth Street
New York, NY 10001
Producer: National Association for the
Specialty Food Trade (NASFT)
Telephone: (212) 482–6440
Fax: (212) 482–6459
Web site: www.fancyfoodshows.com

Pennsylvania

Philadelphia National Candy, Gift, and
Gourmet Show
Location: Valley Forge Convention
Exhibit Center
1160 First Avenue
King of Prussia, PA 19406
Producer: Retail Confectioners Associa-
tion of Philadelphia
Telephone: (610) 527–4259
Web site: www.rcaphila.org

Texas

Dallas National Gourmet Food Shows
Location: Dallas Market Center
2100 North Stemmons Freeway
Dallas, TX 75207
Telephone: (214) 655–6100
Toll-free: (800) DAL–MKTS
Fax: (214) 655–6238
Web site: www.dallasmarketcenter.com

Gift Industry Permanent Showrooms

The showrooms located in these buildings are specifically designed to allow
manufacturers and representatives to
display an extensive line of products,
meet with clients, and complete sales orders. As with trade shows, each building
requires proper identification to enter.

California

California Market Center
110 East Ninth Street
Los Angeles, CA 90079
Telephone: (213) 630–3600
Toll-free: (800) 225–6278
Fax: (213) 630–3708
Web site: www.californiamarket
center. com

L.A. Mart
1933 South Broadway
Los Angeles, CA 90007
Telephone: (213) 749–7911
Toll-free: (800) LAMART4
Fax: (213) 746–1215
Web site: www.mmart.com/lamart/

San Francisco Gift Center and Jewelry
   Mart
888 Brannan Street
San Francisco, CA 94103
Telephone: (415) 861–7733
Fax: (415) 431–2710
Web site: www.gcjm.com

San Francisco Mart
1355 Market Street
San Francisco, CA 94103
Telephone: (415) 552–2311
Web site: www.sfmart.com

Colorado

Denver Merchandise Mart
451 East Fifty-eighth Avenue
Denver, CO 80216
Telephone: (303) 292–6278
Toll-free: (800) 289–6278
Fax: (303) 298–1503
Web site: www.denvermart.com

Georgia

Americasmart Atlanta
240 Peachtree Street, NW
Atlanta, GA 30303
Telephone: (404) 220–3000
Toll-free: (800) ATL–MART
Fax: (404) 220–2450
Web site: www.americasmart.com

Illinois

Chicago Merchandise Mart
200 World Trade Center
Chicago, IL 60654
Toll-free: (800) 677–6278
Fax: (312) 697–5079
Web site: www.mmart.com/mmart/

New York

New York Merchandise Mart
41 Madison Avenue
New York, NY 10010
Telephone: (212) 686–1203
Fax: (212) 779–7105
Web site: www.41madison.com

225 Fifth Avenue Building
225 Fifth Avenue
New York, NY 10010
Telephone: (212) 684–3200

Toll-free: (800) 235–3512
Fax: (212) 684–3203
Web site: www.225-fifth.com

Texas

Dallas Market Center
2100 Stemmons Freeway
Dallas, TX 75207
Telephone: (214) 655–6100
Toll-free: (800) DAL–MKTS
Fax: (214) 655–6238
Web site: www.dallasmarketcenter.com

Magazines

With the exception of *Gift Basket Review,* which caters exclusively to gift basket professionals, all magazines advertise gift basket products, print periodic articles related to gift baskets, and show some helpful designs.

Flowers&
11444 West Olympic Boulevard
Los Angeles, CA 90064
Toll-free: (800) 321–2665
Fax: (310) 966–3610

Gift Basket Review
815 Haines Street
Jacksonville, FL 32206
Toll-free: (800) 729–6338

Gifts & Decorative Accessories
360 Park Avenue South
New York, NY 10010
Toll-free: (800) 309–3332

Gourmet Retailer
3301 Ponce de Leon Boulevard, Suite 300
Coral Gables, FL 33134
Toll-free: (800) 397–1137

Software

FoxE Software Co.
P.O. Box 22205
Lexington, KY 40522
Toll-free: (866) 635–6905
Fax: (859) 276–4988
Web site: www.foxesoft.com
E-mail: foxesoft@compuserve.com
Business software for customer, inventory, orders, and kits. Prints invoices, delivery forms, enclosure cards, labels, postcards, sales, taxes, and items sold. Uses bar codes and works with QuickBooks.

Videos

Gift Basket Basics
Producer: GiftBasketBusiness.com
Telephone: (973) 279–2799
Fax: (973) 742–0700

Web site: www.GiftBasketBusiness.com
Instructional videos for aspiring designers and seasoned veterans.

Learn to Make Beautiful Bows
Producer: Picture Perfect Productions
11664 National Boulevard, Box 340
Los Angeles, CA 90064
Telephone: (310) 838–5624
E-mail: makebows@aol.com

Mary Ann Jacobs Videos and Marketing
      Materials
Telephone: (520) 749–5523
Fax: (520) 749–5436
Web site: www.maryannjacobs.com
Videos on gift basket design, marketing, sales presentations, themes, bows, and business. Complete marketing package available to jump-start your business.

Gift Product Sources

Baskets

Basket Peddler
P.O. Box 44514
Rio Rancho, NM 87174
Telephone: (505) 896–0050
Fax: (505) 891–8988
Web site: www.basketpeddler.com
E-mail: basketpeddlernm@aol.com
A wide assortment of baskets and trays.

Terra
P.O. Box 26400
Akron, OH 44319
Toll-free: (800) 424–6370
Fax: (888) 303–6100
Web site: www.yourterra.com
E-mail: admin@yourterra.com
Baskets, ceramics, plastics, and seasonal items.

A Touch of Baskets
114 Beach Street, Building 5
Rockaway, NJ 07866
Telephone: (973) 983–0333
Fax: (732) 531–3158
Web site: www.atouchofbaskets.com
One-of-a-kind baskets available in various shapes, sizes, and colors.

United Basket Company
58-01 Grand Avenue
Maspeth, NY 11378
Telephone: (718) 894–5454
Fax: (718) 326–3378
Web site: www.unitedbasketco.com
E-mail: helpdesk@unitedbasketco.com
Baskets, trays, bowls, boxes, and "niche" packaging items.

Wald Imports, Ltd.
11200 Kirkland Way, Suite 300
Kirkland, WA 98033
Telephone: (425) 822–0500

Toll-free: (800) 426–2822
Fax: (425) 828–4201
Web site: www.waldimports.com
E-mail: tamibrinley@waldimports.com
Baskets and containers of all types.

Containers

BoxCo
2344 Grissom Drive
St. Louis, MO 63146
Telephone: (314) 567–4990
Toll-free: (800) 654–2932
Fax: (314) 567–4991
Web site: www.boxcoindustries.com
E-mail: sales@boxcoindustries.com
Theme gift boxes, ribbon, cello bags, cocoa, and balloons.

Distributors and Reps

Christopher Brookes Distinctive Foods
7229 212th Street, SW, Unit D
Edmonds, WA 98026
Telephone: (425) 640–2233
Toll-free: (866) 640–2233
Fax: (425) 640–6272
Web site: www.cbdf.com
E-mail: cbdf@nwlink.com
Teas, cookies, preserves, plum puddings, cakes, candies, honeys, soap, sachets, bookmarks, greeting cards. Low minimum and shipping to both coasts.

QCU One Stop Wholesale
3056 Palm Avenue, Warehouses 2 and 3
Ft. Myers, FL 33901
Telephone: (239) 332–2205
Toll-free: (800) 729–2205
Fax: (239) 332–2093
Web site: www.qcu.com
E-mail: info@qcu.com
One-stop product source for the gift basket industry, from the basket to the bow and everything in between. No minimum order; same-day shipping.

Foods and Beverages

Alaska Smokehouse and the Famous
    Pacific Dessert Company
21616 Eighty-seventh Avenue SE
Woodinville, WA 98072
Telephone: (360) 668–9404
Toll-free: (800) 422–0852
Fax: (360) 668–1005
Web site: www.alaskasmokehouse.com
E-mail: customerservice@
    alaskasmokehouse.com
Gourmet shelf-stable smoked salmon, stix, jerky, and cans. Gourmet shelf-stable desserts, cakes, bars, and purees.

American Vintage Wine Biscuits
40-03 27th Street
Long Island City, NY 11101
Telephone: (718) 361–1003

Fax: (718) 361–0204
Web site: www.americanvintage.com
E-mail: americanvintage@aol.com
Gourmet crackers made with wine and pepper, available in three flavors.

Angelic Gourmet, Inc.
24 Mill Street
P.O. Box 127
Naples, NY 14512
Telephone: (585) 374–9783
Toll-free: (800) 294–0947
Fax: (800) 947–5371
Web site: www.angelicgourmet.com
E-mail: angelicgourmet@frontiernet.net
Handmade gourmet foods. Specializing in chocolate-covered pretzels and more.

Chase Collection
14303-B Sullyfield Circle
Chantilly, VA 20151
Telephone: (703) 817–7733
Toll-free: (800) 368–5798
Fax: (703) 817–7755
Web site: www.thechasecollection.com
E-mail: mmorgan@thechasecollection.com
Gourmet, gift, and novelty products from the United Kingdom.

Country Fresh Food & Confections, Inc.
504 Main Street
P.O. Box 604
Oliver Springs, TN 37840
Telephone: (865) 435–2655
Toll-free: (800) 545–8782
Fax: (865) 435–1930
Web site: www.countryfreshfood.com
E-mail: orders@countryfreshfood.com
Country fresh fudge and Papa Joe's Downhome Gourmet.

Delicae Gourmet
1111 East Lake Drive
Tarpon Springs, FL 34689
Telephone: (727) 942–2502
Toll-free: (800) 942–2502
Fax: (727) 942–1837
Web site: www.delicaegourmet.com
E-mail: delicaegourmet@aol.com
Award-winning coffee and tea, jellies, jams, mustards, dips, rubs, vinegars, and many more condiments.

Golden Walnut Specialty Foods, Inc.
3200 Sixteenth Street
Zion, IL 60099
Telephone: (847) 731–3200
Toll-free: (800) 843–3645
Fax: (847) 731–6433
Web site: www.goldenwalnut.com
E-mail: sales@goldenwalnut.com

A full line of cookies, toffee, and cakes in boxes, bags, cans, and tins. Many sizes; great quality.

Maxwell's Gourmet Foods
3208 Wellington Court, #L
Raleigh, NC 27615
Telephone: (919) 878–4321
Toll-free: (800) 952–NUTS
Fax: (919) 878–4325
Web site: www.maxwellsgourmet.com
E-mail: info@maxwellsgourmet.com
Gourmet chocolates, brittles, and nuts in bags, boxes, pouches, and tins.

Morin's Landing
P.O. Box 819
Dayton, OR 97114
Telephone: (503) 864–3958
Toll-free: (800) 945–3603
Fax: (503) 864–3825
Web site: www.morinslanding.com
E-mail: morins@onlinemac.com
Wide variety of award-winning gourmet jams, mustards, sauces, and mixes.

Neighbors Coffee
P.O. Box 54527
Oklahoma City, OK 73154
Telephone: (405) 552–2100
Toll-free: (800) 299–9016
Fax: (405) 232–3729

Web site: www.neighborscoffee.com
E-mail: sales@neighborscoffee.com
Coffee, cocoa, biscotti, and more. Quality products in attractive packaging.

Pasta Shoppe
P.O. Box 159245
Nashville, TN 37215
Toll-free: (800) 247–0188
Fax: (615) 781–9335
Web site: www.pastashoppe.com
E-mail: wholesale@pastashoppe.com
Great gift basket–themed products, including curly and fun-shaped pasta, cookies, snack mixes, biscuits, and soup mixes.

Pride of Alaska
15110 NE Ninetieth Street
Redmond, WA 98052-3524
Toll-free: (800) 386–0008
Fax: (425) 821–8416
E-mail: susano@fishking.com
Smoked gourmet Alaskan seafoods. Kosher salmon, smoked oyster, scallops, and pâté. All products are shelf stable. Great for corporate baskets.

PurpleMoose Products
P.O. Box 7018
Golden, CO 80403
Toll-free: (800) 277–9135
Fax: (303) 642–9343

Web site: www.purplemooseproducts.
com
E-mail: info@purplemooseproducts.com
Makers of Celebration Cakes in short,
round containers with cake mix, icing,
candle, and merry maker. Add water,
microwave, decorate, and celebrate.
More than fifteen themes available.

Stephany's Chocolate
6770 West Fifty-second Avenue
Arvada, CO 80002
Toll-free: (800) 888–1522
Fax: (303) 421–7256
Web site: stephanys-chocolates.com
E-mail: stephanyschocola@qwest.net
Premium handmade chocolates pre-
sented in award-winning packaging.

Tortuga Rum Cake Company
14202 SW 142nd Avenue
Miami, FL 33186
Toll-free: (877) 486–7884
Web site: www.tortugawholesale.com
E-mail: sales@tortugaimports.com
Moist cakes made with a touch of aged
rum. (NOTE: No restrictions on adding
to gift baskets.) Available in six flavors
and three sizes and packaged in beautifully detailed boxes. Coffee, honey,
fudge, sauces, and jellies also available.

Gifts

Distinct Impressions
190 North Arrowhead Avenue, Suite F
Rialto, CA 92376
Toll-free: (888) 345–6331
Fax: (909) 494–4000
Web site: www.aplaceforbaby.com
E-mail: distinctimpressions@
mindspring.com
Quality baby keepsake items and acces-
sories, including handprint and foot-
print kits. No printed catalog; visit the
Web site.

The Home Owner's Journal
2232 North 7th Street, Unit 15
Grand Junction, CO 81501
Telephone: (970) 257–0606
Toll-free: (800) 444–5450
Fax: (970) 257–0333
Web site: www.homeownersjournal.com
E-mail: info@homeownersjournal.com
Complete spiral-bound journal for
homeowners and apartment dwellers to
list their belongings and relevant infor-
mation.

Karen's Keepsakes
11 Anthony Avenue
Edison, NJ 08820
Telephone: (908) 753–5756
Toll-free: (800) 231–9137

Fax: (908) 561–3702
Web site: www.karenskeepsakes.com/gb
E-mail: info@karenskeepsakes.com
Baby's footprint and handprint kits.
Many baby products, Radio Flyer wagons, aromatherapy, pet and adult products. Marketing tips included with order.

A Unique Beginning
2225 Highway 101
Beaufort, NC 28516
Telephone: (252) 504–7244
Toll-free: (888) 551–4747
Fax: (252) 504–7244
Web site: www.auniquebeginning.com
E-mail: spm@auniquebeginning.com
Baby products, including first haircut and lost tooth keepsake boxes, burp cloths, hooded blankets, and more.

Bath and Body/Fragrance

Fleur de Lis Perfumes
26920 West Garret Drive
Calabasas, CA 91301
Telephone: (818) 879–1272
Toll-free: (800) 504–9197, code 00 (zero, zero)
Fax: (818) 879–1272
Web site: www.fleurdelisperfumesstore. com
E-mail: sales@fleurdelisperfumes.com

Bath and body care products, original perfumes, foot care items, scrubs, and more in hard-to-find fragrances and specialty items.

Homespun Naturals, Inc.
195 Bobcat Court
Forsyth, MO 65653
Telephone: (417) 546–5684
Toll-free: (800) 714–1377
Fax: (417) 546–4241
Web site: www.homespunsoap.com
E-mail: info@homespunsoap.com
All-natural aromatherapy bath and body products. Wholesale only.

RainCountry Naturals
P.O. Box 2125
Sisters, OR 97759
Telephone: (541) 549–6816
Toll-free: (800) 543–9133
Fax: (541) 549–6818
Web site: www.raincountry.com
E-mail: jdobson@raincountry.com
A full line of natural bath, beauty, and home fragrance products for all ages.

Enhancements (shred, ribbon, etc.)

Can Creations
P.O. Box 848576
Pembroke Pines, FL 33084

Telephone: (954) 581–3312

Toll-free: (800) 272–0235

Fax: (954) 581–2523

Web site: www.cancreations.com

E-mail: cancreations@mindspring.com

Gift boxes, cellophane, basket bags, shrink-wrap, shred, ribbon, and much more.

Cole & Ashcroft

5631 Brystone

Houston, TX 77041

Telephone: (713) 937–8657

Toll-free: (800) 475–8657

Fax: (713) 937–8578

Web site: www.coleandashcroft.com

Box containers, shrink-wrap, cellophane, ribbons, baskets, tissue paper, shred, and more.

Nashville Wraps

1229 Northgate Business Parkway

Madison, TN 37115

Toll-free: (800) 547–9727

Fax: (800) 646–0046

Web site: www.nashvillewraps.com

E-mail: info@nashvillewraps.com

Over 4,000 gift basket supplies, including cellophane, boxes, ribbon, tote bags, shred, tissue paper, and more.

Advertising Specialties

Impressive Specialties

www.impressive-promotions.com

Imprinting, promotional products, and embroidery services.

Gift Basket Business Web Sites, Classes, and Message Boards

Gift Basket Business.com

www.GiftBasketBusiness.com

Gift Basket Business World.com

www.GiftBasketBusinessWorld.com

Gift Basket Exchange Network

gbexchange.net/mssgbrd/

Glossary

Bill of lading (B/L): A document that establishes the terms of a contract between the shipper and a transportation company.

Buyer's market: An overflow of goods or services, often allowing the buyer to negotiate for lower prices.

Cash cow: A source of an abundance of cash or sales.

Client/customer: Any person, corporation, organization, or institution that has made a purchase. However, a person designated a client may have a more favored relationship.

Consignment: An arrangement whereby a retailer displays and sells products belonging to a vendor in exchange for the promise of a percentage of sales.

Credit: The ability to obtain goods or services in exchange for a promise to pay at a later date.

Free on board (FOB): The point up to which the vendor pays for and has responsibility for the transportation of goods. Also known as freight on board.

List price: The manufacturer's suggested retail price.

Keystone: The markup of a product by 100 percent of the cost paid by the buyer.

Markup: The amount added to an item's purchased price for resale.

Minimum order: The smallest unit of products or sales permitted by a wholesaler, manufacturer, or distributor.

Odd pricing: A merchandise amount in anything other than a round figure (e.g., $9.95 instead of $10.00).

Open account: The sale of goods on credit. Usually obtained when a buyer has proved payment reliability.

Outsourcing: The practice of contracting a firm to provide products or services not available in another company.

Product mix: A selection or variety of goods available for sale.

Purchase agreement: A written agreement, signed by buyer and seller, documenting products or services sold, cost, and other terms of sale.

Stock turnover: The number of times the average inventory on hand is sold and restocked in a given period.

Wholesaler: A person or company that buys large quantities of goods and sells them in small quantities to the retailers.

Index

About the Author

Shirley George Frazier is president of Sweet Survival, gift and gourmet specialists providing a broad range of services to home-based professionals, specialty shops, and department stores. Born in Brooklyn, New York, Shirley writes for trade publications, conducts business seminars and workshops, has appeared on numerous television and cable programs, speaks at trade shows and conferences throughout the country, and is an associate member of the Gift Basket Professional Network.

Shirley lives in Paterson, New Jersey, with her husband, John; her daughter, Genesis; and their dog, Pepper.